In the Shadow of Violence

Mikropolitik der Gewalt – Micropolitics of Violence
Volume 1

Edited by Klaus Schlichte and Peter Waldmann

*Klaus Schlichte* is professor of international relations at the University of Magdeburg, Germany.

Klaus Schlichte

# In the Shadow of Violence

The Politics of Armed Groups

Campus Verlag
Frankfurt/New York

Bibliographic Information published by the Deutsche Nationalbibliothek.
Die Deutsche Nationalbibliothek lists this publication in the Deutsche Nationalbibliografie;
detailed bibliographic data are available in the Internet at http://dnb.d-nb.de.
ISBN 978-3-593-38411-5

All rights reserved. No part of this book may be reproduced or transmitted in any form or by any means, electronic or mechanical, including photocopying, recording, or by any information storage and retrieval system, without permission in writing from the publishers.
Copyright © 2009 Campus Verlag GmbH, Frankfurt/Main
Cover illustration: AK-47 by an entrance to a cave, Afghanistan © Matthew Rambo/iStockphoto
Cover design: Campus Verlag

Printed on acid free paper.
Printed in Germany

For further information:
www.campus.de
www.press.uchicago.edu

# Contents

Foreword and Acknowledgements ................................................................ 9

1. Introduction .................................................................................... 13
   *Armed groups as figurations 13 • The structure of this book 21 • On methodology 23*

2. First Movers: the Formation of Armed Groups ............................. 30
   *Where leaders and staff originate – a statistical overview 32 • From party politics to war: the mechanism of repression 39 • Initiatives of the disappointed: the ad hoc mechanism 42 • Delegated violence: the spin-off mechanism 48 • Conclusion 54*

3. The Shadow of Violence ................................................................. 57
   *The notion of violence: power, immediateness, and trauma 60 • Legitimizing violence in war 65 • Delegitimization through violence 72 • Why violence derails 76 • Conclusion 82*

4. Basic Legitimacy and Charismatic Cycles ..................................... 85
   *Traditional legitimacy and its erosion 90 • The mechanism of basic legitimacy 95 • The cycle of the charismatic idea 99 • Selected affinities: the global timing of discourse 107 • Conclusion 113*

5. Finance and Reproduction ..................................................................116
   *Conceptions and statistics 118 • Economy in war and war economies 123 • Statization, stagnation, and disconnection 131 • Conclusion 142*

6. Hierarchy and Organization ................................................................144
   *Ways to rule and roads to decay 146 • Centrifugal forces and centripetal techniques 154 • The mechanism of patrimonialization 168 • The mechanism of formalization 172 • Conclusion 176*

7. Conclusions: Armed Groups as State-Builders ....................................178
   *The politics of armed groups 180 • Armed groups as state-builders in historical perspective 187 • The politics of armed groups and world politics 194*

8. Notes ..................................................................................................203

9. Appendix: List of War Actors in Data Base ........................................227

10. List of Tables ....................................................................................231

11. Bibliography .....................................................................................232

"It is true that within a group of robbers traits of a human community may develop. But this possibility indicates a fault of the society in which this group develops. In a totally unjust society criminals do not need to be necessarily of less human value, in a totally just one, they would necessarily be inhuman. Single judgements on human affairs only achieve the right meaning in contexts."

*Max Horkheimer*

# Foreword and Acknowledgements

The attacks of 11 September 2001 brought a great deal of attention to political developments that had earlier escaped the consideration of many scholars. Suddenly, states seemed no longer to be what they had been, and warfare seemed to have changed. In public discourse and also among academics who had not worked on non-Western regions, state failure, new wars, organized crime, and transnational terrorism were meshed together into a legitimizing discourse for a new wave of securitization and militarization. This further wave of militarization, as this book will show, will not heal the wounds but will create further problems.

It is a standard mystification in social sciences to do as if results have been reached by lonesome reflection and individual brilliance. I want to stress on the very first page that this book is truly the result of collective action. A somewhat steered, slightly uncontrollable social process of negotiation and debate about single findings and general ideas has shaped this research process from the very beginning. This applies to the content of this book and to its history.

My original interest in armed conflict developed out of the pragmatic decision to bend my philosophical interest in the question of causality into an investigation of the causes of the civil war in Liberia that had just begun when I was still a student in 1989. I stumbled over a group of scholars at the University of Hamburg whose theoretical approach was based on German sociological classics ranging from Karl Marx to Norbert Elias. That approach fits nicely with my inclinations for the philosophy of idealism, but also turned out to be decisive for my later work. It has an undeniable imprint on this book too.

It was only in 2000, that I formed an idea of using a leftover from earlier times itself into a research proposal for the Volkswagen-Foundation: to study the internal politics of non-state war actors. At that time, virtually no systematic knowledge based on comparative research existed on this topic.

When this proposal, entitled "The micropolitics of armed groups" was approved in June 2001, nobody could predict how drastically important this issue would become in just a few months.

However, this is not a book about terrorism. Considering the term "terrorism" as name for certain strategic uses of violence rather than a scientific categorization of actors, I neither intended it to become the focus of this project, nor could I skip the original idea: to study the inner political structures of non-state war actors. Recent events seemed much harder to study than the already challenging subject. The group that began its work in fall 2001 ended up with a sample of cases that can be seen as usual actors in contemporary civil wars, all of them denounced, rightly or wrongly, as "terrorists" by their opponents at times.

Astrid Nissen, Jago Salmon, and Katrin Radtke were these first three PhD-candidates and colleagues I had the pleasure to work with. There is not a single category in this book that has not either fought its way through their challenging criticism with them or was developed jointly in these discussions. I gained from them countless insights on the intricacies of field research under sometimes extremely difficult circumstances, and also the experience of true solidarity that accompanies constructive criticism. This book would not have been possible without not only their written work, stories and assessments. It was their field research in Sri Lanka, Eritrea, Canada, Sudan, Lebanon, Nicaragua and El Salvador that formed the basis of a three-year long discussion in comparative politics. My own research in Serbia, Senegal and Mali would have been much less telling without that contrast.

Teresa Koloma Beck, Daria Isachenko, and Alex Veit joined the group as the so-called "second generation" in 2004 and have commented on every single page of this text. Stefan Malthaner did the same, and laid another foundation for it by editing portraits of eighty armed groups and turning these accounts into a data base. I profited greatly from their expertise and field experiences in the DR Congo, Angola, Moldova, Cyprus, and Lebanon. The "second generation" created a challenge insofar its members represent the combination of post-modern sophistication, historiographical exactitude, the abstract reasoning of social system theory, and the precision of well-founded political science research. Forced to defend my arguments against these four furies I could not but learn and also never felt alone.

Given this background, more than one school of thought comes into play in this book, and more than one methodology has been applied for the research in which it is grounded. In addition to a database, comparative studies and single case studies have been undertaken to minimize blind spots that stem from narrow methodological choices. What is presented in this book is based on field research in 15 countries[1], on interviews with war participants, local experts, and representatives of local populations as well as the analysis of a dataset of 80 cases. The conviction supporting this mixed approach is that neither quantitative factor analysis nor single-case phenomenology suffices in coming to terms with the complexity of armed violence.

Although this book is based on a collective effort, I accept full responsibility of what is said and asserted in it. All errors are mine, I am fully aware of its sometimes brittle basis. My only excuse is that the negligence that political science has shown towards non-state actors for such a long period could not be overcome in a comparatively short period of time. This and my conviction that an adventurous thought is better than none have induced me to say a few more things than high standards would have allowed. But most, if not all books are like this.

My and our greatest debt is to all those who were willing to talk about experiences that were not easy to live through nor to remember. Personally I also want to thank Dejan, Mira and Branka in Belgrad for hosting and aiding me in my regards. Apart from the groups's members mentioned above, Peter Waldmann, Joel S. Migdal, Tom Lewis, Jutta Bakonyi, Daniel Chirot, Kristin Bakke, and Dietrich Jung read parts or the entire manuscript and were not hesitating to contradict. Furthermore I owe a lot to Olawale Ismail and Natalija Basic for discussions and sharing insights that are rarely presented in published texts.

During two conferences in Berlin we gathered critical comments from colleagues. Stathis Kalyvas, Roland Marchal, Marie-Joelle Zahar, Alpa Shah, Marial Debos, Marina Blagojevic, and Pénelope Larzillière had a fresh view on what might at times have looked like an esoteric endeavor. Thank you for the refreshing comments!

During talks at the University of Copenhagen, Zurich, Oxford, Bordeaux, Seattle and several Universities in Germany students and colleagues were supportive and critical as well, a good blend that made me work harder in order to refine the argument and to overcome where necessary the narrow boundaries of political science.

In the same way the working group "Orders of violence" in the German Political Science Association was a constantly stimulating intellectual environment as well. I am extremely grateful to Antje Holinski, Barbara Lemberger, Lisa Tschörner and Meike Westerkamp, Sevda Simsek and Manuel Winkelkotte for their help as student assistants and Tim Wise and Anja Löbert for proofreading the entire text. If it still looks foreign to native speakers, it is certainly not their fault.

Finally, I want to thank Humboldt University at Berlin for hosting the research group between 2001 and 2008, and, of course, Volkswagen-Foundation in Hannover, Germany, for the unique opportunity to work with a young group with means independent from the usual institutional quarrels and for its readiness to allow all deviations and shortcuts in budgeting and research that have been inevitable during the period of the last six years.

Berlin, December 2008

# 1. Introduction

## Armed groups as figurations

"You know, in 1993, in Bosnia, it was a war of everybody against anybody. There were only shaky alliances, like we had only two times. One was near Sarajevo, when we could see from the hills that Muslims and Croats down there would fight each other til the last man would be killed. The Croats asked us whether we would help them and so we did. For eight days I fought together with the Croats although we never trusted each other really. And we had fought against each other for at least a year.

In Bihac, we had an alliance with Fikred Abdic, another militia leader. We were militarily and technically much better, and he had Serbs as officers in his forces. But we were never sure. It was like shooting to one side and looking with the other eye whether the man next to you is still trustworthy. But since we were technically superior, we also rented tanks to the Croats. They paid in coffee, cigarettes, and money, and most importantly in fuel, as we were lacking it because of the sanctions.

Also, at another occasion, Bosniaks and Croats were fighting each other harder than we had ever seen in any war. It was like an extermination. The Croats felt they would be defeated, so they asked us to let them through in order to save their lives. They could only pass through our territory. So we helped them by organizing cars and busses. Later, out of these people, a unit of volunteers was formed in Split. When they were safe and had recovered, they massacred Serbs in an unseen way. Later the unit met in a stadium, about 1,600 men, and the Serbs bombed it with all means we had. It needed to be transmitted through the civilian radio to stop the bombing, as it was no longer possible to do it via the military channels."

(Interview with Serbian war veteran, Belgrade, October 11, 2005)

This short account of the vagaries of war stands like a paradigmatic example of what led many observers to the conclusion that with the end of the Cold War, an age of new wars had begun.[2] What had previously been conceived about the reality of war, the image of well-ordered troops led to the battlefield in hierarchical orders, taking care of innocent civilians, and subordinated to the political will of governments with clear agendas and strategies, no longer seemed to obtain. Instead, rampant opportunism, rapid change of balances, seemingly unlimited violence, and the breakdown of chains of command – all these phenomena which became so evident in the wars of dissolution of the former Yugoslavia apparently indicated the end of an era.

The key explanation that authors of political science, sociology, and other academic fields have offered for this new face of war was that there were now new non-state actors involved in these conflicts who would neither obey the logic of states and routine politics, nor the regulations of warfare.

This book investigates the politics of non-state war actors in wars after 1945. Its focus is on such armed groups' attempts to overcome what I call the "shadow of violence", the de-legitimizing effects of the violence they exert. Converting military power into rule is their ultimate task. The success of armed groups in these attempts differs enormously as two cases already illustrate:

On January 10, 1981, the *Frente Farabundo Martí de Liberación Nacional* (FMLN) launched a general offensive in El Salvador. This alliance of various leftist groups had decided to start a revolutionary civil war after all leftist organizations in that country had suffered severe repression by the state's security apparatus since the mid-1970s. The construction of armed wings had already begun, organized by dissidents of the Communist Party of El Salvador, who no longer believed in the reformist approach of the party which wanted to achieve change through direct participation in elections. In October 1980, five leftist groups founded the alliance, and it was an open secret at the time that Fidel Castro had wielded his influence to coax the groups into this coalition with a unified command.[3]

The FMLN was led by the *Dirección Revolutionaria Unificada* in which each of the five member groups was represented. And while envy and rivalries within the FMLN continued for the next 10 years of warfare, it was holding together throughout that period and eventually became the body from which the FMLN was transformed into a regular political actor, a political party that since 1992 has been participating in elections on various levels in El Salvador.

This success of the guerilla forces was all the more remarkable since during the years of the war, its opponent, the government of El Salvador, became the biggest recipient of United States military aid in Latin America, receiving up to 1.5 million US Dollars per day to fight the insurgency. Furthermore, within the rebellion, rivalries were at work not only at the top level but reached regional and local military commanders as well. Within the guerilla fighters the internal structures of allying groups could not be surmounted and melded into a unified command.

In the first year of the war, these rivalries impeded military success as the groups did not even loan weapons to each other. Only after its retreat to rural areas, the FMLN gained strength and facilitated local self-administration, schools, and education camps. With an overall number of 3,500 troops operating in battalions of 500 men, the FMLN was able to drive government forces out of huge areas, thus controlling up to a quarter of El Salvador's territory.

The FMLN was unable to decide the war militarily, however, even given huge external support. But it was able to attract more and more international support. Financially, it could thus not only draw on assets gained from kidnap ransoms and on taxes levied on coffee-production in areas it controlled, it also benefited from money provided by solidarity groups in Canada and West European countries. Cuba and Nicaragua supported the guerilla groups, and about 1,000 fighters received training in socialist countries.

As government forces were incapable of enforcing a military victory, it resorted to a strategy of counter-insurgency that not only cost thousands of lives but alienated the rural population as well. Given the military stalemate, both parties turned to the United Nations for mediation of the conflict. After successful negotiations in Geneva, several accords were reached from 1990 onwards, and in 1992 the FMLN declared itself a political party that would henceforth compete for power within the framework of regular politics.

As the war in El Salvador drew to a close in 1990, another war was in the making in Yugoslavia. In 1991 the Federation of Yugoslavia dissolved, and with it the question arose of what to do with its military apparatus. In Kraijna, Slavonia, and Bosnia, multiple armed forces emerged, partly self-declared local defense units, partly parastatal forces that would later become state armies as in the case of Bosnia-Herzegovina or Croatia. It was a time of conquering political power by violent means. Also within the Serbian camp there was competition for state offices. Zeljko Raznatovic was one of the competitors. Renowned under his nickname Arkan, he was the son of an air force officer and allegedly already a problematic child. His father had reportedly approached the secret services to assume care of his son, and so Arkan became a child of these agencies. In his twenties, he operated mostly abroad on behalf of the secret service. He escaped several times from prison, thus acquiring the heroic status known in the Yugoslav underworld as *strahopostovanje* – respect out of fear.

Shortly before the wars in Slavonia and Bosnia began, Arkan organized a militia comprised of hooligans from Belgrad's soccer club Red Star. While this was undertaken on behalf of the Ministry of the Interior, this group, calling itself *Srpska Dobrovoljačka Garda*, Serbian Volunteer Guard, soon developed its own agenda. It became independent of the state's command, largely by looting and spoils from black markets that blossomed during the war under conditions of sanctions against Serbia. Arkan was more and more drawn into deals for illegally imported gasoline and he tried to diversify his position. He became the owner of a shipping-company, a radio-station, and a casino. Also, he married Ceca, a singer who had become famous in the early 1990s with a new popular music style known as "turbo folk" that blended traditional romantic lyrics and accelerated beats.

Arkan founded his own political party, but he failed to win elections. Then he fortified his house in central Belgrade, because he never felt safe. And with good reason, as events showed, since in January 2000, he was shot by two men in the lobby of Belgrade's Hotel Intercontinental. Prior to that, following the treaty of Dayton in 1995, his volunteer force, once reportedly numbering between 3,000 and 10,000 men, had withered away. With a pending indictment against him by the International Criminal Court in The Hague, he could not leave the country. Within Serbia, in growing competition with Milosevic's son Marco, Arkan had lost more and more ground in the criminal markets that emerged around the sanctioned regime.

Why are the trajectories of armed groups like the FMLN and the Serbian Volunteers so different? Why do some succeed in establishing territorial control quickly, in building clear internal structures, military capacity, and stable sources of income while others crumble away after brief periods or stagnate for years? This is the central question of this book.

Current academic discourse on these actors has not yet developed an answer. Three arguments can be discerned in that writing. First of all there is the viewpoint that asserts a new wave of disorder, of chaos and anarchy, in which ecological crises, unemployed youth, and increased criminality were causal factors in the new outburst of brutal and apolitical violence.[4] A second position, formed around rationalist utilitarian arguments, states that civil wars were largely to be explained by the greed of actors who want to gain control of state resources. "Rebellion is large-scale predation of productive economic activity" as Paul Collier, one of the main proponents of this position, expressed it. Finally, a third position argues that in the 1990s we were witnessing entirely new wars. Martin van Creveld (1991) and Mary Kaldor (1998), for example, believed that they observed a growing brutalization of warfare and a depoliticization of its ends.

As stimulating as this thesis is for the debate on contemporary warfare, it cannot as such explain why the politics of these groups differ so enormously. While these suggestions triggered interesting debates and stirred public interest in the subject, they did not delve deeply into explaining divergent trajectories of war actors.[5] As a result, the politics of armed groups, the intriguing interaction of violence and political structures of which insurgents are agents and objects, was overlooked. This was also due to the lack of a theory with which such a task could have been approached. Political sociology, I argue, offers such a theoretical perspective. Using this vocabulary I want to show that it is the de-legitimizing and legitimizing effects of violence that are at the core of the dynamics which decide about an armed group's fate.

In this book, armed groups are conceived as figurations, that is smaller social settings, groups and less structured collectives, and as ensembles of interdependent individuals. These individuals are linked by asymmetric power balances, as they exchange favors or commodities, as they maintain emotional ties, and even as they fight. Many things can thus be sources of power in these relations that become balances. But these precarious balances are not equilibria. They constantly shift and are almost never truly balanced, due to the persistent action of actors and due to acts of contestation and acts of consent.[6]

This understanding does not intend to reduce the political to either intentional actions of individuals or to the structure of societies or systems, but to stress the relations between individuals as the forming element which constitutes the subject of sociology. Norbert Elias started his study of figurations in his work on the royal court in European history (1983) in which he showed that the figuration of a royal court society was reducible neither to the king's decision, nor to abstract structures of absolutist societies. The architecture of Versailles, the rules of life at the court, and the habits of its officials – all this, Elias found, was part of the court society as a figuration. Kings' rule did not differentiate between private and political issues, and all members of court society felt obliged to the ruling dynasty by personal ties. And although the figuration of the court does not yet know the many distinctions between codes and spheres which characterize modern political systems, absolutism already achieved the monopolization of taxes and of the legitimate use of violence, at least in its external relations. Even more remarkably, the politics of courts surpassed the logic of personal relations insofar as the death of one incumbent did not necessarily entail the crumbling of the figuration. As shaky as the succession might often have been, dynastic principles remained largely unaffected.[7]

Elias' main point in his analysis of court society as a figuration was the argument that this system cannot be understood in terms of modern political language and conceptions. The symbolic world of the court, its economic basis, the royals' "ethos of status consumption", as well as its ceremonies and etiquette were all part of a pattern of interdependencies between the court societies' members. This totality can only be understood through the study of these particular interdependencies.

Armed groups can be studied in a similar vein. They also crystallize around nodal points and consist of interdependent individuals linked by asymmetric power balances. Like a royal court society, they produce their own symbolic world and work as socializing institutions for their members. By focusing on relations and interdependencies, the concept of figuration allows us to abstract from individual peculiarities and idiosyncrasies without losing sight of them. What matters are the relations, the unstable power balances. Using the noun "balance", Elias' intention was not to maintain that these relations are equal or even just in a normative sense. On the contrary, he stressed the continuing struggle in these relations and the never ending game between those involved in finding the "balance". The expression "balance" strikes the right note in view of the fact that power relations are never exclusively dominated by one side.[8] Of course, the relations that constitute figurations are not among equals. There is a difference in the ability to exert power, as those more powerful dispose of more means or resources than the less powerful in this relation. But power is never total or absolute. It is always limited in space and time and also in its social reach. This applies to armed groups as well as any other set of social relations.

Another reason to perceive armed groups in this way is the fuzziness of their boundaries. It is almost always impossible to draw a clear line between members and non-members of insurgencies as forms of participation differ appreciably. Contrary to terms like organization or group, the concept of figuration does not presuppose such clear boundaries, rendering the concept more appropriate than any other for the study of armed groups.

Every figuration has a history. Armed groups also emerge in a broader given social context, and they bear traces of earlier phases of this context. And as much as new forms and practices may emerge in figurations, they are always a combination of the new and the old. They do not differ in all regards from their environment.

Furthermore, as the two entry stories have shown, armed groups are dynamic. The interdependencies that constitute them change when any of the other relations is changing, for example when new resources become available, when somebody involved in a figuration loses a capacity, or when new agents enter a figuration. Figurations continue when their constituting power relations can evolve into forms of domination, but they can also be weakened, erode to mere power relations, and eventually dissolve altogether. This happens to armed groups as readily as any other figuration.

In this regard, armed groups differ little from other social organizations. Their main quality, however, stems from the physical violence they employ. Violence casts a cloud on social relations that is due to the short timeframe it introduces and its psycho-physic effects. Violence cuts short, it interrupts, it inflicts pain, and it has lasting effects. This "shadow of violence" falls on each single organizational aspect of armed groups.

Moreover, violence is power. Insurgents need to turn this power into more stable relations and ultimately into domination. Max Weber's distinction between power as "the probability that one actor within a social relationship will be in a position to carry out his own will despite resistance", and domination as "the probability that a command with a given specific content will be obeyed by a given group of persons"[9], is the second foundational theoretical distinction of this book. The politics of armed groups oscillate between mere power and its institutionalized form, domination. Armed groups need to gain legitimacy in order to turn the power of violence into legitimate rule. However, the power of violence remains ambivalent: it almost always legitimizes and de-legitimizes political actions and actors. In the chapters that follow, I will discern mechanisms at work within and around armed groups that either favor or impede legitimization of power positions that armed groups acquired using force. The "shadow of violence" is key in all of them, as violence can legitimate power, but it can also have de-legitimizing effects.

Violence, power, and domination are core concepts of political science. By using them as the key variables at work in figurations, I want to develop a theoretical viewpoint that surpasses the reductionism of economic approaches and the murkiness of culturalist essentialism. My central argument why some armed groups succeed in their quest for political domination while so many others fail concerns the politics of armed groups. The key variable that explains this issue is legitimacy. Only those groups that achieve a minimum of legitimacy among their ranks, in their community, and in the international community are able to establish and maintain political domination.

There are, of course, countless reasons why armed groups fail. Most are related to the inability to meet simple organizational requirements that emerge in organizing armed violence and territorial control. Armed groups differ from other organizations by the fact that physical violence is an integral part of their mode of operation. And as the exertion of violence always has both legitimizing and de-legitimizing effects, it is particularly hard for armed groups to succeed. Being de-legitimized by violence is the main danger on the way to domination. This "shadow of violence" is cast on all relations armed groups maintain or want to establish.

With this argument, I offer an alternative to prevailing explanations built on a *homo economicus* model, especially on the role of resources in civil wars. By bringing back a truly political theory of insurgency, I argue that it is the "shadow of violence" and the ensuing dynamics of legitimacy that largely explain the particularities of the politics of armed groups.

## The structure of this book

The aim of this book is not an all-encompassing theory of violence or war but to reintroduce political sociology into the debate on contemporary warfare. This shall allow us to go beyond an understanding that limits itself to utilitarian rationalism. The claim connected to this reintroduced perspective is that it is able to explain more features and varieties in the life of armed groups in a theoretically coherent manner. At the same time, I do not claim to explain every aspect of the politics of these figurations. The proclaimed task of this study is rather to reveal the most fundamental mechanisms of these politics.

In the second chapter, three mechanisms of how armed groups come into being will be distinguished. It is a thesis running through this book that the context from which armed groups evolve plays an important role for their trajectories. This can be seen first in the three mechanisms distinguished here. Insurgent groups are formed either as a result of violent repression, as ad-hoc groups formed by excluded members of the political class, or they spin off from authorized state violence. In any event, state agencies play an important role in the production of armed groups, as will also be shown by a statistical overview of biographies of leaders and staff members. In these biographies, the shadow of violence can already be observed in the sheer number of previous experiences of violence.

Doing interviews with veterans forces one to acknowledge that the experience of organized violence made enormous difference in their lives. The experience of violence, having both exerted it and been afflicted by it, becomes pivotal in the biography. As well, the organizational life of armed groups is heavily influenced by the practices of violence the group exerts. These practices, their explanation, and their outcomes are the subject of chapter three. The relation between violence and legitimacy is complex, but three elements seem to be essential. First, organized violence by armed groups needs to be legitimated. How this is done is dealt with in the first part of this chapter. Second, violence can legitimize outcomes as well as actions and it has the tendency to lead to further legitimizations of violence. And the third aspect is de-legitimization through violence. The wounds and the scars, the suffering and the traumata, both of perpetrators and victims have long lasting effects on social and political orders and their possible justification. The organization of armed groups is closely linked to these effects of violence. Already, the mode in which armed groups are formed has an impact on the types of violence they practice. Moreover, violence derails quite often, threatening the legitimacy of a group both within its ranks as well as in its environment. This chapter thus investigates the causes and effects of derailing use of force, based on a concept of violence that tries to explain its contradictory effect of being able to legitimize as well as de-legitimize actors and political structures.

The fourth chapter, on discourses and ideas, deals with the workings of legitimacy in a wider perspective. The de-legitimizing effects of violence threaten the success of insurgencies. But there are countervailing forces to this threat. First, armed groups can benefit from forms of basic legitimacy that can accrue to them if they achieve the ending of open violence. If they are also able to maintain an acceptable degree of order, the momentum of ordinary life may help to restore normalcy which in turn stabilizes their position. In order to bolster these crude forms of acceptance and turn them into legitimacy, armed groups deploy political programs and narratives that put their political project and their rule into a series of political necessities. Any of these programs, as I will show, is bound by the cycle of charismatic ideas.

It is through these policies that armed groups can also alter their sources of income. In an economic environment that is increasingly marked by the shadow of violence, capital stock will devalue, and armed groups must develop strategies to deal with that challenge too. These strategies, with their limits as well as their consequences for the organization of armed groups, will be the subject of the fifth chapter. Armed groups can either stagnate or be disconnected from their social environment, or their economic strategy can lead to para-states in which insurgent groups act like governments. Many armed groups, however, discover new sources of funding, albeit not always by strategical decision but in an iterative manner. This chapter will show what the conditions of these strategies are and what factors limit or allow their use.

Conditions necessary to create legitimacy and limitations on developing means to fund their war are the main structuring elements in the organizational life of armed groups. Both in turn can be explained by contexts and structures in which armed groups move. However, there is room for maneuver, and as will be shown in the sixth chapter, some armed groups are more apt to deal with the endless challenges their violent politics create. As far as I can see there are two main pathways to institutionalization by which the power of arms can first turn the armed group into domination within the figuration and then within its social environment. One is the way of patrimonialization, marked by central redistribution and clientelist structures. The other one, formalization, is more difficult to achieve. But there are also armed groups that develop bureaucratic features. How this comes into being and is maintained, depending again on the structures, the composition of the group, and the habitus of leaders will be seen. The central argument includes centrifugal tendencies within the groups and their centripetal techniques that determine the outcome.

The last, conclusive chapter again assesses the theoretical concepts of this book and connects the politics of armed groups with larger debates on world politics and the formation of states. The shadow of violence, finally, is also cast on state policies that include violent means. Armed groups maintain dynamic interactions with these states. The last question addressed in that chapter is whether the politics of armed groups can be seen as processes of state formation.

## On methodology

The methodology of this book is first and foremost comparative in nature. Using the terminology of political sociology, comparisons were made with a small sample of groups, including semi-structured interviews with war actors, close observers, bystanders, and political office-holders in the respective countries. Large-N sample statistics were only marginally employed on the basis of a database of 80 group descriptions that contain narrative sections as well as coded organizational features (cf. Malthaner 2007).

The main research on which this book is based is the collective discussion of a group of seven PhD-candidates and the author as its supervisor. Each of the candidates spent at least six months of field research in the years between 2001 and 2007. My own research during this period was carried out in Serbia, but I also draw on earlier field research in Uganda, Mali, Senegal and Liberia. These different experiences and cumulative reading were the fruitful background of comparative discussions of cases concerning all the general issues evoked in this book.

This approach has its basis in certain peculiarities of this field of research. Wars and armed conflicts since 1945 have so far not been documented to a degree which makes sound quantitative analysis possible. Some wars and smaller armed conflicts have not even become the subject of thorough descriptions. And for those cases in which good and dense descriptions are available, the authors have used a wide variety of theoretical orientations, focusing on various issues. As a consequence, these studies are not cumulative but often need synthesis from further theoretical viewpoints.

Within the academic debate there is not even an established understanding of what the term "armed group" includes and excludes. The operational definition of armed groups in this book refers to non-state actors active after 1945. It is evident that the empirical record of this is vast. Using the database of wars after World War II that the "Study Group on Causes of War" at the University of Hamburg established, there have been 206 wars in the period between 1945 and 2000.[10] Given the fact that most groups in wars often show dynamics of fractionalization and splintering, it is plausible to assume that the number of non-state actors in these wars will amount to almost 1,000. The number of groups which might have begun with low levels of violence and withered away after first encountering repressive action is unknown. They, of course, never documented any war statistics. Finer scrutiny began only recently. The "Military Balance", issued annually by the London based International Institute for Strategic Studies, lists 332 armed groups in 2005 which were active in 28 armed conflicts. India alone, according to this list, had 49 groups fighting within its borders, whereas in Iraq for that same year 26 were listed. These numbers lead to the assumption that in the period after 1945 several thousand groups might have been active. Only of a few of them we have consolidated knowledge. The data that is available and used here for comparative discussion is restricted to cases that are comparatively well documented. This results, of course, in a selection bias which relativizes inferences from this data set. However, with the current state of knowledge on this subject, I do not see a viable alternative to this combination of methodical approaches.

It is always a difficult task to delineate armed groups from mere criminal gangs and also from one another, since one of the early insights we derived from our study of armed groups is their extreme volatility. There are always kernels around which armed groups crystallize and almost always certain centers of authority and forms of hierarchy. But to delineate membership is a tricky task. People, mostly men, join armed groups not only for different reasons, but also in different forms and functions often for very short periods. Seasonal war-participation, loose collaboration, and permanent shifts of allegiance render it extremely difficult if not impossible to establish a sound empirical register of armed groups. The sheer informality of armed groups makes it too difficult and too intricate an endeavor to attempt such a record, since the result will always be unreliable. As a consequence, there is no all-encompassing list of these groups as most records either do not include all conflicts or indicate boundaries between groups that could be contested with good reasons. A complete register of armed groups is not available, and it is doubtful whether one will ever be compiled, given the low level of documentation of post-colonial states, especially in their early phases.

There are further reasons why it is dubious and unsatisfactory to base an inquiry on armed groups merely on a statistical approach. They involve the quality of the data. The most important reason data on wars are chronically disputable is that these numbers and the information on which they are coded are themselves political. Apart from the usual problems of reliability associated with any data on social life, this political factor renders data on wars problematic, as the case of numbers on war victims might most clearly show (cf. Leitenberg 2006). Numbers on wars are always contested and often construed not least because violence is a subject intricately bound up with morality, and this has the consequence that many aspects of war violence are hidden by secrets and taboos by those involved. Individuals and organizations alike often do not want to give accurate accounts due to feelings of guilt, shame, or fear.

Secondly, the record of wars and armed conflict in that period is incomplete. Many wars are not documented at all, so even the number of conflicts and actors involved is contested in academic debate. This incompleteness is even more dramatic when it comes to information on persons involved and on the interactions within and between warring parties. As a consequence rumors abound and are often taken as reality. Furthermore, media coverage is selective, following other imperatives than to give a thorough account of global events. The peaks and lulls of certain political events and crises also influence the volume and intensity of reporting. While some subjects attract international journalists for long periods of time, others go almost unnoticed.

Thirdly, available information is scattered in archives, books, reports, and not least crucially in memories, in different languages, and in different conceptions. In each case it will likely require the work of generations of historians to establish reliable accounts. This is even harder, if not outright impossible, for all those cases in which no sources exist other than personal memories with all their fallibilities.

Despite these reservations it is possible and recommendable not to forego any attempt to numeralize aspects of warfare. Single case studies and comparisons of smaller numbers of cases carry the danger of exaggeration. Larger numbers of cases, however, can normally only be compared with some degree of numeralization. Taken with care these numbers can thus give at least some indications and help to distinguish stereotypes and good guesses from well-founded theses. That is the reason a minimum of quantitative analysis is indispensable. But it must not become the sole universal tool.

Instead of creating a treacherous numerical soundness by restricting the investigation to statistical analysis, this book draws on additional methodological ideas. Starting with the concepts of political sociology and a number of excellent case studies at hand,[11] the politics of these groups have been conceptualized and further investigated through field research in different contexts. The output of theses from these experiences was then checked with available knowledge on other, similar and dissimilar, cases.

Despite differences in methodological orientations, the literature on armed groups is complementary. Macro-quantitative studies prevail in political science. They draw on rationalist assumptions about combatants' behavior and try to disentangle the intricacies of armed violence by statistical means.[12] Correlation analysis and regression analysis are the major tools of this research school that apparently conceives its aim in mathematically sound theory, born out of calculations on "factors".

Similar rationalist assumptions underlie recent attempts to discern "micro-foundations" of violence. These attempts, however, also include methods such as ethnographic field research and archived data collection.[13] While sharing rationalist assumptions with macro-quantitative approaches, this newer branch of research focuses much more on the interpretation of actual practices of force, attempting to discern the "logics of violence".

Such rationalist abstractions, I argue, need to be counterbalanced by finely tuned accounts of single events and cases. These accounts can most accurately be founded on extensive case-related reading and direct interaction with the actual actors. Case descriptions are much more apt to deal with these differences. Such detailed case studies on single wars or armed actors are normally written by either sociologists, historians, or anthropologists who usually do not share rationalist assumptions. As a consequence, their writing is extremely insightful for the understanding of single stories, but seldom amounts to more general or comparative statements, and frequently omits any theoretical claim.

The literature in political sociology in turn, which would be the most appropriate candidate for this end, has so far not dealt with armed groups. From its inception it focuses instead on modern societies and their institutions.[14] Still, by using the ideas and conceptions of the latter discipline this book attempts to contribute to such an analytical language and to offer testable and contestable theses on the politics of armed groups. The works of Max Weber, Norbert Elias, and others were used for the basic vocabulary for the project of which this book is a result. This theoretical choice has its roots in the conviction that the terminology of this strand of social sciences is the most appropriate to come to terms with an analysis of armed groups' complexities.

Interviews with former war participants and people who experienced violence in their immediate surroundings differ from standard situations of social research. Not only is it almost always impossible to make audio recordings of interviews on these often still highly political issues, this kind of research also entails security issues for both the interviewer and the interviewee as well as other informants. More than once we reached the limits of our intellectual capacity to come to terms with complex and confusing accounts and narratives. The effects of violence were almost palpable in interview situations, be it by the aura of secrecy, the taboos surrounding particular issues, and foremost in the very conspicuous traumata of our interviewees.

Of course, whoever undertakes such a project does not remain unaffected by its subject. The closer one gets to things, the more likely one is to become involved. This is true even for comparatively sedate research topics like administrations or constitutions that do not ordinarily excite passions. But it is even more probable for scholars dealing with violent political processes. And in fact, a huge amount of literature on this topic displays various forms of implications and involvement in the political maelstrom that encircles violent conflicts. Writings of military and strategic experts tend to sympathize implicitly with state forces, whereas authors who are political activists in their respective home countries – but strangely also Western authors, though fairly remote from the actual fighting – often tend to romanticize armed movements in seemingly exotic surroundings.

This book tries to abstain from comments in this regard. Its aim is not to counsel state agencies or international institutions on how to combat violent actors or to help organize such movements, although the author cannot rule out either usage. Ultimately, it is the reader's decision how to utilize the knowledge he or she has acquired. The main intention of this book is grounded in the academic interest of knowing more about what is actually happening and how it works. The only other normative interest connected to it is the conviction that violent politics remain dilemmatic: They create more problems than they solve. The resort to arms does not lead to redemption. However, confronted with violence, political actors often see no alternative to taking up arms themselves. I see it as the scholar's task and responsibility to discern this dilemmatic situation.

Dealing with the subject of political violence, the scholar's task is to remain neutral whenever possible. To understand relations between causes and effects, to discern pathways and their interdependencies with political contexts is the main objective of research in this field. However, the scientific investigation of political violence is not without ethical implications and relevance. One result of the research for this book is the insight that the use of violence creates vicious circles that seemingly perpetuate violence although the opposite was intended. The production of violence expertise, almost if not always undertaken by state agencies throughout the world, is a typical example for such a circle. There are countless stories of how the use of violence did not lead to a final regulation and peaceful transition of conflicts but triggered later rounds of violent fighting instead.

The study of the politics of armed groups may help to develop alternative forms to break with the tradition of reproducing the shadow of violence that in so many instances is rather reinforced and leads to the legitimization of further violence. The immediate lessons for the current political situation, discussed in the last chapter of this book, hint to the importance of local surroundings for the establishment of promising alleys for true political instead of military "solutions". The differentiation of pathways of how armed groups develop, a better understanding of the politics they employ and the problems they encounter is a necessary step for any political design that would not just be another application of a "one fits all" scheme, bound to fail as it reacts rather to external expectations instead of giving specific answers to specific challenges.

This book is also driven by the insight that stories in seemingly remote areas are actually not confined to just these local arenas. The politics of armed groups are in many regards related to the politics in so-called "peaceful" parts of the world. They are affected by decisions taken elsewhere, and they react to them, creating repercussions for those living outside the immediate realms of warfare. The shadow of violence is thus cast on all of us.

# 2. First Movers: the Formation of Armed Groups

"No one knows who is who right now," a New York Times journalist quoted Adil Abdul Mahdi, one of two vice presidents of Iraq in May 2006. The proliferation of armed groups that has been taking place since 2003 surpasses any earlier experiences of the spread of organized violence in Iraq. A "galaxy of armed groups" (Filkins 2006) has evolved, each with its own loyalty and agenda. At the time, in addition to the police and the army, state agencies such as the Ministry of the Interior maintained their own military apparatus, with the Oil Ministry alone having a force of 20,000 troops. Party leaders also had their own militias, mostly recruited along confessional lines. Left uncounted were the rogue units among the 145,000 police officers, commandos, and other officers that have emerged since 2003.

How does this come about? How do armed groups come into being? In the case of Iraq this question might be relatively easy to answer, as the dissolution of Iraq's national armies during Operation Iraqi Freedom led to a power vacuum. According to prominent political theories, this inevitably leads to the emergence of self-help systems which, in the case of Iraq, would presumably consist of regrouped units of the disbanded army.[15] In other cases the background of such stories is less well known. Why and how are armed groups formed in the first place? The perilous acts of organizing a violent subversive group, the refusal of safer alternatives, the danger of being killed – all these risks tend to make the occurrence of armed groups rather unlikely. And while research on motives of recruits has produced various insights[16], the logic of the formation of armed groups remains somewhat enigmatic.

As this chapter will show, there are at least three mechanisms by which armed groups come into being. Based on a statistical overview, on single case stories, and, most importantly, on systematic comparison, these three mechanisms also allow explanation of many features of the further trajectories of armed groups.

First is the mechanism of repression. Violent repression, exerted by government forces, causes political opposition to evolve into armed action. Leaders of these groups are usually not militarily experienced but instead are politicians who have acquired their positions through descent, formal education, and long political activity. Groups that emerge out of this mechanism become armed, as groups they are older.

Second is the ad hoc mechanism. It is activated when neo-patrimonial settings experience crises. Single individuals who feel excluded from clientelist networks of a political class begin to organize violent actions against state agencies. Groups formed through this mechanism are new creations that can include older modes of organization but have difficulty becoming stable due to the vagaries of war. Normally their primary purpose is to overthrow the regime in power, although at times they connect this aim with a broader political agenda.

The third mechanism is often linked to situations of open political violence. This spin-off mechanism is tied to state policies, but its main characteristic is that the group's activities become free from state control. Originally, the formation of these groups is a state project. In times of war, governments or single state agencies often employ informal, non-regular armed forces they can deploy for objectives that regular forces are unwilling or unable to achieve. International law and a loss of external legitimacy might discourage governments from disclosing official orders involving such operations, or at times the professional ethos of military officers and regular soldiers might be an impediment. Very often military stalemates induce officials to create informal armed capacities. In many cases, these informal troops are initially under government control but later develop a life of their own.

These mechanisms have been generated by systematic comparison between 80 cases described in the database. And although they do not cover all cases with the same precision, it is obvious that they delineate pathways that repeatedly appear in the empirical record. In the form they are presented here, they are rather ideal types. Emblematic stories will be used to illuminate the causal relations at work in each of them, followed by a short discussion of similar cases in order to outline the consequences of these formative processes for the figuration's life. Depending on the mechanism of formation, organizational features of armed groups begin to differ as they build divergent figurations. There is also a relation between methods of funding their activities, and thirdly, practices of violence by these figurations seem to be related to the way they come into being. However, as shown in later chapters, the mechanisms of formation do not predetermine the figuration's fate.

## Where leaders and staff originate – a statistical overview

Nobody rules alone, and only very simple forms of political domination can do without staff. Gerontocracy and primary patriarchal forms are among the only figurations in which specialized personnel is not required, as the rulers themselves suffice to enact and enforce their decisions. But any political setting, in which social relations surpass immediate and face-to-face interaction needs some sort of support staff, that is people who reliably acquiesce to general procedures and obey orders of political leaders. This staff is usually augmented by followers and lower ranks. The distinction between leaders, staff, and followers allows the development of rough initial ideas about the foundations and development of these internal relations within armed groups as figurations. The ways in which armed groups form reveal a great deal about their eventual odds of gaining legitimacy, both within their ranks and in the eyes of external observers.

One problem for the analysis of armed groups as figurations is to find a good starting point: What could be an appropriate but preliminary conceptual tool to look at the formation of armed groups? Like other organizations, they might be created by the initiative of individual persons, but they soon become collective endeavors. In most cases the process of foundation involves pre-existing political groups or entire political parties. As they quickly encompass more people than can be controlled by direct contacts, all armed groups soon develop internal stratifications that for want of better alternatives can analytically be separated with the threefold distinction of leader, staff, and followers. Before going deeper into statistical findings, a few elucidations might be helpful in order to alleviate understanding of this Weberian vocabulary and its linkages to the issue of legitimacy.

What can be seen from a rough statistical analysis using this distinction is that states are deeply involved in the emergence and logic of armed groups. This becomes apparent when examining the most frequently shared biographical characteristics of leaders and staff. Also, the ties between leaders and staff members, with few exceptions, pre-date the onset of armed violence.

According to Weber, obedience of staff members is typically based on four sources. First is local customs, defined as those rules that are not yet conventions or law but have somehow developed and are followed with little reflection and with no debate or discussion (cf. Weber 1978, I: 29f.). Second are motives of affection, with the leader's personal attraction and voluntary submission of the staff seen in cases that come close to the ideal type of charismatic rule. The third motive, now widely discussed, in which economic motives are seen to underlie everything, is the chance of financial gain that a position as staff member offers. And fourth, in Weber's distinction, are idealistic motives, or "value-rationality" to use his terminology.

The problem with these motives is that they can rarely be empirically observed in pure form. The "subjective meaning"[17] why single staff members in political organizations usually obey is a mixture of these four elements. The relative weight of these elements varies, but customs and material interest are dominant in most forms. However, if these two reasons alone form the motive for political personnel to follow commands, the figuration is rather instable.[18] The core element of Weber's theory of domination calls for stabilization of relations between leaders and staff, and that constitutes the idea of legitimacy. Both within the figuration and in its external relations, insurgencies need to overcome the costs of violence which consist first and foremost in its de-legitimizing effects.

The argument here is not only that all rulers strive to rouse and groom belief in the legitimacy of their rule. For stable rule it is necessary that at least staff members believe in the legitimacy of the respective order. It is by the type of legitimacy that political forms can best be distinguished. This, as I will argue through the rest of this book, also holds true for armed groups. Their inner functioning, their internal dynamics, and also their external behavior can best be understood and explained by the role and quality of legitimization within the figuration. All three ideal types of legitimacy, charismatic, traditional, and legal-rational, can be found in various blends in these figurations.

It has often been said that it is extremely difficult to empirically ascertain legitimacy. Empirically, hypocrisy can often be observed in hierarchical relations and might be wrongly taken for legitimacy. Also, personal interest, weakness, or helplessness prompt people to follow a given order. Indeed, all these motives are empirically observable in figurations such as those of armed groups. But no political figuration can endure for long without a certain degree of legitimacy, at least in the eyes of its staff. Furthermore, it is not probable that such weak motivations as indifference or helplessness could explain participation in an armed group in its early, most dangerous phases.

It can also be shown that in fact many armed groups that were able to fight in civil wars for extended periods had strong forms of inner legitimacy. It is likewise implausible to assume that a group could keep its organization intact through long periods of fighting connected with suffering, hardship, and huge costs in so many regards without such inner bonds.

The formation of armed group is the process by which such kernels of figurations are formed. As will be seen in the three mechanisms, this formation always takes place within a context. There are always rules, relations, and meanings on which the formation's initiators can draw. This does not necessarily imply that the formation will be successful. An uncounted number of armed groups never surpassed their early stages. The pre-existence of these ties, however, means that there is a foundation on which to build first attempts toward legitimization. As will be seen in many examples, this inner legitimacy provides essential cohesiveness for the internal hierarchies of armed groups. Loss of legitimacy leads to a group's ultimate failure.

The form of legitimacy matters not only for the analytical purpose of distinguishing political organizations. It also reveals a great deal about the entire internal logic of any political organization. The main distinction here is between rule-based authority on the one hand and personal authority on the other. Whereas the former can be identified, for example, in bureaucratic forms of rule, the latter either involves charismatic legitimacy - the belief in a "specifically exceptional power or qualities" (Weber 1978, I: 241) of the incumbent, or the belief in the sanctity of old forms and ties, that is on traditional legitimacy.

As will be shown in later chapters, all these forms of legitimacy, rule-based and personal ones, can be found in armed groups, although never in pure forms, but always blended to varying degrees. Nevertheless, the distinction not only allows tracking changes in the inner organization, it is also fundamental to discern varieties of their original formation.[19]

One way to start the investigation of relations within a figuration is to look at numerical distributions of biographical experiences of leaders, staff, and followers. Bearing in mind reservations regarding statistical approaches to the study of political violence, some quantitative findings can be given on the "foundational personnel" that are worthy of discussion despite these restrictions. They indicate – of course very tentatively – some features of the processes of armed groups' formation. A first look at leaders of armed groups, for example, shows a surprising number of shared features in their biographies:[20]

Table 1: Biographical characteristics of leaders
(N=80; insufficient data: 8,8 %; multiple selections possible)

| | |
|---|---|
| Former professional oppositionist | 73% |
| Academic education | 61.6% |
| Former detainee of state prisons | 46.6% |
| Military education | 43.8% |
| Violent oppositional actions | 43.6% |
| Formerly exiled | 39.7% |
| Education abroad | 37% |
| Academic professional | 31% |
| Member of the ruling political class | 23.3% |
| Military professional | 16.4% |

Source: MAG database

Given the disclaimers above, there is a danger of overstating what can be seen here. One could, of course, develop unique hypotheses for each of these findings, and then all these theses would deserve further scrutiny. No specific profile can be deduced from this list. However, one can see that states, in many ways, are involved in the "production" of the armed groups' leaders. It is supposedly within state institutions that core skills needed for armed rebellion are transmitted. The high percentage of academically educated, for example, suggests that skills such as abstract reasoning and knowledge of bureaucratic and organizational techniques are important preconditions for becoming an armed group's leader. Also, some degree of military expertise, usually acquired in state institutions, is a characteristic of the profile of many armed groups' leaders. And finally, the experience of violence in state prisons and prior political conflicts also suggests a causal relation between encounters with state violence and the resort to arms as a political strategy.

The data also leads to the assumption that conflicts in which armed groups are involved are indeed political. This is suggested by the high percentage of those leaders that have been active as political opponents before they became leaders of violent political groups. Furthermore, it is interesting to note that in opposition to what it is often stated in academic as well as the media discourses, few armed groups' leaders have criminal backgrounds (6.8%) or religious education (9.6%). The "crook" and the "mullah" do not rank prominently among those who instigate and organize armed opposition against regimes in power. A second look at comparable data for staff members of armed groups also leads to some counter-intuitive indications. The following characteristics have been reported on staff members of armed groups:

*Table 2: Features of staff members of armed groups*
(N=80; insufficient data: 30%; multiple selections possible)

| Military education | (66%) |
|---|---|
| Academic education | (55.4%) |
| Former professional oppositionist | (53.6%) |
| Violent oppositional action | (42.9%) |
| Formerly exiled | (41.1%) |
| Education abroad | (35.7%) |
| Professional military | (33.9%) |

Source: MAG database

Of course, staff members attract far less attention than leaders in international media coverage of armed rebellion, and information on them is even scarcer. However, as these numbers suggest, they share a number of features with their leaders. Many have a record of earlier political activity, and their lives were not confined to "national arenas" as shown by the considerable number who left the country as exiles or to pursue education abroad. Academic education also figures prominently.

Within the staff of armed groups there is a much higher percentage of professional military men and a lower percentage of former professional oppositionists than among leaders. This would seem to be the outcome of strategic decisions by leaders to supplement their own skills, which are apparently more often political than military. But it could also be that professional military men are simply less apt to become leaders of armed groups and thus are more often found among staff members than among leaders.

Further findings hint at relations between leaders and staff that are not purely instrumental, as the literature suggests that only interest in personal enrichment induces people to participate in armed rebellion.[21] But greed is an insufficient explanation for what drives the formation of an armed group. Much more conclusive evidence about the mechanisms of how armed groups are formed comes from information on shared experiences of leaders and staff. Table 2 points out that a very high number of staff members share experiences of political battles. Many have the same ethnic background, and in an equal number of cases staff members and leaders know each other from attending the same educational institutions. In 50 out of 56 cases in which there is sufficient information on the matter, there is at least one example of ties between staff members and leaders such as a shared political past, a common ethnic background, or socialization at the same school. This does not prove that personal material interest plays no role in the process of armed groups' formation. These figures do suggest, however, that there are further explanations how armed groups crystallize and function. Other elements of these relations might be of at least equal causal importance.

There is not much data on shared biographical data of leaders and staff members in armed groups. But the evidence at hand shows that quite a number have common backgrounds and shared experiences. We know of 28 groups out of a sample of 80, that leaders and staff members had been active in the same political organizations before the armed group was formed. In 17 groups of the same sample, leaders and a number of staff members went to the same schools or universities, and there are also many cases in which both share the same ethnic background or even have parental ties.[22]

Data on characteristics of followers suggest that these close relationships do not structure entire armed groups. Although material on regular fighters and supporting milieus is particularly rare, the existing literature on the groups investigated suggests huge socio-economic differences between leaders and staff on the one hand and followers on the other. Table 3 at least hints at this difference. It is implausible to assume that members from rural areas would have as high a percentage of academic education as staff and leaders. Nevertheless, in at least half of the cases, students form part of the follower community, and this can be caused by mobilization within the same urban milieus from which many staff members and leaders come. But this certainly cannot be the entire story.

Table 3: Milieus of followers
(N=80)

| Rural population, peasants | (80.8%) |
|---|---|
| Students | (52.1%) |
| Identical ethnic groups | (45.2%) |
| Urban subclasses | (41.1%) |
| Members of other violent groups | (32.9%) |

Source: MAG database

The data given in these tables is useful for preliminary speculation on how armed groups come into being. As such, however, they are not informative of the processes by which formation of armed groups take place. Further evidence is needed for reconstruction of these evolutions. Based on the intense case studies and the comparative discussion of these findings with accounts on additional cases, it is possible to construct the three mechanisms of armed groups' formation discussed in the following.

These mechanisms do not cover all cases of formation. The claim here is that most cases can be explained by one of these mechanisms. The three mechanisms of formation will be elucidated in the following by giving typical stories that will render their causal connections more ostensive. Evidence from further cases will then bolster the claim that formulation of these mechanisms is not merely an unjustified generalization of single instances.

## From party politics to war: the mechanism of repression

In the 1970s and 1980s the Philippines saw explosive economic growth that was partially a result of the boom in nearby Hong Kong, Taiwan, and Japan, but was also transmitted by a calculated strategy of export-led industrialization by the Marcos regime. The ensuing social mobilization complicated a political situation that was already marked by intimidation of oppositionists and illicit techniques to maintain semi-feudal political order (cf. Sidel 1999: 71ff.). During this highly dynamic phase of Philippine history, the Muslim Independence Movement (MIM) emerged.[23] The commercialization of agriculture, migration towards cities, and increasing levels of education all fueled the political dynamics of which formation of the MIM was a part.

Up to the 1950s and 1960s, the Muslim minority in the Philippines was integrated politically through its old social elite's role in the semi-feudal system of rule. The situation began to change when two processes intertwined. First, the Philippine state started an active cultural policy to modernize the Muslim region that was allegedly lagging behind the rest of the country. Part of the plan was to allow Muslim students' enrollment at universities from which they had previously been excluded.

At about the same time, foreign actors began to engage with the same group. Two hundred young Muslims from the island of Mindanao were given grants by Gamel Abdul Nasser in Egypt, allowing them to study at the famous Al-Azar University in Cairo. However both groups that acquired academic degrees, whether in Egypt or the Philippines, could not use them at home because the old elite was still controlling the access channels and excluded the "Moros" as Muslim Philippinos were called since Spanish colonial times. The path up the social ladder was closed. As a consequence a political party was founded whose main goal was autonomy for the Muslim regions of the country. Simultaneously, due to a land shortage in the early 1970s, Christian gangs attacked Muslim farmers, as a consequence of which Muslim gangs formed and took revenge on Christians. The government reacted by declaring a state of martial law. This turned the political party MIM into a guerilla movement called Moro National Liberation Front (MNLF) which launched its first attacks in 1970. Its existing contacts in the Middle East alleviated its situation by quickly beginning to serve as channels for foreign support.

Within months, hundreds of thousands fled from rural areas into cities. The war between government forces and the MNLF ended in 1976 when, in the Libyan capital Tripoli, a peace treaty was signed that contained provision for legal autonomy in the Muslim regions. But because the Philippine government repeatedly delayed its implementation, a splinter group formed that has since negotiated several peace agreements: the Moro Islamic Liberation Front (MILF). Furthermore, another group split from the MILF in 1991, the Abu Sayyaf Group (ASG), who were not at all inclined to political concessions.

At the top of the Muslim opposition were men who started out as politicians. Nur Misuari, the first head of the MNLF, had been active in a communist youth group and studied political science. Being a typical politician turned *guerrillero*, his political skills were useful in the late 1970s for negotiation of a peace agreement. But as the new governor of Mindanao he was unable to prevent dissatisfaction among younger MNLF members and staff persons when implementation of the peace agreements failed.

Salamat Hashkim, the leader of the splinter group MILF, had once been Misuari's deputy and belonged to the group of Al-Azhar graduates. After his return he worked as a librarian but was also politically active organizing Muslim cultural circles in his home area. Through these activities in the late 1960s he came into contact with disgruntled Muslim politicians who had lost their status in the clientelist networks of the Philippine oligarchy.

Both leaders proved to be politically apt and able to negotiate complex treaties encompassing the regulations of autonomy for some southern regions of the Philippines. These treaties also encompassed the integration of thousands of fighters into the military and police forces. Despite multiple rounds of negotiations, the conflict was not brought to an end until 2006, partly because defecting factions like the Abu Sayyaf Group (ASG) disrupted peace agreements and partly because internationalization of the war as a part of the post 9/11 War on Terror aggravated the conflict and led to further military escalation.

But it is not the possible ways of settling a war that are of interest here. It is rather the MILF's process of formation revealing typical elements of the mechanism of repression. Governments in societies that have become unstable are overburdened with tasks that result from these changes. If they represent an old oligarchy, these regimes lose their legitimacy in a rapidly changing social and political landscape.

In order to preserve their privileged positions, these regimes often resort to violent repression of their opponents. This measure usually has more unforeseen consequences than planned ones. It supports hard-liners in oppositional parties and does not encourage attempts to find peaceful solutions. Political activists feel threatened and abstain from political activity or go underground. This renders non-violent politics even less likely, as could be seen in the case of the MIM which became an armed liberation movement after state repression had set in.

The radicalization of existing parties is alleviated by the fact that state repression is often indiscriminate. As Stathis Kalyvas (2006: chap. 6) has convincingly shown, this is always the case when information on opponents is scarce. This typically occurs when government troops are deployed in areas they are not familiar with and thus cannot tightly control. When rebellious forces offer at least partial protection, civilians shift their support towards them. This has been the case in Mindanao as McKenna demonstrates with a number of individuals' stories about why they joined opposition forces (1998: 176ff.). Indiscriminate government repression made the option of joining the rebellion a more rational alternative than flight and non-action. The young fighters, mostly between the ages 15 and 25, were largely reporting that they joined the rebellion to defend themselves and their families against the Philippine government.

In contrast to armed groups that emerge as ad hoc formations, the MNLF could draw on pre-existing structures. The earlier political activity of the MIM had secured not only a broad network of politicians, but it was also backed locally within the Muslim communities of Mindanao and other islands in the southern Philippines. The political experience of its leaders enabled it to hold a political line throughout the years of war, even if during negotiations and implementation of the agreements these structures proved too unstable to endure internal disputes resulting from disappointments and envy among its leaders and followers.

Armed groups formed by the mechanism of repression do not always fragment like the MNLF. Many succeed in keeping their organizational boundaries and build strong bonds of inner legitimacy. The Liberation Tigers of Tamil Eelam (LTTE) in Sri Lanka are a case in point. Having been formed in much the same manner as the MNLF, the LTTE did not falter but became one of the biggest and best organized armed groups with complex internal organization and strong transcontinental branches (cf.

Radtke 2009). Furthermore, most leftist guerilla groups in Latin America have been shaped by this mechanism. More often than not they were formed under oligarchic rule with strong militarist traditions. Similarly, colonial rule often reacted with repression against what was called at the time "liberation movements". The "Frente da Libertação de Moçambique" (FRELIMO), the beginning of the anti-French "Front de Libération Nationale" (FLN) in Algeria and the foundation of the "Viet Minh" during Japanese occupation of French Indochina are identical in this regard. The usual sequence of the repression mechanism of the formation of armed groups can be summarized as follows: [24]

*Rapid social change* → *overstrained regime* → *political exclusion* → *organized opposition* → *repression* → *radicalization* → *armed rebellion*

The common features of armed groups formed through the mechanism of repression thus do not extend throughout their entire life-span. Other mechanisms, dealt with in later chapters, can alter their fate in many directions. The fate of groups that emerge via this mechanism is thus not preordained. As will be discussed in later chapters, they seem, however, to be more successful in gaining political power than armed groups on average. This might have its basis in their social ties and organizational forms that exist prior to widespread armed conflict. Legitimacy is established before violence sets in. Furthermore, the practices of violence they exert differ from those employed by groups which come about through the two other mechanisms presented below. Also, these groups experience different forms of violence. More often than in the groups of the other two kinds, indiscriminate violent repression such as massacres and collective punishments continuously characterizes the conflicts in which these groups engage. Hence, the last stages of the mechanism are seen repeatedly during wars, constantly producing violent resistance.

## Initiatives of the disappointed: the ad hoc mechanism

The National Patriotic Front of Liberia that pushed this West African county into a civil war, lasting with brief interruptions almost 15 years, was led by a bona fide opportunist.[25] Charles Taylor, born in 1948 in marginal Nimba County, traveled to the United States in 1972 and earned a degree in economics. After returning to Liberia he became a senior official in the People's Redemption Council, a junta that had just toppled the regime of Americo-Liberians which had controlled politics in Liberia since its independence in 1847. Taylor did not stay long in a government position. Just three years later, he was charged with embezzlement of 900,000 US Dollars and escaped to the United States. There he was arrested, but escaped under cloudy circumstances from a prison in Boston. Shortly afterward he began his rally for support through West Africa, apparently considering organizing an armed rebellion that would unseat the sub-officer turned president Samuel Kanyon Doe.

Between 1986 and 1989 Taylor traveled through all of West Africa before finding in Blaise Compaoré and Houphouët Boigny, the heads of state of Burkina Faso and Côte d'Ivoire, respectively, two powerful supporters for his plans.[26] They introduced him to Colonel Ghadaffi of Libya who provided training grounds and military expertise to aid formation of the first troops of the NPFL. Taylor also made contacts with businessmen from France and other foreign countries who desired access to Liberia's rich mineral deposits and other valuable natural resources (Prkic 2005).[27]

The main Liberian support Taylor had for his plans came from exiled politicians, driven out by Doe's tactics designed to protect his own power. This group, however, was not homogenous. Indeed a number of Taylor's early supporters, it became clear, had their own agendas. After a few months this led to the first divisions within the NPFL.

Among these exiled politicians was Moses Duopu, a former minister in Doe's government and main recruiter of the first round of members. Duopu had a joint past with Charles Taylor as student activist. Tom Woewiyu, a long-standing opponent of the Doe regime was yet another old friend from student days and became the Defense Minister in Taylor's shadow cabinet. Both later challenged Taylor's position, although with different personal fates. Duopo was killed in June 1990, while Woewiyu survived.

Certain others of Taylor's early companions were included as he needed military expertise to succeed. Prince Yormie Johnson had been trained in military police duties in South Carolina, and had the reputation of being a severe disciplinarian. In 1985, Johnson had been involved in an attempted coup d'etat and was perhaps the most experienced in this regard. But he left Taylor's NPFL in March 1990, three months after the first attack in

Nimba County. His newly created Independent National Patriotic Front of Liberia (INPFL) attracted world-wide attention when it captured President Samuel Doe in August 1990 and later videotaped his torture and execution. Prince Yormieh Johnson had a force of well-trained fighters under his command when the NPFL forces seized the initiative and attacked first (Ellis 1999: 82).

Elmer Johnson, who had served both in the Liberian army and in the US Marine Corps, became acquainted with Taylor when both studied in the United States during the 1970s. Like his namesake he tried to turn the NPFL fighters into a disciplined organization, and in the process aroused suspicion about his loyalty. Elmer Johnson was killed in an ambush on June 4, 1990, not even six months after the rebellion had started. Rumors circulated that he was killed on Taylor's orders as Taylor thought Johnson would use his well-disciplined units to seize the seat of government before he could (Ellis 1999: 81).

Thus within six months, the NPFL was split into subgroups, and it was only through general mistrust and ruthless internal violence that chains of command could be maintained. Although Taylor's plan had worked as intended in so far as indiscriminate violence by government troops drove thousands of fighters into his ranks, the ties within his ad hoc formation were not strong enough to turn this support into a coherent organization, or to contain the competing interests of its most powerful members.

The formation of the NPFL thus shows in an extreme manner the crucial problem of armed groups formed by the ad hoc mechanism. Typically, they consist of members of the political class who have been driven from power during severe crises of post-colonial regimes. Ad hoc groups are created exclusively for the purpose of taking power by force without relying on existing social or political organizations. They might try to borrow legitimacy from older traditions and to impress external observers by using satellite telephones and press officers, but such tactics cannot disguise their chronic instability.

In Weberian terminology, ad hoc groups are "voluntary associations based on self-interest" (*Zweckvereine*) (1978, I: 41), that is their inner logic is the shared assumption of its members that military success is necessary to seize the spoils of power. This shared interest is the weak bond holding the initial group together. Only the charisma of the leader would be a viable source of legitimacy that could overcome this fatal weakness. But in Taylor's case it was the intervention of West African states that prevented him from immediately conquering Liberian state power. The ultimate source of warrior charisma, sudden miraculous success, was thus beyond his reach.

Structures of these groups are chronically endangered as any change in the situation might give incentives for members to exit the shaky coalition. This is the primary reason ad hoc groups fragment as frequently as they do. All members who act with strategic views closely observe any change of options. They leave as soon as they have enough supporters to project a chance to get a bigger share through acting independently. Another problem of ad hoc groups is lack of internal control, leading to uncontrolled violence with its de-legitimizing effects on the group as a whole.

This fragility accompanies ad hoc formations from the very beginning. They have sharply limited time frames to organize a wide range of skills in order to take best advantage of their first military strikes. In the case of the NPFL, for example, it seemed vital that they avoid postponing action as the regime of president Doe was still cut off from official external support. According to unconfirmed reports, the International Monetary Fund and the World Bank were about to resume services to the Liberian regime. Such a step would have increased Doe's options considerably. The most important competencies required to organize this early phase are the ability to raise funds, to organize political support, and to build sufficient military strength. When these competencies cannot be combined in one person, as was the case with the NPFL, centrifugal tendencies are strong from the beginning. Taylor disposed of the political connections to heads of states of neighboring countries and had access to the informal business networks that ruled Liberia's economy. But for military expertise he had to rely on others.[28]

The ad hoc mechanism can be summarized as follows: when neo-patrimonial regimes – or any political systems in which clientelist networks structure political life – come under serious strain, members of the political class will be selectively barred from the spoils of power. An increase of export profits or the loss of international monetary credits can lead to this effect.

Those who are excluded tend to organize armed violence when they find propitious conditions like sanctuaries offered by neighboring regimes willing to offer support. If the central figures are able to enlarge their group's competence by the addition of military expertise, the likelihood that exclusion from clientelist rule will eventually lead to armed opposition increases.

*Political crisis in neo-patrimonial systems* ➔ *selective exclusion from political class* ➔ *leader initiative* ➔ *search for military expertise* ➔ *armed rebellion*

Armed groups produced by this mechanism often become structured along patron-client lines themselves. Two reasons account for this. First, their economy does not differ from the political economy of the system in which they operate. William Reno's account (1998) of Taylor's predecessor makes this point very clear: the economy of extraversion that underlay Doe's rule, this strategic mix of fees for business concessions and rents from plantations plus mineral exports, development aid, and political loans was and would continue to be the basis for the rule of Taylor or any other president of Liberia. Apart from the political loans, Taylor already had control of such an economy in his para-state, "Taylorland" (cf. Prkic 2005). So even when ad hoc groups succeed, they are doomed to replicate the structures they fought in.

This in turn means that their future rule will be threatened by the same dangers they created for their predecessors. Only to the degree the leaders are able to form much deeper and more stable lines of allegiance in their newly conquered territory can they diminish the risk of being overrun by future challengers to their power. The need to create legitimacy first and foremost among the followers does not vanish with the success of these groups' leaders. It is merely postponed.

Furthermore, it is not accidental that ad hoc groups typically develop in settings where systemic change like decolonization has triggered a long-term process of appropriation of inherited institutions, which defines the post-colonial situation. The states of sub-Saharan Africa are one main theater of these processes. Charles Taylor's NPFL in Liberia and Foday Sankoh's Revolutionary United Front (RUF) are not the only salient African cases. Laurent Kabila's *Alliance des Forces Démocratiques pour la Libération du Congo* (AFDL) [29] follows much the same pattern. Supported by governments of neighboring states, single particularly ambitious politicians organized exiled members of the political class and enlarged that kernel by including further personnel with military expertise.

There are striking similarities with processes that developed in states of the former Soviet Union in the course of its dissolution. Here again, the appropriation of new states included violent confrontations between armed groups that formed almost randomly around certain persons. Many of them did not even have sufficient success to receive attention from Western media as Georgi Derlugian (2005) and Valery Tishkov (2004) have demonstrated in the Northern Caucasus. The difference, however, is that in post-Soviet states the patrimonialization was not yet accomplished: the violent conflicts that flourished in the early 1990s have to be seen rather as escalations of the struggles concerning who would appropriate and patrimonialize the newly independent states, whether the old *nomenklatura* would master the transition or which faction from the emerging opposition would succeed in the battle for state power.[30] As in sub-Saharan Africa, intellectuals played an important role in these situations. In Georgia, for example, a specialist in English literature, Zwiad Gamsadchurdia, became president in 1990. He was overthrown by the Mchedrioni, a self-declared militia guided by the sculptor Tenghiz Kitovani and the film critic Djaba Ioseliani. The secessionist movement in Abchasia was led by the erstwhile student of proto-Hittite mythology, Vladislav Ardzinba (Derluguian 2005: 61f.).

Intellectuals appeared as well in African cases of ad hoc formations. Not only was the Ugandan head of state, Yoweri Museveni, a former student of political science. He also supported the leader of a Congolese rebellion in the late 1990s, Ernest Wamba dia Wamba, the unsuccessful leader of the *Rassemblement congolais pour la démocratie* (RCD) who in turn had taught history at the University of Dar-es-Salam before becoming a warrior (Balancie/ de la Grange 1999: 428).

The prominent role of intellectuals in ad hoc groups, but also in armed groups that come about by the mechanism of repression, has much to do with the close relationship universities maintain with the political field throughout the world. Universities not only reproduce a state-class of bureaucrats and technocrats. Especially in times of political crises and growing social contradictions, they are also hotbeds of political opposition. As Derluguian pointed out (2005: 61), what matters are not only the academic skills, such as the ability to formulate political programs, to address a Western public in a foreign language, or to set up an organization. Of equal importance are the contacts, the social capital in Bourdieu's terms, accumulated during the long years in the cultural milieus that are part of the individual's resources. Skills, cultural capital, contacts, social capital are necessary requirements for successful leaders of armed groups.

In the faltering years of the Soviet Union, such intellectual networks often merged with violent entrepreneurs chasing opportunities in weakened states, and sub-proletarian militancy rendered violent escalation in these situations more likely. That the ad hoc mechanism is not restricted to the post-Cold War period can be seen by a number of further cases in which the mechanism occurred in almost its ideal-typical form. A perfect example is Uganda's National Resistance Movement (NRM), formed by the current president of Uganda, Yoweri Museveni, when he was defeated in contested elections in 1980. The NRM also started with a few dozen fighters in February 1981, who were soon joined by those who were, or feared becoming, victims of indiscriminate repression by government forces. At the end of the year 1981, the NRA already had 1,000 members and began to reject volunteers since they did not possess enough guns (cf. Schubert 2001: 78). Initially formed as a group of left-wing oppositionists in neighboring Tanzania, some of the NRA's leading members had learned guerilla tactics in camps of the FRELIMO, which at the time was fighting Portuguese colonial troops in Mozambique. But apart from a rather rhetorical leftist jargon and some signs of Maoist guerilla strategy, the NRA was not determined by the usual Cold War tactics of the time.[31]

Armed groups that came into being by the ad hoc mechanism are thus not a product of narrow periods of time. There are structural histories behind their emergence, and these structures extend into the inner workings of these groups. They rely on inter-state rivalries, and they usually appear in patrimonial regimes. For their emergence this institutional setting is causally much more important than the fluctuations of global politics. The same applies, it seems, to the third mechanism.

## Delegated violence: the spin-off mechanism

One of the most renowned militias of the former Yugoslavia was clearly a state creation. It was the *Srpska Dobrovoljačka Garda* (SDG, Serbian Volunteer Guard), led by Željko Raznatović, also known as Arkan. Raznatović was born in 1952 as the son of an air force officer. He was a problematic child, and his father had reportedly approached the secret services to request they assume care of his son who then became a member of secret units of various federal agencies. In the 1970s, Arkan operated mostly abroad and had arrest warrants in several Western European countries. He escaped from prison several times, for example in Belgium and the Netherlands, allegedly with the help of Yugoslavian secret services (Judah 2000: 184-186). Throughout the 1970s and 1980s he was almost certainly under the protection of these secret agencies (Milivojević 1998).

In 1990 Arkan was again arrested, this time by local police forces in Croatia for having smuggled arms into the Krajina region. Once free, he founded his Serbian Volunteers Guard. Much earlier, Arkan had become a member of the fan club *Delije* (Heroes) of Belgrade's famous soccer club Red Star. This job was also reportedly undertaken on behalf of the Ministry of the Interior, as the members of this club had become hooligans and were seen as a problem for public order. Arkan, who at the time was officially just the owner of a bakery, invited fans on tours in other countries whenever Red Star played matches in the European leagues, and thus he soon became a hero among the Heroes. Most members of this fan club seem to have come from the *banlieu* type neighborhoods of Belgrade where the social contradictions of socialist modernization were particularly hard felt. High unemployment rates among youth, sinking household incomes, and a constantly deteriorating supply of staple goods marked life in the areas of Novi Beograd. But when the SDG was founded in 1991, recruitment for Arkan's guard was not restricted to socially deprived youths, but included people of all ranges of age and education.[32]

The Serbian Ministry of the Interior provided Arkan's militia a training camp in Erdut in East-Slavonia, and he was in constant contact with Radmilo Bogdanović, Franko "Frenki" Simatović, and Radovan "Badja" Stojičić. The first two were high-ranking officials in the Ministry of the Interior, while the latter was the Interior Minister himself. Certainly with their consent, if not on their order, the SDG participated in the siege and capture of various cities in Slavonia and Bosnia and soon gained a reputation for particularly brutal treatment of non-Serbian civilians (Silver/ Little 1996: 185, 222), as one of the main instruments of the policy of ethnic cleansing.

Among Serbian paramilitaries the SDG was well-equipped with light artillery, trucks, and arms from barracks, including tanks according to one source (Balkan-Institute 2003: Fn. 14). Although there is diverging information concerning estimates of its size, ranging between three and ten thousand, it seems likely that altogether around ten thousand men underwent training in Erdut,[33] and that in most cases war participation was not longer than one or two years, while many members stayed only a couple of months.

According to various sources, Arkan introduced a rigid hierarchical structure in the SDG, with corporal and capital punishment for its members included. Recruits for the SDG not only had to swear an oath of allegiance to their leader, they also wore uniforms and were organized in a military style hierarchy. In its internal structure the SDG was thus not much different from a modern army, apart from the fact that it was led by a patriarch with further ambitions. Other characteristics were that he distributed looted goods among his followers, that the SDG paid for the gravestones and funerals of its members killed in action, and that widows of combatants received pensions "as long as he could afford to do so" – all this is still remembered among former members of the SDG.[34]

During the years of war and particularly after the Dayton Agreement in 1995, Arkan had tried to diversify his position. Erdut, the location of the SDG's training camp, became the brand name of a wine company owned by Arkan, and he became the owner of a shipping company, a radio station, and the casino in the Hotel Yugoslavia. His main economic activity, however, developed under the embargo during the war years. Apparently in growing competition with Milosevic's son, Marko, Arkan tried to monopolize the illegal import of petrol and derivatives from Romania and Bulgaria. Other sources also report his activity in further criminal markets, partly in cooperation and partly in competition with Kosovo-Albanian networks (Judah 2000: 187).[35]

Arkan increasingly became a political entrepreneur, making efforts to improve his parliamentary career. His Party for Serbian Unity (*Stranka srpskog jedintsva*, SSJ), founded in 1992, however, did not fare well, and he failed to gain a seat in the Serbian Parliament after 1993. Three years later Arkan became the owner of Serbia's first league soccer club *FK Obilić*. Politically, Arkan had failed, and his erstwhile power base was eroding after the war in Bosnia-Herzegovina had ended. With a pending international arrest warrant and growing competition from rival mafia networks with closer contacts to Serbian authorities, the lives of Arkan and his wife were almost restricted to his fortified house and the lounges of Belgrade's international hotels. In January 2000, he was killed by two men in the foyer of Hotel Intercontinental.

The trajectory of the SDG is typical of armed groups that start out as state militias, and easily become independent of their sponsors. Seemingly, one condition for the fact that many delegated violent organizations develop a life of their own is that the political situation becomes murky as was the case in Serbia during the 1990s. Another is that leaders of these groups have political ambitions and use the power they assemble as a stepping stone to an independent political career.[36]

The desire for personal enrichment, whether by legal or illegal means, was definitely a strong character trait. But even Arkan had shown another face. Many of his actions reveal that his ambition was not just to enrich himself and to prove his masculinity in combat. His eagerness to appear in the media, as well as his attempt to build up political support, suggest further motivations. Arkan's political career, however, was not successful, and his appearances as a statesman might have been instrumental for opportunities that were accessible only through public positions. But his desire for public recognition cannot be overlooked. He succeeded in this regard insofar as his image among militaristic nationalist circles comes close to that of a *hajduk*, those outlaws that served, during the long periods of foreign rule in the Balkans, as a positive role model of social bandits.[37]

Whereas spin-off groups such as that of Arkan are not without imprints of local historical traditions and political cultures, the main mechanism that leads to their creation is state bound. In situations in which governments feel they cannot exclusively rely on their army, they tend to either tolerate or deliberately create other informal armed forces. One reason for this can be that the chain of control is interrupted due to deep political crises and stalemate situations, as was the case in Lebanon in the mid-1970s (cf. Salmon 2006: 110). Parts of the armed forces then become focal points for the creation of militias. In these cases it becomes difficult to judge the extent to which creation of such militias is in fact a state project.

Another reason, probably more often the case, is the deliberate decision of governments or single state agencies to create a second layer of organized violence because the regular forces are seen as either not sufficiently forceful or not trustworthy to fulfill missions which are in violation of international ethical standards. Perhaps for this reason, militias and paramilitary troops created in this manner are particularly prone to commit severe human rights violations in civil wars: they feel legitimized to cross moral boundaries since they know they have state backing, and these transgressions are seldom if ever sanctioned.[38]

Very often, regular forces are not trusted to be ruthless enough to commit these deeds, given their ethos as professional soldiers. The creation of paramilitary forces is thus always the result of individuals' ambitions and strategic decisions within state organs. Exactly how these causal moments mix in each case is a question that can only be answered by empirical investigation. Nevertheless, judging from the similarities between cases, the main elements of the spin-off mechanism can be summarized as follows.[39]

Spin-off groups form in wars or war-like situations. Politically motivated violence is already openly visible, and for individual reasons or in order to support the official state forces, the commander of the state military delegates the right to exert violence to newly created groups. When these groups are successful in the sense that they form, organize, and succeed in combat, their leaders potentially accumulate enough warrior charisma and resources to sever the chain of command to official superiors.[40] The newly formed group then gains its own momentum.[41]

*War* → *informalized state* → *delegation of violence* → *own momentum* → *separation*

Spin-off groups usually encounter several problems not shared with groups emerging through the mechanisms outlined above. Spin-off groups typically do not stand in an openly hostile relation to state forces, although the relation is never an easy one. Not only did many officers of the Yugoslavian army (JNA) detest the militias created by the Serbian Ministry of the Interior.[42] But also the "cossaks" who participated as informal troops in the short war that led to the separation of the Transdniestrian Republic from Moldova in 1992 were viewed with contempt by Alexander Lebed, the commanding general of the 14th army, then stationed in Tiraspol (Lieven 1998: 244).[43] The uneasy relationship between spin-off groups and formal state forces is somewhat ameliorated by personal relations and the fact that they share elements of the same military habitus.

Perhaps even more importantly, spin-off groups become political competitors even if they are deliberately created as auxiliary units by contested regimes. Arkan was a perfect example in this regard. Not only did he come into conflict with Milosevic's son Marko over dealings in the criminal markets. Even more dangerous were his political ambitions. His lack of success at the polls probably saved his life for some time.

Secondly, it is typical for the organizational development of spin-off groups that they desperately lack popular support. From a sample of nine such groups only one reportedly enjoyed considerable popular support, whereas for the overall sample of armed groups popular support was reported to be more than 50 per cent (MAG-database).

Several case stories provide evidence why this situation is found. The creation of the *Resistencia Nacional Moçambicana* (RENAMO), for example, was undertaken by the governments of Rhodesia and South Africa who, in the mid-1970s, wanted to destabilize the neighboring regime in Mozambique which in turn supported the opposition in these two countries. RENAMO was perceived as a foreign power and relied heavily on forced recruitment, mostly of children. Its ultimate success in becoming a partner in the national government in 1993 was only due to the fact that the ruling FRELIMO regime had estranged the rural population with modernization policies whereas RENAMO left local power structures untouched and allied themselves with the colonial chief system.

Thirdly, spin-off groups are much more inclined to use ruthless violence with resultant high costs to their legitimacy. This might be related to the fact that their staff usually includes high numbers of military personnel. Among the nine cases investigated more closely, six leaders have a military education, whereas the overall rate for the entire sample is 43 percent. Also, in six of the nine cases at least some staff members came directly from positions in states' armed forces. In the entire sample of 80 armed groups, this applies to only one third of them. Although spin-off groups become increasingly independent from state control, they might still feel legitimated by the power originally invested in them by state agencies.

Like the other two mechanisms by which armed groups form, the spin-off mechanism is not inevitable. It can stop at any point if conditions for its unfolding are not sufficiently developed. Most of these groups do not survive the regime that has produced them as they are unable to attract sufficient support with their rather vigilante and nationalist rhetoric. Extreme violent practices characterize them in comparison to the two other types. Their programs and rhetoric seems to be overshadowed by their violent practices. However, the case of Abdurrashid Dostum as depicted in chapter six, can be seen as proof that spin-off groups are not always doomed to failure.

## Conclusion

The three mechanisms of formation outlined in this chapter produce slightly different pathways for the future development of the armed figurations they bring about. And although these mechanisms do not determine the odds of these figurations to institutionalize and turn their violent power into domination, the divergence of structural conditions nevertheless accounts for different probabilities.

Groups marked by excessive violence from repressive regimes seemingly do not suffer noticeably from legitimacy deficits. Repressive states de-legitimize themselves, and in turn, targeted groups can garner popular support, especially if they provide effective protection. These groups also generally benefit from social ties and legitimate forms of organization that precede the outbreak of violence.

Ad hoc groups, in contrast, usually have weaker ties at the beginning. They usually consist of connections that are products of circumstances rather than relations cultivated over time. Consequently, their internal functioning is precarious. Shared interest alone does not suffice to create stable organization, and ad hoc groups are therefore more prone to fragmentation and decay. In propitious settings, such as strong support by other states, they can institutionalize and defeat government armies.

Spin-off groups typically consist of organized kernels, relying on state resources during their beginnings, accompanied by respective organizational capacities. While internal hierarchies initially remain uncontested, spin-off groups have enormous problems overcoming the de-legitimizing effects of the massive violence they often inflict. Their retrogressive discourse is seldom able to raise popular support.

Despite differing outcomes, these three mechanisms as processes have many features in common. All three processes of formation of armed groups are, for example, to some degree internationalized. Other states are often involved, or the experts in violence have partly acquired their skills in institutions abroad. Furthermore, political ideas around which a group's program is centered have a long-standing international history, and even the very act of founding an armed group sometimes takes place on another continent or in another country. Also, world historical timing plays apparently a role in these processes.

However, the formation of armed groups always takes place in a local arena, as large and far-reaching as the internationalization of these processes might be. While the political project might be connected to events in other states, it is first and foremost aiming at political change in single states. The most important shared feature of all three processes is perhaps that all of them germinate during political crises. It is certainly not enough to point to particular features in the political economy or to material interest to explain the formation of armed groups. The more challenging question is how and under which conditions these groups form. The three mechanisms distinguished in this chapter share the common feature that these formations often occur in critical situations of post-colonial states, in either a crisis of distribution due to a shortage of resources or in a crisis in which exclusion and political violence already play a role. These situations can be seen as culminating phases of deeper structural change, and through the three mechanisms it was thus possible to say more about the situational and structural background of the formation processes.

Secondly, in all three mechanisms it became clear that these processes are always highly political, although perhaps not in the sense that political has been understood in the Western tradition throughout the 20th century, that is in the divide between left and right, with a liberal position somewhere in between. The politics of armed groups, and this applies to their formation, is political in the much broader sense that it is both an outcome of power and at the same time the organization and exertion of power.[44]

It also has become clear that the formation of armed groups is genuine social action in the sense that it has identifiable actors who act intentionally. There is always somebody who makes decisions regarding the creation of armed organizations, be it in reaction to state repression, to being driven from the ruling class, or in a situation perceived as desperate enough to permit the creation of unlawful armed forces. The resort to arms, as legitimate as it may seem to the individuals involved, is always based on a decision. It does not happen without it.

A third major commonality concerns expertise in exerting and organizing violence. It is overwhelmingly within state institutions that future insurgents learn how to fight by military means. Rough aggregated data presented at the beginning of this chapter alluded to the state itself as a main source of this capacity. The exemplary stories delivered further evidence for this interpretation. Particularly those armed groups that originate through processes resembling the second or third mechanism sketched above involve personnel that has acquired its knowledge of how to use arms and how to organize armed forces in state institutions.

Fourthly, the formation of armed groups seems to be bound to pre-existing milieus, locales, and micro-arenas. When studying the accounts of various armed groups it is astonishing to see that inevitably there is a structure from which groups develop. Oppositional milieus, universities and armies, prisons and schools appear to be the institutional settings in which focal points crystallize that start the formation of armed groups. The reason for this is certainly the simple organizational requirement that shared interest does not suffice for an organization to emerge. There must be other social ties that allow for the aggregation of interest. This is even more evident when high-politics such as incumbency of power positions is at stake, and when the outcome is settled by violent means.

Milieus and institutions are necessary as it is within them that focal points occur which serve as the basis of armed groups. At the center of these figurations are ties that stem from shared experiences such as many years in armies, schools, prisons, or in exile, or having seen the same things and undergone the same or similar experiences. This creates *Gemeinschaft*, to phrase it in old sociological terms, community based on sympathetic understanding which is based on intimate mutual knowledge, "resemblance in constitution and experience", transmitted via shared language, "its true organ in which it develops and unfolds its being" (Tönnies 1991: I § 9).

Yet the decision to form an armed group is in any case not simply explained by communal ties based on shared languages or regional descent. The role of shared experiences of violence and repressive regimes seems crucial for this decision and the strength of ties among the initial group. In this regard the formation of armed groups is just a further example of Max Weber's dictum that: "The community of political destiny, i.e., above all, of common political struggle of life and death, has given rise to groups with joint memories which often have had a deeper impact than the ties of merely cultural, linguistic, or ethnic community" (1978, 2: 903).

The mechanisms of formation sketched here do not explain recruitment generally. As the next chapter will show, parts to the mechanisms, however, occur repeatedly also during the course of a war. That repressive violence by government armed forces drives more and more people into the arms of opponents is a truism and does not need further elucidation. The ambiguous relation between violence and legitimacy, dealt with in the next chapter, remains fundamental for dynamics of armed groups once they have been formed.

# 3. The Shadow of Violence

Violent figurations such as armed groups share many problems with any organization that is founded for a specific goal. Internal communication must be established, different departments with diverse activities require coordination, and the acquisition of funds for the provision of staff is necessary. The very particular character of armed groups, however, originates in the fact that they employ violence as a means of attaining power. As will be shown in this chapter, this choice entails peculiar challenges, since the exertion of violence leaves its effect on the organization. Any attempt to theorize about the use of violence by war actors suffers from the fact that, hitherto, social sciences have not delivered any well-grounded theory of violence.[45] This chapter does not aim to present such an all-encompassing theory as a task of this nature is much too large to be solved in the framework of this book. Instead, what will be done here is a combination of perspectives that will help answer questions related to the contradictory practices of violence of armed groups. At the center of these reflections is the linkage between violence and legitimacy. Organized violence needs to be legitimized, while at the same time it inevitably has delegitimizing effects. This ambiguous relation creates enormous problems for armed groups as the control of violence exerted is crucial for the political success of the group.

Whereas theoretical essays about irregular warfare stress the importance of good relationships between insurgents and local populations, even a superficial study of evidence shows the ubiquity of force in these relations. Violence, it is argued here, spoils these relations, and the shadow of these practices dooms many armed groups to failure. The violence of armed groups derails, and this often decreases the chances of victory.

The current debate on contemporary intrastate wars has so far not delivered a convincing explanation for this phenomenon. The debate that revolves around the dubious dichotomy of "greed" versus "grievance" as explanations for civil wars does not explain why and how violence as a form of behavior comes into play, and the thesis of barbaric violence that has been promoted by several authors only states that these practices of violence occur without giving any coherent explanation why, particularly over the last 15 years, such an outbreak of random violence should have occurred.[46]

Methodically, this chapter deviates from the preceding and following ones. Practices of violence in civil war have only recently attracted serious scholarly attention. There is consequently only a limited number of theoretical ideas based on a fragile empirical basis. This is also due to numerous methodical and ethical issues connected to this subject. Here, I will draw on theoretical contributions and on evidence from a variety of case studies in order to bring these ideas in a systematic relationship, organized along the question of legitimacy and violence.

To focus on the link between violence and legitimacy is certainly not the only way to think about the violence that armed groups exert or are afflicted by. The choice of legitimacy as the main perspective on this manifold topic relates to the general idea of the theoretical perspective of this book. To view armed groups as political actors, as figurations within which relations shift constantly between mere power and domination, necessitates a focus on the concept of legitimacy as the key variable.[47] From such a vantage point, I argue, it is possible to understand the specific dynamics of armed figurations. Their emergence, their rise, but also their fall and decay would remain inexplicable without the vocabulary of political sociology.

This chapter begins with a short elaboration of the understanding of violence in this book. This is based on the works of the phenomenological sociologist Heinrich Popitz who conceived violence as "action power", as a form of power that is situational, observable, and instantaneous. As such it is ubiquitous as an option. Different from other ways of action, violence is always available, even if the concrete forms of its organization and deployment are always limited. In this sociological perspective, physical violence has two main qualities. First is its *immediateness*, the diminishing of the future wherever violence is exerted. It enforces short-term thinking, it devaluates reflection on long-term investments, and it cuts short strategies and patterns of behavior.

The second quality of physical violence is more enigmatic, but is key to understanding many phenomena connected to it. Violence is somatic, and it causes traumatic experiences. This can be seen in the tales and gruesome memories that shape the lives of victims long after the moment or the period when they are injured. It is even conveyed in the fright that comes with stories about violent events, whether they are criminal or political. Violence moves into bodies and minds, and it cannot be easily removed. It is remembered not only in thoughts and narratives, but also in wounds and scars. What I want to indicate by the term *trauma* is that despite the precipitous nature of violence, it can profoundly affect the life and world of individuals and collectives in an instant. The shock that accompanies it will be remembered in an almost physical way. The long-term effect of violence, its particular moral quality, seems to be closely related to these somatic effects of violence, situating it far apart from other practices of power. Violence is marked by its immediateness and, simultaneously, by its deep long-term effects.

But the exertion of violence is always framed. As universal as organized violence seems, historically, its exertion is bound to moral orders that allow and restrain it at the same time. How violence is legitimized in war is thus the subject of the second section of this chapter, in which three constitutive parts are elaborated. The argument that will explain how the use of violence is legitimized first draws on the idea of moral orders that make a fundamental distinction between insiders and outsiders. Further mechanisms contribute to the actual, concrete legitimization of the use of force in practice. First is the warrior habitus, centered on the concept of honor. Second are collective interpretations and narratives that legitimize the use of violence. Thirdly, violence can also be legitimized by personal violent experiences that in turn fuel further violence.

The shadow of violence consists of its traumatic effects. Moral orders do not remain unaffected by the violence exerted. The third section of this chapter deals with this other causal direction, the effects of violence on legitimacy. It contrasts the theoretical ideal of irregular warfare with the empirical findings on the practices of violence that can be observed. The "shadow of violence" is cast upon its practices also due to derailing violence that is seemingly inseparably linked to its organized exertion. Apart from the incalculable effects of intended and strategically applied violence, situational mechanisms, delineated in the last section of this chapter, will help explain why these unintended consequences of military force occur so often.

## The notion of violence: power, immediateness, and trauma

In March 2003, when for the first time I met veterans of the wars in the Former Yugoslavia, it was in the office of a veterans' association in a suburb of Belgrade. This office was located in the local administrative building, and around a table loaded with stacks of stapled papers sat three men and – behind a typewriter – one woman. We were shaking hands and starting a conversation, partly in Serbo-Croatian, partly in English and German. While the woman left to prepare coffee, the men offered me Slivovitz and cigarettes, and I had a chance to study the room's decor. On the shelves one could see more files, but on top of it were a UCK-uniform hat, a broken grenade casing, as well as a small US flag. "These two are war booty", the secretary general explained to me, while the flag was a gift from a US army officer who came once to exchange war stories. "Yes, we were fighting each other. But after all, we are both fighters", the secretary general declared. Next to the shelves were a calendar showing Ratko Mladić, at the time wanted by the International Criminal Court of Justice in the The Hague, and newspaper clippings. One of them showed a photograph in which, as was revealed in our conversation, the association's secretary general, wounded and lying on a gurney, was being decorated by a high-ranking Serbian general.

The small group around the table, it became obvious, was assembled in order to present the visiting German academic a sample of veterans who remained engaged and eager to tell their versions of events, "the truth" as they called it, being well aware of what was thought and said about Serbia's role during the Yugoslav drama in German and other Western media.

The next thing I was shown was an illustrated book – you would not call it a coffee-table book although similar in size – that contained dozens of photographs of war victims, heads cut off, mutilated bodies littering the streets, corpses both in uniform and in plainclothes. The book had been published in Sweden in the early 1990s and was intended as a documentation of war crimes committed against Serbian army members and civilians during the war in Slavonia and Bosnia-Herzegovina. The pictures were shocking. But my reaction to the brutality depicted was not shared by the veterans who continued to converse avidly on the topic of the injustices world opinion inflicted on them in making Serbia the scapegoat for all crimes that had happened during the early 1990s and then later in Kosovo. As a final proof of their suffering, one after another removed his shirt and explained to me the scars on their chests and backs. The marks of war, I thought, were limited neither strictly to the narrated nor to the physical. The trauma that had affected them in their inseparable function as doers and victims consisted essentially in a multi-layered complex of words, thoughts, feelings, and physical pain.

Violence is understood in this book as a form of action power that consists of the willful injury of the physical integrity of a person by individual or collective actors.[48] Exerting violence is exerting power. In Weber's definition of the term, "power" – the chance to assert one's will against resistance – is not restricted to violence, as there are endless other forms of power. But violence stands out as a particular form of it, with particular consequences. The reason for this is an anthropologically given fact, the vulnerability of men (Popitz 1992: 25). According to this view, violence does not necessarily rely on existing relations. It might not even aim at establishing a relation between an actor and a victim. Its main feature consists in its character as an action. According to Popitz, the vulnerability of human beings is the anthropologically given fact that allows this form of action power.

In war, violence does not happen without forewarnings. It is organized, it announces itself. There is a front approaching, rumors abound, and people flee or hide. But still, even these strategies of avoidance prove its first essential quality. Violence casts a shadow of immediateness. This comes to the fore in almost all eyewitness accounts of war.

"Whatever I do now, I always get my hands dirty, like when I tried to repair my oven yesterday", notes Margret Boveri, a German-born journalist, during the last days of Nazi rule in Berlin in April 1945. Soviet troops were entering the city, fighting their way street by street, house by house, against the remnants of the German *Wehrmacht* and the *SS*. Both armies were spraying artillery fire over the not yet conquered areas.

"The reason for this permeating dirt is that due to all the hits of shells and the concussions the air is filled with dust. Just yesterday another door on my storey was hit. [...] None of us is thinking about the fact that world history is happening here, right now. We can only think of the most immediate things, and this is first and foremost that our house is not hit. Nobody has any inclination or time to reflect on what will happen later".

(Boveri 1970: 58)

It is a recurrent pattern in accounts of concrete war experiences that short-term thinking prevails. The exertion of violence creates the primacy of *immediateness*. The danger of being even more severely injured or killed on the part of the victim, the danger of retaliation or of a change in the relation of forces on the part of the perpetrator makes it risky to continue for both. Short-term thinking in violent war situations therefore is in no way related to cowardice or stupidity. For most people exposed to war violence it becomes a vital necessity to think in terms of immediate consequences, of short-term chances to escape from a situation, or of raising defense levels.

This, of course, does not mean that violence cannot be planned long in advance. In modern societies armies and police forces are created specifically for that purpose – to organize the use of violence and to stand ready to deploy it. Also, traditional warfare is planned, insofar as training and raids do not happen spontaneously but with long-term preparation including the training of fighters. But quite differently from other means of power – for example the mills of bureaucratic rule – violence is action power, and as such it creates its own temporality once it begins. It creates emergencies, immediate dangers.

Action power, as Popitz describes it, can take on different forms among which violence is only one. Any sudden utterance or display of power differences can be seen as action power as it enforces immediate reactions. But violence is a specific form of action power since it has another quality that, oddly, has particular long-term implications. The feeling of pain, the fear that is experienced on sight of the means of violence is not ephemeral. Violence will be remembered due to this physical dimension. Wounds, scars, and losses remind one what has happened. Narratives and discourses about violent events prolong this memory and reiterate the questions of guilt, shame, and honor. This is the reason physical violence also has an almost timeless quality. It de-borders regular temporality; it tends to perpetuate the state of emergency in minds and social relations created by violent means. This primary effect of violence, exerted or threatened, is the *trauma*.[49] This expression shall indicate that the particular character of violence as a form of power stems from the existentiality that its exertion always implies.

Both qualities of violence have consequences for politics that go far beyond the actual situation in which violence is used as a means to change power relations. The specific temporality of violent politics renders the construction of domination extremely difficult. First, as the power effects of violence are short-term, they require reinforcement by other measures in order to change them into something more stable, more enduring. The task of transforming the momentary power effect of violence into a longer lasting political form is equivalent to the challenge of changing power into domination, a dynamic that a successful armed group has to master in the same way as any conquering army.

The second political consequence of exerted violence is that perpetrators need to overcome trauma and fear. Victims of violence will for a long time remember their experience. Fear is, therefore, the immediate successor of trauma, and the historical record is replete with examples of how trauma and fear have been used as instruments of political rule. But systems of rule, if they are to have any chance of longevity, cannot rely on these principles alone. The almost insurmountable task for armed groups, therefore, is to change trauma and fear into toleration or even support. In this regard, the politics of armed groups resemble the task of state-building as they need to draw on moral codes for the legitimization of violence.

Independent of actors' intentions, large-scale organized violence is thus a political phenomenon *sui generis*. It directly affects political institutions and rules. It changes boundaries; it destroys social ties, and creates new communities of fate. A huge part of political history revolves around these changes, induced by organized violence, and resulting in new moral orders which legitimize and restrain the use of force.

How violence is framed and organized differs enormously. Currently, the development and global spread of statehood as a political form has become the frame, reference, and evaluation for the conceptual discussion of violence. Historically, however, it has been only one form among others of the organization of violence. Empires, cities, tribes, clans, or families also have a moral order that distinguishes between the rules that apply for insiders and those that apply for outsiders. Violence normally marks the border.[50]

Political entities form, in the words of Norbert Elias, "survival units"[51] that distinguish between an insider and an outsider morality. Modern states institutionalize standing armies and police forces as special agencies for the use of physical violence.[52] Both underlie specific regulations. At least theoretically, armies and police forces base their troop training on rules derived from textbooks and according to accumulated experiences of how violence can be deployed in a coordinated and efficient manner. Military training and separation from civilian life have been used as techniques to control troops' use of violence and to enforce rules about how and when it is put into action.

In reality, rules of different forms might overlap or contradict each other since social change affects the organization of violence and its legitimacy. Layers of historically different moral orders contradict one another, and the boundaries of the legitimate use of violence remain contested. Even in most modern states there is still political argument about the legitimacy of state agents' authority to decide the moral orders of private homes, as discussions about the consequences of domestic violence prove. But whatever the relevant laws might be in single contexts, violence today is mostly a question of states. The organization of violence is monopolized and regulated. They established patterns and procedures of when and how these organizations are employed and set into motion. These regulations constitute orders of violence that change over time due to challenges to their authority.

Within each of these orders, whether state-like or not, violence thus is morally framed. Some practices appear legitimate, others do not. Where the line between legitimate and illegitimate practices is to be drawn varies historically and across cultural settings. What is universal in this regard is the distinction between moral codes that apply within survival units and those that apply to their external relations. Violence is legitimized in different ways, depending on whether it is exerted against outsiders or insiders. This fundamental difference between insider and outsider morality is that outsiders can be treated "callously, opportunistically, or in any other way, but they are not subject to demand for ritual conformity" (Collins 1986: 215).[53]

The formation of armed groups as it was outlined in the preceding chapter is the creation of such a survival unit that distinguishes between what is allowed inside and what is legitimate in regard to external opponents. This distinction between insider and outsider morality is the essential source for the legitimacy of violence. As could be seen in all three mechanisms of the formation of armed groups, the creation of these boundaries usually draws on existing institutional boundaries and rules. As will be seen, these demarcations move due to the violent politics of armed groups.

## Legitimizing violence in war

The logic of insider and outsider morality is one means to understand the legitimization of violence in a very general way. It builds the broader framework of dynamics in which shared or individual emotions are of equal importance to the nested circles of violence. The concept of social honor, closely related to such emotions, helps to explain how violence in war is rendered legitimate and how it is regulated. Numerous anthropological, historical, and sociological studies have demonstrated the fundamental importance of these codes of honor in the social organization of violence.[54]

Three elements seem to be crucial here. Traditional and modern forms of the warrior habitus centered on a concept of social honor constitute the first. Collective interpretations of violence are the second, and individual experiences of violence are the third. These three elements usually constitute the legitimization of violence both within armed groups as well as for the constituency they attempt to mobilize.

Along the lines of moral orders as they are embodied in states or other political organizations, legitimate violence is seen as serving the maintenance or expansion of political organizations. On this institutional level, the organization of violence is thus not only tolerated but openly supported by the respective morality of this organization. The range of these discursive forms extends from heroic tales to symbols, speeches, textbooks, and sophisticated doctrines concerning the rationale and structure of modern armies. Particular national experiences, often narrated as historical "missions", form the basis of orientation that a professional soldier learns during extended periods of systematic instruction received in the military.[55]

This doctrine is supported by the official accounts and narratives that each state teaches in schools and that are often reiterated in public discourse. The exertion of violence by soldiers of modern states is thus deeply embedded in the public discourse regarding the value of nationhood, modern democracy, and other elements of the self-understanding of modern societies.

Similar patterns of legitimization appear in the discourses of armed groups that have a communalist program. But the literature on armed groups confirms that there are other moral orders than those of the nation. These share, however, the same moral dichotomy. Ethnic solidarity, for example, based on shared languages or faith is in this regard the same as communities of settlers or of fate. While their boundaries, of course, are never totally fixed and move over time[56], there is always a distinction between the rules that apply to the group and those that apply to non-members. Particularly in the course of wars, these boundaries harden and become stereotypes and rigid moral orders that in turn allow for further violence. "In the context of militia politics", Thomas Scheffler summarizes, for example, in regard to the war in Lebanon between 1975 and 1990, "religion was used less as a spiritual or ethical guide of life but rather as a kit of symbols which could be used a) to strengthen exclusive demarcation lines between virtual political groups, and b) to legitimize the monopolization of communal leadership by secular militia bosses" (1999: 175).

In civil wars as in international wars one can always observe the debordering of violence mostly in instances when violent actors operate outside the contexts of their constituency.[57] The legitimacy of violence is thus always related to such a moral order. The ensuing obligations seemingly necessitate the individual's contribution to the protection of a community to which he belongs. As a result of these moral decisions, the distinction between insider and outsider violence is then reinforced in the course of a war and often radicalized as it becomes a self-fulfilling prophecy.

*The warrior habitus and moral orders*

The case of Lebanon is instructive as an example of how a more abstract moral order translates into more subjective forms of legitimate violence. As it goes hand in hand with role ascriptions, such a moral order defines who, under what circumstances, is entitled to act violently. The "men in arms" during the Lebanese civil war not only looked back on a long tradition of communal self-defense, they considered their violence legitimate as it epitomized social ideals like family solidarity, belief, attachment to the land, and bravery (Picard 2002: 322). This "ethos guerrier" combines the insider morality with duties and rights in the exertion of violence for the defense of the community. This warrior habitus is the point where personal ambition and social codes of honor coalesce.[58] Such codes of honor are universal but not stable. They change with forms of social organization but are not bound to certain religions or other specific belief systems (cf. Peristiany 1966).

It is an almost historically universal observation that abstract moral orders have their equivalent in a specific habitus of those segments of societies that are legitimized as violent agents towards strangers. Not surprisingly, the moral framing of the "warrior" has strong structural similarities across contextual borders. This habitus, centered on the concept of honor, appears as the ethos of the professional soldier, of the medieval knight, of the *guerillero*, and of the traditional warrior.

Although the extent to which traditional warfare has been imagined as rule-bound by anthropologists might be exaggerated[59], the use of violence has definitely been limited by codes of honor that can be seen as functional equivalents to legal regulations on warfare of modern states. The *lex talionis*, institutionalized as blood revenge, is one example of this. Among Balutschis in Pakistan, for example, such a code is still more powerful than state law.[60] Examples from other contexts confirm that the traditional heroic warrior habitus was still alive in late colonial phases. During the mid-20th century, Tuaregs in the French Sahara exhibited a wide range of reactions to the encroaching colonial state. One clan leader, Alla, still opposed to the French administration, attacked French officers and their allies in occasional raids with a dozen of his fighters. His cause was lost from the beginning, but he gained open admiration by the majority of the local population. "Some considered him a rebel; others thought he was just after personal advantage. But the majority thought he was doing this simply to prove his bravery, to show everybody his courage" remembers a clan member (Ag Acheriff 1993: 209).

Although the regulation of warfare by the codes of honor in stateless societies seems to have been exaggerated by early political anthropology, practices like raids display patterns of regulation that developed over time, whether by repeated experiences, discovered costs, deliberate agreement, or as self-regulated systems (cf. Bollig 1991). These codes also changed over time. In European history, they merged with the professional ethos of the soldier which in turn was incorporated into the institutional order of post-colonial armies.[61] Changes in forms of political rule seemingly also affected the ethos of violence specialists. The British colonial administration used the tradition of cattle rustling for the conquest of East Africa and later tried to transform the traditional warrior ethos into the newly created colonial army, the King's African Rifles (Mazrui 1977: 252). Norbert Elias relates the enormous prestige of military personnel in Imperial Germany, particularly in Prussia, to the creation of the violent German state in the late 19th century (Elias 1990: 63).

The habitus of the warrior that appears in its tribal form or in its transformation of the ethos of the professional soldier can thus be seen as the subjective specification of the moral order of political communities or organizations. It reappears in different, historically shaped guises in contemporary armed groups. In the wars of the Former Yugoslavia, "heroic role models" (Allcock 2000: 391) were inspired by the tradition of *haiduks*, the social bandits of the 18th and 19th century. They fought in the Balkans, partly for their own advantage and partly against Ottoman rule. These images survived in the region due to the long history of an irregular military. In the 1990s, they were mixed with modern importations of movie characters like Mad Max, Rambo, and Ninjas (ibid. 407).

Similarly, during the wars in the Northern Caucasus in the 1990s, the ideal of the free "men in wars" was revived and competed with the image of the regular soldier. It created legitimacy for a number of leaders of armed groups that had no military experience and had worked as drivers, technicians, or intellectuals before intrastate conflicts became violent (Gordadze 2003: 379).

The recourse to older, often more fabricated rather than genuinely historical forms of the warrior ethos, does, however, not automatically produce a stable organization of armed groups. Two reasons stand opposed to this. First, the very fact that fighters in armed groups rely on such images is evidence of the lack of coherent and valid alternative forms. The habitus of the irregular warrior can be a supplement to the ethos of the disciplined soldier, but it is not a functional equivalent. Intrastate wars generally indicate a crisis of legitimacy of the political order. The moral order of armed groups that challenge the state's moral code usually cannot rely on a ready-made alternative. This code, as most life-stories of armed groups show, is often constructed during the fighting. That older forms and symbols as well as modern icons and heroic models are drawn on for the self-identification of fighters is proof of this precarious ongoing construction.

Secondly, the exertion of violence has counterproductive effects dealt with later in this chapter. Derailed violence spoils the image of the warrior as the ethical, heroic guardian of the community. Warriors do not escape the shadow of violence, the fact that it generates honor as well as guilt and shame. Furthermore, the successful warrior who accumulates charisma through his military achievements might destabilize a precarious hierarchy in an insurgent group by countering the traditional authority of elders or political figures, thus endangering the political structure of an armed group.

## Collective interpretations of violence

Violence is remembered by individuals as well as by collectives, and it has become almost a banality in historical theory that there are few forces that shape collective identification as much as shared experiences of violence.[62] And although simple descriptions of these collective imaginations might cover a broad and highly disparate range of memories and narratives, no serious scholar of history would deny that wars generate images of the past and evaluations of the present.[63]

States in particular create master narratives of what has happened, what the causes and the results were in terms of political structures and rules justified by "historical reasons". The victorious days of decolonization movements, for example, are celebrated annually in order to reanimate the political order that has been the result of this liberation from foreign rule. In cases like Algeria and Yugoslavia these narratives remained uncontested for at least a generation. But eventually, the appeal of all these master stories begins to fade. They can no longer conceal the fact that new injustices have developed and that the old guard can no longer minimize these fissures and dynamics by reiterating its historical sacrifices and merits. In Algeria, it was the Islamist banner under which the challengers of the old guard gathered in the early 1990s. Thirty years after the victory over French colonialism, a politically stagnant regime that had fostered its image as an erstwhile violent rebellion, legitimate and politically rewarding, was now facing a younger generation eager to seize power and not reluctant to employ violent means when open competition was denied to them (Martinez 1999).

In Yugoslavia, the victory of the Partisans over the German army during World War II also became an almost mythological narrative. The legitimacy of political violence was not only implicit in the appraisal of Marshall Tito's military genius. It was also institutionalized in numerous military organizations and in the general esteem of the preparedness for violent resistance in this historical border zone (Colović 2002).

In the foundational myths of most states, violence is justified *ex post*. It is also celebrated and glorified as a liberating force. This applies to the period of Democratic Kampuchea (Hinton 2004: 165) as well as the wars of independence (Allcock 2000: 383). The historic legitimization of political violence as "heroic" seemingly allowed for transpositions into current situations. If it was just and effective then, why not now? The intellectual operation needed for this step is merely the construction of an analogy. Former enemies are replaced by the current one, and victims of today are equated with those of earlier times.

Thus, when armed groups emerge in surroundings that are "charged" with violence, in the sense that large-scale violence has taken place less than a generation ago, the legitimization of violence is just a question of integrating experiences and interpretations of the past with perceptions of current situations. The symbolic entrepreneurs in armed groups, its "organic intellectuals", need only relate current situations in causal-mystical ways to what has happened earlier (cf. Apter 1997). The trauma and grief that still linger then fuel the action of the day.

*Personal experience of violence*

Personal experiences of violence, of course, shape behavior as much as collective memories and political attitudes. In this regard, the field of violence is the same as any other domain of social action. Psychological research has repeatedly confirmed that there are mechanisms through which violent experiences are transmitted across situations and extended periods of time. The popular saying, "violence produces violence" refers thus to an meanwhile accepted scientific truth.[64]

However, violence on the individual level cannot be explained solely by reference to violence encountered earlier, nor is this always the most important factor. Not all leaders or members of armed groups have experienced physical violence in earlier phases of their lives. But an overview of these biographies given in the preceding chapter reveals that many of the subjects apparently had close contact with forms of organized violence, even if they had not become victims themselves. First are those who have received military training and who might consider the use of violence legitimate whenever they see their personal or their communities' existence endangered. Second are those who have experienced repression in one form or another. Counter-violence against threats will certainly look much more legitimate to those with a background of such experiences. Typical in this regard is detainment for political reasons. Sometimes, both experiences are combined. Josip Broz Tito is a classical example in this regard. He acquired military experience in the Austrian army during World War I, was scattered by the vicissitudes of war into Russia, made contact with Bolsheviks, and later became co-founder of the Yugoslav communist party. When he was arrested on political charges in the 1930s, his prison became the social space in which close ties between future Partisan leaders developed.[65]

In international and civil wars not only leaders but entire segments of populations may experience large-scale violence, possibly over extended periods of time. Their personal experiences and collective interpretations are usually inextricably interwoven in the legitimization of further violence. Many of these forms of violence do not initially come to mind, but the history of armed groups and biographical material contain so many instances that patterns become apparent. Deportations, enforced settlements, indiscriminate repression by other groups or state forces, detention in refugee camps, the loss of family members through political or criminal violence – the long register of such experiences is at the same time a list of sources that make the occurrence of violence more likely. A complete register of social settings where physical violence is more probable to be experienced has not yet been produced. We know, however, that war itself produces innumerable experiences that would presumably defy any attempt at complete categorization (Nordstrom 2004: 9).

Armed groups can draw on such personal experiences as a matrix for the legitimization of violence. But the inclusion of traumatized people into such a precarious organization might cause more problems than it solves. When motivations are predominantly emotional, the probability is low that an armed group will succeed in establishing an enduring internal order. Uncontrolled anger and the lust for revenge threaten to spoil the decisive moment when the opportunity exists for military superiority to be converted into legitimate rule. Local populations and also external bystanders will resent any violent act that transgresses what might still be perceived as necessary in the course of military operations.

Military organizations have taken notice of this problem, and consequently, the management of emotions has become a major field of social techniques in modern armies. These skills are used to enhance "fighting capacity", but at the same time should be controlled in order to avoid derailed violence that would disrupt the functioning of a highly regulated army with a complex division of labor. Armed groups also need to manage emotions, and as with armies they need to control emotions that are connected with the exertion and affliction of violence. As will be shown in the last section of this chapter, the dynamics of violence on the emotional level play a crucial role in the inconsistency of violence exerted by armed groups.

## Delegitimization through violence

"We captured ten AFL soldiers in Old Road. They put their hands up and we killed them. We cut their heads off. I don't feel good killing. I have knife-proof. But he is my enemy. I wear my charms – they are Sonkaley-Goa. I have my medicine. It is Seke. I am not sure what's in it. It was given to me by a medicine man from Saklepie. If you take the medicine than you can't have sex or eat raw cassava or palm oil. If you do, the medicine will spoil. I keep the medicine because everybody know I'm a rebel. I wear a ring and two fetishes on rope around my neck. If you are my enemy, my ring will burn me. If somebody is my enemy at the checkpoint, then I will know because my ring will tell me. If somebody is my enemy I will take him on one side. People beg. The say 'Please, don't kill me!' But I don't trust them. There are in my territory. I have killed fifty people. I cut off their heads or shot them. They begged for their lives, but I didn't trust them. My people in my area like me. I did things for them. If I think about the war I feel bad, because here's my own country and we have damaged our country. Now everybody has an enemy."

(Elija Mccarthy, NPFL soldier, Monrovia, quoted from Huband 1998: 107)

"While it moves forward, the Islamic Resistance Movement repeatedly reminds all the sons of our people and the Arab and Islamic peoples that it does not seek fame for itself, material gain or social status. [The movement] is not directed against anyone or our people to compete with him or to take his place. Nothing of the sort at all. It will never be against any son of Muslims or [against] Non-Muslims who are peaceful toward it, here or elsewhere. It will support only those associations and organizations operating against the Zionist enemy and those in league with it. The Islamic Resistance Movement accepts Islam as a way of life. It is its faith and its [normative] standard. Whoever takes Islam as a way of life, whether it is here or there, be it a group, an organization or a state, or any other body, the Islamic Resistance Movement is its soldiers, nothing less. We ask Allah to guide us and to guide (others) through us and to decide between us and our people with truth. O Lord, do thou judge between us and our nation with truth, for thou are the best judge (Suara 7, al A'raf, v. 89). Our last prayer is praise for Allah, the Lord of the universe."

> (The Charter of the Islamic Resistance Movement (Hamas), conclusions, quoted from Mishal/ Sela 2006: 199)

On first impression, the sources presented here stand in no relation to each other. Whereas the first is a spontaneous statement of a Liberian rebel given to a British journalist during the war in 1990, the second is part of a carefully considered document that contains many scholarly references, published by the highly organized Palestinian armed group Hamas, aiming at generating support in the presence of powerful competitors. However, the two texts may stand symptomatically for the fundamental challenge of armed groups in contemporary civil wars. The dynamics of violence that have been triggered in Liberia apparently overwhelmed the single rebel who is torn between an obligation felt to communal belongings and total mistrust towards anybody else.

The Charter of Hamas, a group that is known for its extremely strategic use of violence, has a national agenda but also strives for support from outsiders. It presents its project as a clear cut and difficult task, without taking into account the dynamics of violent actions in a volatile environment. Whereas the Liberian rebel no longer pretends to have an agenda other than his own survival amidst turmoil, Hamas cultivates an impression of utter decisiveness and self-assurance. While the former is simultaneously the doer and the victim of derailed violence, the latter maintains that it has total self-control.

The dynamics of violence account for this gap between clear strategy and political ambition initially and the eventual total loss of control and the absence of a political agenda other than preserving one's own life. What becomes evident here is a fundamental problem for all armed groups: The unpredictable effects of physical violence render the projects of armed groups extremely precarious. The micro-dynamics of violence run counter to efforts to control and contain the use of violence. The underlying cause for this can be found in the delegitimizing effects of violence that are so difficult to control. While all armed groups attempt to establish full command of the violence they exert, many fail to do so due to counterproductive micro-mechanisms that wartime violence entails.

Of course, many violent acts committed by armed groups may be categorized as elements of the general image of wars: attacks on patrolling soldiers, ambushes and onslaughts, or the indiscriminate killing of state employees and competing armed groups' members. These actions are always intended as communicative acts in the sense that they demonstrate to the constituency and to political opponents the power of the respective group. Although these acts can have disastrous consequences for the legitimacy of an armed group, generally they follow what most theorists of irregular warfare claim to be a proven plan for success. [66]

This theory or strategy of irregular warfare, however, stands in striking contrast to the evidence in most empirical cases, especially in regard to the use and forms of violence. While according to this strategy the relationship between insurgents and local populations is crucial in order to change the power of violence into real and more effective domination, most armed groups threaten this legitimacy by practices of violence that have devastating effects on their political credibility. The empirical evidence of the violence that armed groups wield throughout their life-cycle is irritating. Numerous practices openly contradict the ideal of irregular warfare. Rebels apparently cannot confine their violent practices to strategy as it is presented in theory. A short overview of this necessarily fragmentary empirical record will be briefly discussed here.

*Table 4:* Reported violence of armed groups against civilian population (1945-2005, in percent)

|  | All groups (N= 80) | Repression (N= 48) | Ad hoc groups (N= 41) | Spin-off groups (N=9) |
|---|---|---|---|---|
| Non-sufficient data | 2.5 | 4 | 5 | 0 |
| Bomb attacks | 24.4 | 30.4 | 23.1 | 100 |
| Massacres | 28.2 | 21.7 | 38.5 | 77.8 |
| Corporal punishments | 24.4 | 39.1 | 41 | 55.6 |
| Systematic terror | 35.9 | 30.4 | 41 | 66.7 |
| Evictions | 32.1 | 26.1 | 41 | 55.6 |

Source: MAG database

Two main observations can be made from this overview. First is the finding that armed groups use violence against civilian populations to an astonishing extent. Media reports and case literature on which this overview is based state that all three forms of armed groups use methods of indiscriminate violence against civilian populations. While spin-off groups apparently rely more often on such practices as massacres, systematic terror, and evictions, ad hoc groups and those groups that were created by the mechanism of repression do not abstain from these practices. To a considerable degree these acts might be explained as strategic violence that is addressing potentially hostile elements of the civilian populations. Evictions, for example, are strategic steps in numerous civil wars that are symbolically framed in ethnic terms.

Second, and even more striking, are the respective findings on the three sub-types distinguished here. These findings can be interpreted first, as a confirmation of general ideas about the moral order of armed groups and their constituencies and second, of the suppositions of the inner working of groups of these sub-types. The formation of armed groups, as might be concluded from this data, does not solely determine the type and amount of violent practices. Connected with the argument on moral orders that limit the use of violence among insiders and legitimize the use of it against outsiders, the three different mechanisms of formation described in the preceding chapter help to explain a number of differences.

Spin-off groups, as can be deduced despite the low number of cases, are according to this interpretation more inclined to transgress moral boundaries as they practice violence with the implicit permission and legitimization of state authorities. They may therefore view themselves as less concerned with winning the populations' hearts and minds. Furthermore, they might find it necessary to employ less disciplinary violence as a considerable proportion of their members have received previous military training. Their rather military-like character would also explain why their military acts are relatively conventional when they attack state forces.

On the other end of the spectrum are groups that exert violence in reaction to state repression. For these, one could argue, it is crucial that they attract popular support, and very often they might feel bound by the moral order of the social context in which they move. And indeed, these groups are less inclined to use violence against civilians than spin-off groups. And yet, one-quarter of them reportedly evicted parts of the populations, and one third systematically used terror methods in order to attain control. Here, state violence is much more pronounced, whereas the strategy of the armed groups against the state more closely follows the classical theory of guerilla warfare.

Ad hoc groups largely resemble those armed groups that resorted to violence as a reaction to state repression in their violent practices. They show slightly higher levels of violence against civilian populations. Ad hoc groups might attempt to gain legitimacy in the eyes of local populations, but as instrumental and mixed as their formation is, they are less hindered by shared moral orders of shared origin.

What remains to be explored is the enormous amount of violence that targets civilian populations. Even if one admits that there could possibly be a strategic rationality in certain forms of violence from a military point of view, this finding is counter-intuitive to the lessons of the theory of irregular warfare. Even in hostile surroundings, it is essential that insurgents eventually gain acceptance in order to avoid endangering their subsequent victory. The next section of this chapter claims that part of the explanation for this counter-intuitive insight is to be found in unplanned violent acts. These acts are also part of the shadow of violence as they inevitably follow the practices of organized use of force to the detriment of the perpetrator's legitimacy.

## Why violence derails

It is an old observation, made repeatedly, that the actual experience of war violence does not resemble what political speeches, newspaper editorials, and glorifying fictional accounts tell us. In the trenches of World War I, soldiers from all the countries involved had the experience that their national ideals and celebrated national histories and missions were not only demystified, they evaporated in the emotional stress of combat and the paltriness of everyday life in wartime.[67]

Not all experiences of violence have such immediate delegitimizing effects. Violence in war can also be welcomed, for example when dangers and threats from opposing forces are driven out of an area, or when final victories are achieved that bring the fighting and suffering to an end.[68] The typical situation, however, is that nothing is decided, and current changes are open to various interpretations. Then, violence might be judged neutrally by observers as its outcomes are still unclear, or the violence of both sides is seen as equally illegitimate by the populations. And beyond the devaluating effects of the hardship that is connected with the endurance of war, there are particular mechanisms that are likely to become established even when violence is organized and strategically exerted.

There are several ways in which experiences of violence can diminish the reputation of an armed group.[69] Some of them can be summarized as micro-mechanisms that are bound to specific situations rather than being of a general, over-arching character. Partly, these mechanisms are cognitive, partly they are rather emotional. First, there are two cognitive mechanisms that help explain why armed groups such as armies experience information problems. If they act in social contexts in which they are not deeply rooted, there is a high incentive to use indiscriminate violence in order to establish control, as Stathis Kalyvas has argued (2006). The reason for this is not only that hidden loyalties to the enemy would endanger this control, but also that armed groups almost always conceive any form of loyalty other than to themselves as a competition if not a threat. They therefore try, at minimum, to monopolize political power in the areas they control. The ensuing uncertainties result in violence against civilians, and this violence is detrimental to the insurgents' legitimacy.

Second, there are situational micro-mechanisms that have neither strategic nor tactical background but rather stem from situational dynamics that are impossible to control. The immediateness of violence and its emotional extraordinariness (*Außeralltäglichkeit*) create an endless number of constellations in which violence is often simply "happening" rather than being employed in an instrumental, reflected way. This is what Reemtsma (2008: 116) calls "autotelian violence", forms of over-reactions that seem to elapse any rationalist explanation. The following four mechanisms are just a first approximation, based on other authors' work, cross case reading, and reflections on field notes. Sure, this is not enough. It remains an unfulfilled task of research to attempt an all-encompassing typology of these sorts of situational mechanisms.

Much of the actual transaction of war might reside in such situational dynamics that as yet have not received significant attention in the analysis of civil war. Only a long-term phenomenological research program could possibly shed more light on these dynamics. Some mechanisms are hypothetically sketched here in order to come closer to an explanation of derailed violence that is so widespread in the politics of armed groups. It is possible to disentangle at least four basic forms: information problems, revenge, fear, and shame. All four can negate strategic concerns in various situations and trigger delegitimizing violence. They all result in extending the borders of violence. Violence derails and enters into causal cycles, while the cognitive and emotional effects of violence become causes of further violence.[70] As such, these micro-mechanisms open ways for explaining delegitimizing violence.

## *Diverging interpretations and lack of information*

Beneath the overarching "master cleavage" in any civil war, there are a myriad of things occurring that have become possible in the shadow of violence and to a large extent shape its outcome.[71] These forms of sub-violence have to do with spontaneous self-enrichments, with the settling of old accounts between neighbors and competitors, and other mundane affairs. They threaten to spoil the political effects of violence exerted by armed groups and their enemies likewise, as they lead to erroneous ascriptions of who did what and why.

The list of things that happen in a war and influence its outcome, contrary to anybody's intentions, is probably endless. Dense descriptions from anthropologists on single theaters of war repeatedly show that the master cleavage in a civil war is not often the driving force behind events. This has been particularly true for those cases that had been interpreted as "proxy wars" during the Cold War. Christian Geffray (1990), for example, has shown in his study of zones near the frontlines in Mozambique during the late 1980s that it was not the ideological divide between "Eastern socialism" and "Western Democracy" that most people viewed as the source of the conflict. Rather, it was the often brutal collectivization of farms that spurred resistance and gave the ruthless Renamo rebels a niche for their anti-government discourse. In his groundbreaking book dealing with the war in Liberia, Stephen Ellis (1999) stressed the perception of the civil war by the local populations in a syncretistic spiritual symbolism that had little or no relation to what was thought and said about that war in Western media.

Disjunctions between the center and periphery, local conflict potentials not anticipated by warring factions, and differences in the frames of interpretation of war actions are sources of derailed violence that threaten the legitimacy of armed groups and state forces alike. This is also true for information deficits that, according to Kalyvas (2006: chap. 6) underlie indiscriminate violence. There are at least two ways in which this develops. First, when an armed actor has no relationship with the populations that is close enough to allow the collection of information needed for selective violence, it would employ indiscriminate violence in order to obtain control. But indiscriminate violence is most likely to produce resentment, ascriptions of guilt and shame, and will be detrimental to the legitimacy of the armed actor (Kalyvas 2006: chap. 7).

The second way in which this mechanism might become established is during a self-defense situation that emerges when frontlines move quickly. Incomplete information regarding the situation can then trigger reactions that look like mere panic. Actors lacking information will expect an aggression and organize their defense. They are prone to over-react to any sign seen as part of the feared aggression. Witch hunts or pogroms might be the consequence (Elwert 2002: 339). This has been the logic of widespread roadblocks in African civil wars, but known also from the early phases of the wars in the Former Yugoslavia. The familiarity of armed groups – and state forces alike – with local circumstances is here again crucial for the success not only of military operations but also for the anchorage of the organizations in order to bridge the problem of insufficient information (Chaliand 1994: 27).

*Revenge*

A fundamental emotional mechanism of derailed violence in war is revenge. The distressing feeling of being dishonored and humiliated by the violence somebody else exerted spreads into planned or spontaneous counteracts that contradict the strategic use of violence aligned with the group's ambitions (cf. Waldmann 2000). Often, to external observers the degree of violence seems to lack any benefits. Psychological theories suppose that power-equalizations are the aims of acts of revenge, and seemingly this can be one motivation. Another one is the restoration of individual or collective honor as it is codified in moral orders. Revenge serves the restoration of self-esteem and honor (Frijda 1993: 270), and its motivating feeling can persist over extended periods of time.[72] The convention of the Balutchi, mentioned earlier in this chapter, is a case in point. Systems of regulated violence, as in the form of *lex talionis*, are connected with feelings and strong emotions, but at the same time they are embedded in codes that limit and regulate violence. As such, revenge survives the dissolution of traditional forms of social organization and can be found in rather modern contexts as well. "[M]any American men in the Civil War era were quite capable of reconciling Christianity and vengeance, just as they were to suspend the Commandment, Thou shall not kill, for the duration of the war" (McPherson 1997: 148).[73] According to this finding on the Civil War in the United States, vengeance that is situational can prolong itself into retributive cycles. It can become an "infinite, endless process" that can threaten the social cohesion of a society (Girard 1977: 28).

Especially in war situations in which moral codes of honor are at stake, revenge can lead to derailing violence. The violence exerted is no longer commensurate with the political aims, but attempts to control it fail. Vengeance also spills over into legitimizing narratives about past wars, in which the legitimacy of violence resulting from revenge remains uncontested, as these words of a Serbian veteran show:

"War is the greatest stupidity men can do. I am no longer interested in questions of responsibility, who did what and why. It always comes down to ordinary people slaughtering each other. But politicians never send their kids. Today, it is simply about pressing a button for them. But they will see their Gods one day, Tudjman and all the others. And also, I must tell you, Serbs never started anything. They were just harsh doing revenge, they never started to kill anyone."

(Interview Belgrade, October 2005)

*Fear and protection*

A vast amount of violence that takes place in a civil war also seems disconnected from the master cleavage as it is also an effect of threats and violence. The approaching front line or the expectation of possibly becoming a victim leads, in all wars, to violent acts as anticipated defense. In times of uncertainty that precede open violence in civil wars bystanders face a security dilemma (Posen 1993) and are turned easily into belligerents. Fear or the need for protection is a frequent motivation for joining an armed group. In his study on the Moro National Liberation Front (MNLF) in the Philippines, McKenna observed that the insurgents he interviewed rarely made spontaneous mention of either the "Moro" nation or Islamic renewal as a motive for joining the MNLF (1998: 186). Instead, the fear for one's own life or the need for protection of families and communities facing an unregulated army was reported by virtually all the insurgents as a primary motivation. This was also a primary motivation of many who joined informal forces in the wars of the Former Yugoslavia.

"I joined the forces when it was about the liberation of Dubrovnik. It was a beleaguered city and Serbs had nothing to do there. I think they were actually Montenegrins there besieging the city. What did they think they were doing? What was going on in their heads? Did they want to loot or what? They plundered whatever they could get. What did they want to do with the city? Occupy it? Keep it? That's nonsense. So we had to de-block it".

(Interview with Croatian volunteer (Bašić 2003: 279))

Closely in line with the legitimization of violence according to the moral order argument presented above, fear and protection can also spur irregular violence, as well as many other actions. "I only had one idea in my mind – the tanks must not enter the camp", explains a staff member of the Islamic Jihad as his motivation to buckle dynamite around his waist and wait for the tanks that were approaching the gates of a refugee camp in Jenin in August 2001 (Larzillière 2004: 129).

*Shame and humiliation*

David Keen, in his analysis of violence during the war in Sierra Leone, hints at the dynamics of shame and humiliation. Anger at being excluded from real life chances created, among unemployed youth, a feeling of humiliation (2005: 38), and the imposition of extreme humiliation and shame on the victims became a particular feature of this war (2005: 59). According to this interpretation, humiliation was used in the war in Sierra Leone by combatants to assert their superiority in a society from which they had felt excluded during peacetime. In turning the society into a "perverse universe" during the war, by forcing men to commit crimes and act against all moral codes, this estrangement was made even more pronounced. Humiliating their victims by the most outrageous acts proved the rebels' desire for respect and recognition (Keen 2005: 79).[74]

Even taken together these mechanisms do not constitute a full-fledged theory that can explain all the transgressions of violence so often triggered during war situations. They provide, however, an avenue of thought and research that promises to lead to more thorough explanations of the inner dynamics of war violence than enigmatic statements regarding the barbaric violence criticized above.

Further systematic research on causes of derailed violence would also encompass investigations about more general conditions that increase or decrease the likelihood of such situational dynamics. Mechanisms of revenge, honor, shame, and fear may not exist in all circumstances. They are, for example, more likely to spoil the rationale of armed groups when the group itself has experienced violent repression. Then the wounds are fresh, the fear of being hurt again is alive, as is the grief for family members and communities. Many armed groups then fail because they are unable to control the specters of earlier violence, the trauma. As a result of this lack of control, fighters cross the line of what is allowed, not only in the realm of outsider morality, but also of insider morality. The consequence of this is the loss of the group's legitimacy, both internally and in the eyes of external observers. The shadow of violence is thus cast on any future political or military step.

## Conclusion

The shadow of violence is cast on many aspects of the life of armed groups. It is part of their internal policy, their disciplinary techniques aimed at forming individuals into well-trained warriors.[75] The shadow also falls on the emerging or hardening lines of stereotypes and the destruction of social institutions as well as biographies. And it creates an environment in which war has not yet arrived but is threatening to come. Furthermore, the shadow of violence is cast on the relations war actors can possibly engage in with local populations, and it is, finally, following the course of strategic use of force as a trail of delegitimizing deeds and excesses.

The argument that was constructed in this chapter is that the oppressive effects of the use of force can best be understood when violence is conceived as a form of action power aiming at hurting the integrity of human bodies and characterized by immediateness and ensuing trauma. Both of these qualities account for the fact that violence is so difficult to contain, that it produces aberrant outcomes, and that its effects are long-lasting.

In all societies, it was then argued, violence is subjected to rules and customs, which draw a distinction between insider and outsider morality. These moral orders create the distinction between legitimate and illegitimate violence. The legitimization of violence by armed groups is therefore bound by these antecedent structures. The actual legitimization of the organization of violence by armed groups, it is argued, draws on at least three distinctive elements. One is the warrior habitus as an ensemble of values and traditional patterns, centered on the notion of social honor. Secondly, collective experiences that are embedded in narratives and myths contribute to the social acceptance of organized violence whereas, thirdly, personal experiences of earlier violence constitute another abetting element in that process. The trauma of violence thus also has a function in the legitimization of further violence.

The violent practices of armed groups, as was then demonstrated by a statistical overview, however, do not follow a model that has been spread globally as the theory of irregular warfare.

While it is plausible to assume that the mode of guerilla or "people's" warfare has been adopted and adapted by most armed groups, there is the fact asking for explanation that their violent practices are not congruent with what this theoretical model proclaims. The shadow of violence can be seen here in the excessive violence that is apparently triggered by situational mechanisms based on emotions like fear, revenge, and shame, as well as on information problems. Beyond the delegitimizing effects all acts of violence can have, the violent politics of armed groups are prone to lead to additional excessive and even more delegitimizing acts of force.

What could hopefully be shown through this chapter is that violence and legitimacy are inextricably linked. This ambiguous relationship forces armed groups to avoid practices and instances of violence that endanger their legitimacy. Violence has the tendency to derail, to turn bystanders into opponents, and both tendencies would destroy the legitimacy of an armed actor who strives for military and political success.

The violence of armed groups thus does not break the cycles of guilt, shame, and honor that surround political violence and structure the interpretation of history. But beyond this shadow of violence that is cast for extended periods of history on the self-imagination of societies, armed groups must deal concretely and immediately with another effect of their action. They must turn the power that they exert as violence into something more enduring in order to defeat an opponent with higher organizational capacities. The legitimacy that armed groups require in order to reach their goals must always overcome these immediate detrimental effects. Part of this change is simply a function of time. The particular policies armed groups implement in order to gain legitimacy, both in discourse and in practical regards, will be analyzed in the next chapter.

# 4. Basic Legitimacy and Charismatic Cycles

In 1990, when the Sudan People's Liberation Army rebels in Southern Sudan had advanced after eight years of warfare, the government in Khartoum began to devise new modes of delegating violence. It not only supplemented the army with ethnic militias in the South, it also, using Islamic rhetoric, created the People's Defense Forces as a volunteer militia for Northerners. Large PDF campaigns were mounted when the conflict, now under the regime of the National Islamic Front, was renamed a jihad. In this way, even Sudanese who were not members of the ruling Islamist party could be mobilized. The PDF used Islamic mystical symbolism rather than the rationalized discourse of Islamic legal interpretation. The "miraculous feats" celebrating the martyrs of the PDF were broadcast nightly. Government newspapers in the early 1990s published stories about the PDF in connection with prophetic dreams, sweet smelling corpses of martyrs, and supernatural assistance by animals. Yet within a few years, volunteer mobilization declined, and the government linked tuition-free study to prior service in the PDF. Later, students receiving military training escaped from camps and staged demonstrations in the streets. The PDF's battlefield losses were high, and in order to increase the militia's size, the government had to offer more than symbolic benefits for participation in the PDF, such as free education, health care, and housing for the families of the "martyrs". Eventually, in August 2004, foreign dignitaries attended a staged public ceremony during which 500 PDF members surrendered their weapons.[76] The attempt by the regime to create a militant movement had officially failed.

Yasir Arafat will always be remembered as seen in a photographic image which he carefully designed. Being a symbol himself, his attire, his weapons, and his body language in the picture constitute a perfect mise en scène of the struggle. His checkered scarf was the traditional headwear of rural

Palestinian men, and it became a symbol itself during the rebellion between 1936 and 1939 against British rule and Zionist land seizure. Arafat, having grown up in an urban milieu, wore the symbolic headwear to bridge the gap with rural Palestinians. At official occasions and in photos, Arafat wore one end of the scarf across his right shoulder so that the lowest lappet formed the shape of Palestine. Contrary to these local symbolic icons, Arafat's camouflage uniform, his pistol, and his three-day beard were imprints of a modern, international symbolic canon. In this way, he signified continuity with all other "people's liberation armies" of the period, and made allusions to the attire of Fidel Castro or any other committed revolutionary working with untiring and soldierly discipline for the new state. Finally, on many occasions Arafat was seen making the victory sign and borrowed from Winston Churchill who had popularized it during World War II. Here again it symbolized steadfastness and courage.[77]

What comes to the fore in these two examples is an expression of the need for armed groups and governments to communicate their activities and viewpoints to one another. While the shadow of violence is cast on them, they would benefit from employing other, additional means to gain acceptance for the power they have acquired or want to acquire. This discourse is an ensemble of symbolic techniques that help overcome the lack of legitimacy that results from acts of violence.

As violence and legitimacy are inextricably linked, armed groups suffer from the same dilemma as many armies: it is important that exerted violence which serves political purposes be legitimated, while at the same time it inevitably produces delegitimizing effects. So, how do armed groups overcome the delegitimizing effects of violence?

The answer to that question, as developed in this chapter, is based on the observation that most armed groups are somewhat aware of these dynamics. They try to bolster their position while constantly threatened by the effects of violence through deeds and discourses that address a threefold public. First, these discourses are internal. They are established in order to streamline the figuration in the sense that the group functions despite the distractions and centrifugal dynamics of war events. This is why many armed groups hold meetings or, at later stages, party congresses, during which they communicate statements describing their missions, trying thus to mobilize their followers anew, settle internal disputes, and solidify their organizations.

Second, by a combination of actions and rhetoric, armed groups also try to establish their authority in social realms that are not their original constituency. Part of this public is the local population on whose support, whether of an overt or covert nature, any armed group depends. Armed groups draw on norms and values of their social context, and they create narratives of the past and present in order to justify their political claims, thus framing the ongoing conflict.

And third is the international public, consisting first and foremost of governments of powerful states whose influence has grown since the end of World War II. It is counterbalanced and intermediated by what is awkwardly referred to as "global public opinion", the mass media images that have gained considerably greater importance in that same period. As will be seen, many armed groups are very capable of using the tactic of pitting governments' policies against global public opinion and vice versa.

The first section of this chapter deals with first forms of legitimacy many armed groups can draw on, that is, *traditional legitimacy*. While it is a sociological truism to state that traditions are never permanent, the legitimacy of armed groups can often rely on established patterns of authority. Parental ties or ethnic orders often constitute such first forms. Due to the dynamics of violence, however, they have the tendency to erode over the course of a war. As will be argued, there are two predominant forces which erode the value of traditional patterns of domination within armed groups. One is the generational change that affects the internal life of armed groups, and second is the "charisma of the warrior", the rise of the reputation of successful fighters.

In the following section, this chapter contains the *mechanism of basic legitimacy* that contributes to the success of armed groups within a given local political context. It may begin whenever an armed group gains territorial control, and it rests on the group's ability to restore some degree of preliminary order and bring an end to open warfare. Whether it can fully unfold, however, depends on a number of steps that do not proceed automatically. Basic legitimacy is a crude first form of finding acceptance among a population that is not necessarily involved in the political struggles within which armed groups emerge. It does not streamline or structure a social space. But basic legitimacy allows for more and further steps in the project of transforming the conquering figuration into a ruling body.[78]

The use of ideas and programs, as will be shown in the second section of this chapter, is undertaken by armed groups in an attempt to enlarge and foster basic legitimacy. However, this new foundation is chronically unstable as these ideas also undergo life cycles. The *cycle of the charismatic ideas* delineates a second mechanism of ways in which armed groups gain legitimacy. It is based on initial growth later followed by the decreased appeal of political ideas promoted by armed groups. In the discourse of insurgencies, projects such as national liberation or social emancipation figure prominently. They convey a temporality that transcends the moment of single battles, and of mundane interests and needs. This "extraordinariness" (*Außeralltäglichkeit*) renders them charismatic.

The related argument is that armed groups benefit from legitimizing their actions through political projects that proclaim a renewal of politics, if not of the entire society. These projects may unfold into a great mobilizing force, but usually they are not fully realized. Ideas become dangerous as soon as the actions they express are no longer being fulfilled. Part of this banalization is the need for *Realpolitik* that armed groups are forced to practice, not only by violent means but also in agreeing to compromises or by not reaching the promised ends. The promise of the ideas then seems to be betrayed. The cycle of these ideas is completed when new challengers draw on similar charismatic ideas.

In a last section, this chapter will address the globally embedded nature of this strategy since the discourses of armed groups, their political programs and speeches, are simultaneously both genuine productions and parts of global political processes. As can be seen in almost any history of armed groups, the processes of societies encountering stalemates in which the organization of anti-government violence becomes more probable are already highly internationalized. This applies not only to decolonization movements, but to revolutionary movements as well. And it is also valid for numerous armed groups whose symbolic language is rather inspired by religious ideas. The last section of this chapter will show how armed groups attempt to attract external support by linking their agendas to larger, regional or international politics, and what consequences this strategy entails. Programs and political ideas thus function as links between local and international politics. The outcome of these connections may be very different, as the history of the Cold War teaches us.

These theses on changing legitimacy are based on material which is sometimes dense and rich, sometimes scattered and rather anecdotal in character. The construction of all mechanisms is inspired by established ideas of political sociology and the interpretation of the discourse of armed groups, and unsurprisingly, the main ideas and programs reflect global tides of political ideas. The idea of national self-determination and programs of social emancipation predominate in these discourses. However they should not be taken at face value, as it is often difficult to ascertain how much of this discourse reflects true political ambition and how much is rhetoric aimed at garnering external support.

Nevertheless, even on this superficial level there are a few remarkable differences that follow the lines of the mechanisms of formation. While nationalist and social-revolutionary agendas prevail among groups that came about through the mechanism of repression, the second category is absent among spin-off groups. Yet even spin-off groups are inclined to bolster their political ambition by declaring political objectives.

*Table 5: Political programs of armed groups*

| Program type | All | Repression | Ad hoc | Spin-off |
|---|---|---|---|---|
| Nationalist (irredentist/separatist) | 33.8 | 60 | 40 | 55 |
| Social revolutionary | 21.3 | 40 | 19 | 0 |
| Vigilantism | 2.5 | 0 | 2 | 22 |
| Mere regime change | 15 | 0 | 22 | 22 |
| Others | | 0 | 18 | 0 |
| N | 80 | 27 | 41 | 9 |

Source: MAG database

The attempts of armed groups to legitimize their political objectives with political programs linking them to global norms and political arenas certainly do not prove that the majority of members or even a considerable number of followers, staff members, or leaders deeply believe in the political projects and theories that underlie those ideas. But as will be shown in this chapter, the consequences of these programmatic choices are real, and it cannot be denied that a number of members at various levels must grant a measure of credibility to the political agendas connected with these ideas.

## Traditional legitimacy and its erosion

Armed groups do not emerge in vacuums. They always come into being in given social contexts, and they share imprints and traditions of their origins, as contradictory and problematic as these meanings, norms, and traditions may be. Of course, such traditions are never immune to change. Contrary to the associations the expression evokes, there is ample academic literature on the issue that demonstrates how volatile and innovative so-called traditions may be.[79]

However, from a historical perspective, change is rather slow, often unnoticed even by contemporary observers. The *longue durée* of institutions, habits, and customs is the regular case. Armed groups, like all other political actors, can build on these forms. They do not operate in a social void. By virtue of the fact that they consist of individuals who were born and raised in the same context, numerous ties and loyalties can be advantageously utilized from the very beginning of the formation of armed groups to aid in their growth. This relation is not purely instrumental. Most of these links to tradition are rather habitual. Merely by being raised in the same context, armed groups' leaders can use patterns of behavior, social norms, and habits to assist their efforts to recruit potential followers: their social habitus renders this possible.

Traditional legitimacy is one of the major sources for the early internal structuring of insurgent groups. As will be seen in this section, this applies first and foremost to those groups that emerge in semi-traditional settings. Parental ties, neighborhoods, and communal belongings are quite frequently inherent elements of their hierarchy. In the cases of Kurdish movements in Iraq and Iran, militias in Lebanon, and also various clan-based figurations in Somalia or other Sahel states, the role of traditional legitimacy becomes particularly evident.

Traditional legitimacy comes under pressure from at least two sides, and this is an important part of the internal politics of armed groups. First, its usual patriarchal nature is questioned by political ideas held by younger, intellectualized members. The ensuing conflict is often between generations, which equally characterize the social environment of insurgencies.

Second is the conflict that arises from violent dynamics. Successful warriors accumulate "warrior charisma" (Weber 1978, II: 1115), and their growing reputation within an armed group entices successful fighters to threaten the established hierarchy. Many of the internal splits within armed groups are related to these competing sources of legitimacy.

*The power of Big Men*

The internal splits and dynamics of the diverse Kurdish national movements are particularly illustrative of the problems traditional legitimacy can entail for the politics of armed groups. While Kurdish nationalism began developing in the 19th century among the urban intellectuals, its acceptance and legitimacy among the largely rural Kurds was always broken or intermediated by tribal and familial factions, led by Big Men who either joined this political project or refuted it, aligning with regimes.[80]

Tribal cleavages among the Kurdish populations in Iraq, Turkey, and Iran have been fostered by the clientelist politics of regimes, in order to maintain delegated power in remote areas by a divide and rule policy. Up until the present, Kurdish nationalist movements in these three states have been unable to overcome the political power of established local authorities but needed to co-opt them for the mobilization of fighters and as local vectors of support.[81]

The changes of loyalties among the Kurdish people are a result of broad socio-economic developments. Only during the 1960s could nationalist movements build an urban constituency strong enough to deliver constant political support. During that period, most nationalist parties in Kurdish areas adopted a Marxist-Leninist discourse. As the most prominent ideological reference for competing groups in what was then referred to as the Third World, this program allowed explication of the crisis of an unemployed urban middle class, excluded from the spoils of state agencies, albeit having diplomas and degrees. And as Hamit Bozarslan (1997: 126) has noted, this orientation provided the traditional order with an alternative, namely the single-party model, transposing hierarchical forms into a more depersonalized form of power. The single-party model also legitimated the use of violence against dissidents or fighters of competing organizations.

With the decay of real-world socialism since the late 1980s, Marxist orientations lost appeal for challenging states and Kurdish traditional authorities at the same time. Instead, religious discourse gained importance, as it did in Algeria, Lebanon, and other countries with predominantly Muslim populations. Still meshed with nationalist agendas, recourse to religious ideas is anything but traditional.[82] However, neither has this programmatic development entirely broken the traditional authority of clan leaders whose legitimacy often cannot be separated from entrenched religious orders.

While the erosion of traditional legitimacy can be observed in numerous instances, the power of Big Men thus remains a major political obstacle for armed groups' attempts to structure a social space as well as their own internal organization. The power of Big Men is often enough to prevent unification of armed movements with similar agendas in identical contexts, but the fact that armed groups continue to operate and thrive is also indicative of its erosion. It is an ironic twist in many armed groups that despite their leaders' official intention to modernize a social space with revolutionary politics, their rule often leads to a re-enactment of traditional forms of rule, incorporating many features of traditional practices such as patriarchal behavior and patrimonial distribution. Partly, one might think, this could be an adaptation to the engrained habits and expectations of local populations, thus shaping political rule in a rather traditional way, with leaders acquiescing to customs despite originally having different ideas.[83]

*Generations and programs*

Migration and flight are two of the major social phenomena that lead to this erosion. With growing urbanization and diminished integrative capacities of clientelist inclusion, alternatives to traditional forms of social order become more appealing. It is widely known that urban youth particularly, but marginalized rural youngsters as well, constitute a high percentage of followers of armed groups.[84] The emblematic stories used in chapter two to illustrate the three mechanisms of formation of armed groups offered concrete evidence for these processes. In the case literature, further support for this observation abounds.[85]

The politics of armed groups are often heavily influenced by this dynamic, as the conflict of generations is taking place within their midst. This is often a consequence of rapid growth of the group's ranks. Within the National Resistance Movement in Uganda, for example, such a conflict arose when the group grew from the initial 35 members to several hundred in a span of two months. The National Resistance Council that directed the movement with its Army Council as a subcommittee was not accepted as being adequately representative by the new members. The commanders, coming predominantly from the southwestern parts of the country, were not sufficiently legitimized in the eyes of locally recruited Baganda followers and urban intellectuals who had also joined the movement. Already in its first year of armed fighting, the NRM held a gathering in which a new organizational form was set in place. The newly created National Resistance Army Council represented all battalions and administrative sections of the movement. With the parallel system of Political Commissars, in charge of political education and the maintenance of discipline, the leadership ensured its control beyond the enlarged representative bodies.[86]

But ordinarily, organizational learning in armed groups is difficult to manage. There is always an inherent contradiction between an established leadership that wants to keep its power position, and the need for more participation of new members. Very often, this contradiction cannot be resolved or mitigated. As a consequence, competing legitimacies constitute a fault line along which armed groups may fragment.

*Charismatic competition: the honor of warriors*

The most visible form of leadership competition within armed groups is a sign of another mechanism of the erosion of traditional legitimacy. Other forms of legitimacy threaten the traditional one of established leaders. Most prominent is the charisma that accrues to violent actors as well as to politically successful leaders.[87] Military success can lead both to a charismatic appeal of the group as a whole as well as to the appeal of single individuals or parts of armed groups.

It has repeatedly been noted by Weber and other sociologists that charisma is sharply opposed to bureaucratic and traditional authority. Extraordinariness is its particular quality, and neither routines of bureaucratic rule nor strict rules of tradition can coexist with it.[88] As will be elucidated later in this book, there is, however, the inherent tendency of charisma to lose its power, as followers strive for continuous provision. Sporadic spoils of war are not adequate in the long term, and any charismatic leader must eventually assure followers that his successes translate into stable positions and offices. But this is a later dynamic that follows the emergence of charisma as a challenge to traditional legitimacy.

The split that occurred in the *Mouvement des Forces Démocratiques de Casamançe* (MFDC) illustrates such a competition between charismatic leaders. The foundational discourse of this group, active since the early 1990s in the south of Senegal, was formulated by the catholic priest Diamancoune. His charisma as priest, but also his traditional descent from a local royal lineage, practically preordained him for such a role. While Diamancoune led the movement until his death in 2007, the group's military operations were led by Sidy Badji, a former officer of the French colonial army and later of the Senegalese state forces. By 1992, a split had emerged between a Southern Front led by the charismatic priest and the more pragmatic military leader Badji, followed by fighters from the Northern Front. This split could never be overcome. Mistrust continued between these two fragments, leading to violent attacks between the two.[89]

This fate of the group is almost a textbook version of what Weber had stated concerning the dynamics of charismatic competition:

"The genuine prophet, like the genuine military leader and every true leader in this sense, preaches, creates, or demands new obligations. [...] Recognition is duty. When such an authority comes into conflict with the competing authority of another who also claims charismatic sanction, the only recourse is to some kind of a contest, by magical means or an actual physical battle of the leaders".

(Weber 1978, I: 243f.)

In the case of the MFDC, dealt with in more detail later in this chapter, the two leaders certainly were not purely charismatically legitimized. The case demonstrates, however, that within the leadership of armed groups legitimacy is not always uniform and does not necessarily create unity. Especially when political leaders and military commanders are not interchangeable, there is a constant threat of fragmentation for which there is then no peaceful solution.

While traditional legitimacy is thus endangered both by the social dynamics within and around armed groups, as well as by the production of charisma in battle, it always maintains a structuring role for armed groups and their inner functioning. No group, or any other political organization, can entirely overcome the power of customs and tradition, and to a large extent its future is dependent on its observance of these rules and settings.

## The mechanism of basic legitimacy

When armed groups conquer an area, the first moment is also the most dangerous. Neither does the conquering group know much about the local structures and the attitudes among the population, nor can the population be certain about the policies of their new rulers. Violence can resume at any point. It is only through interaction that these uncertainties are eventually overcome as patterns emerge. Over time, the mechanism of basic legitimacy takes effect. It can be described as a sequence of steps that contribute to the establishment of an order that is not yet legitimate in the Weberian sense of "a belief in the justification of a given order". Instead, these crude forms of acceptance could rather be conceived as forms of initial stabilizing toleration.[90]

The first element of this mechanism is the impression of force. If those who experience the force of the conquering armed groups accept the *supremacy of their violence* and do so without armed resistance, the possibility exists that the next steps will be taken. There is already an element of basic legitimacy in this first stage: the very fact that those subdued capitulate to the superior force gives an armed group a relative advantage since this means that the old order of things is deposed. At the same time, the new power holders are seen as capable – even if not yet morally justified – of establishing a new order. Of course, this tenuous advantage can be overshadowed by the resentment resulting from aggressions by armed groups. The shadow of violence is usually still present, but ascriptions of guilt and shame that result from it might not become a serious obstacle until later phases.

The second step of the mechanism of basic legitimacy is founded on the simple fact that conquering armed groups might establish something resembling order. This step, the *precarious order*, consists of very elementary changes: when shooting stops and micro-boundaries of everyday life become stable, at least temporarily, this is appreciated by everyone concerned as it allows the activities of everyday life to resume. This might, paradoxically, go hand in hand with arbitrary behavior by the rulers. Recruitment for forced labor or the requisition of items and commodities may affect anyone. Such measures can still be perceived as "rigid, but just", as any popular reaction to law and order politics proves. The value of this precarious order is appreciated even more when it occurs after long periods of civil strife and open violence in streets and villages.

The account of Abdurrahman Pahwal, an Afghani intellectual from Nimroz, on the first period of the Taliban's rule in his home region illustrates this point well. Despite a hostile overthrow, as Pahwal's account shows, the preservation of basic rules is often unexpectedly appreciated. This appreciation overcomes the effects of the alien character of the invaders:

"the first period of the Taliban's rule differed in a number of regards from the second. In the early stages of their conquest, they respected the peculiarities of locals and did not attack their customs and habits. One can say that the Taliban knew about the particularities of our region or that at least they were very reluctant in the beginning. Their ranks consisted of young men who came from the old province of Ghazna or from areas in the Northeast. Most of them were very open-mined towards books and sciences. They liked to read, and the public library of Nimrod also had a number of Taliban among its users in this period. It seemed as if they were really "taliban-i 'ilm", students of science, and not "taliban-i 'tufang", students of guns. [...] Therefore the deep mourning of the people of Nimroz could not be stilled when a number of Taliban were murdered by brothers of Abdulchaliq. Quite the contrary. People disliked the murder and said it contradicted the rites and customs of this region that is so rich in stories of heroes and their tales".

(Quoted in Rzehak 2004: 20)

The third step of the mechanism relies on the ability of the new power holders to employ force in order to assure that people take certain actions. It is their *organizational capacity* itself which contributes to the strengthening of their position. They are the ones who are able to organize forced labor, and at least in retrospect this is often seen as legitimate. Numerous armed groups, for example, had established taxation systems by which they were able to finance a series of public services. An even larger number, such as the GAM in Indonesia, the LTTE in Sri Lanka, or UNITA in Angola installed courts to resolve conflicts between neighbors and to settle communal disputes and thus become functional equivalents to states.[91]

For those who benefit from measures taken by the new incumbents of power, these activities foster the legitimacy of the new situation. And for those who are bystanders there is a demonstration effect, the experience that things are moved and that the new power is not only able to kill and to destroy but to build and invest as well. At least potentially, those not benefiting now can entertain ideas of materially benefiting later. The fourth step lies in the *participation effect* the new, even if precarious, order has. Any action that does not contradict the claim of the new rulers is at the same time a silent agreement. People invest time, labor, and money in things that become part of the new order. To restart businesses, to cultivate fields, or to join the administration is a means of investing in the new regime. These investments stabilize the new power structure. To some extent, the effects of this fourth step are therefore a simple function of time. As time elapses, more and more investments are made, and more and more social relations are built on the premises of the new order, rendering it more solid.

This is not only true for the much debated war economy that has often been portrayed as prolonging a conflict. The economic policy of Charles Taylor's NPFL-state, for example, created a broad range of business relations within Liberia and beyond its borders. Although it largely followed the old pattern of a concession economy, any business relation concerning the exportation of iron ore, timber, or rubber was also an investment in the rule of the NPFL as another change of power would have endangered investments made in gaining these concessions.[92] And although these investments are purely profit-driven, they create bonds since a change of the political situation would require another investment to regain the same concession.

Participation in the economy, however, is not restricted to direct relations with armed groups. Its more important sources are the routines of everyday life. When people resume their normal routines, when schools are reopened, and when traffic gains in density and reliability, predictable daily routines also contribute to the stability of the new order. Not only rich businessmen or officials, but everyone continuing a regular life under the new order becomes a "subtenant of power" (Popitz 1992: 227). The participation effect is even stronger when armed groups are able to recruit collaborators. It is a well-known insight from studies of the sociology of colonization that even when culturally foreign powers conquered a territory they used existing voids and structures to integrate themselves into their new system of rule.[93]

A general condition that either hinders or favors the evolution of basic legitimacy is the cultural proximity of insurgents to the population they encounter when conquering territory. When armed groups stem from the same cultural area as the local population they can draw on the shared image of "we" against "them". Commonalities start with simple issues such as shared languages and the ability to formulate claims and directives that are comprehensible. This kind of belonging creates a raw form of solidarity allowing communication that would otherwise be much more challenging. The argument of the moral order presented in the preceding chapter also has a binding effect on rulers. As Georg Simmel, in his essay on the stranger, has remarked, cultural aliens easily become targets of negative ascriptions. For them it is much more difficult to find acceptance of their customs and language, as the general public is aware that they are not bound by the local moral order (Simmel 1950: 766).

Cultural belongings, however, are constantly in motion. Acculturations take place not only top-down but also bottom-up, and they allow for the overcoming of barriers over time. The lesson of colonialism once again is intriguing here. In many instances colonial administrators adapted lifestyles and moral values of the social systems they were intended to alter, and the history of colonialism generally can be seen as a process of mutual adaptation.[94]

The mechanism of basic legitimacy can, of course, stop or derail at any moment. The recurrence of violence, the waning of resources, derailing violence, or a new outbreak of fighting can interrupt the sequence of these four stages. The mechanism is thus not an automatism. It can come to a halt at any point, due to practices that overload the problems facing the population, or due to a failure to bring violence under control. Generally, the task of territorial control poses a wide variety of challenges to armed groups as well as to invading armies. Basic legitimacy, in these cases, is not enough. Even if armed groups succeed in gaining all available men and materiel, there is still a wider need for increased support, particularly if military action is ongoing in other areas. When in danger of being militarily defeated, armed groups feel forced to exploit local economies, to recruit personnel, and to assure that desertion and treason do not devastate their precarious position.

In these phases, the delegitimization of government forces through the violence they exert might temporarily counterbalance the failure of armed groups to construct effective protection.[95] Insurgents can gain from charismatic strikes, for example, deterring government forces by impressive single acts. But as warfare continues, both sides face legitimacy costs. For government troops these costs are a result of the trauma they inflict by indiscriminate violence, whereas for insurgents costs are incurred through failure to protect their supporters. Like the charisma of the warrior, the gains of spectacular strikes depend on repetition, otherwise they are short-lived. Especially for armed groups that do not possess any kind of traditional legitimacy, the problem arises of how to achieve relations with its environment that go beyond mere toleration and basic legitimacy.

One means to enlarge the short temporality of basic legitimacy is to mobilize with a political program, to design and formulate a political project that is able to justify the injustices that are inadvertently connected with warfare and that also helps to legitimize the armed group's rule. A number of armed groups, particularly those oriented towards the ideals of social-revolutionary warfare, use schools and training for "political education" in order to strengthen their legitimacy by inculcating an ideological dogma.[96] Radio and TV stations, websites, newspapers, books, and videotapes are used for transmitting the messages to a broader audience.

Such programs and political ideas, however, also have limited life cycles as will be shown in the next section. Their function to transform the charisma of violent success into traditional legitimacy by embedding the group's project into larger normative frameworks can fail for various reasons, one of which is that these charismatic ideas do not survive the everyday life of rule.

### The cycle of the charismatic idea

During a period of cease-fire in the summer of 1994, the Abbot Diamacoune, leader of the *Mouvement de Forces Démocratiques de Casamance*, was placed under house arrest by the Senegalese government. At that time, the MFDC had been waging a small insurgency in the southern province of Casamance for four years. While researching the causes of the rebellion, I had been attempting for quite some time to arrange an interview with the Abbot, who was typically presented in scholarly and press accounts as the charismatic leader of the small secessionist movement. The MFDC was unable to gain territorial control over parts of the Casamance, only achieving close proximity to the provincial capital Ziguinchor on a few occasions. After street fighting lasting a few hours, it was invariably repelled by the Senegalese army. The remainder of the time, it used thick forests and swamplands at the southern fringes of the province, and of neighboring Guinea-Bissao, as a sanctuary for their attacks on government installations.

On my second visit to the house in which the Abbot was confined, the guarding officer of the Senegalese army allowed me to enter and speak to the leader's entourage. They agreed to an interview on the condition that I provide a list of questions beforehand. After I had met this demand, the interview was scheduled to take place in a few days time.

First, my Senegalese assistant and I had another lengthy conversation with one of the Abbot's aides. He presented himself as a teacher who had lost his position as a result of his involvement with the MFDC and was now selflessly serving the Abbot. After this introduction, we were guided into a room with closed shades in which four men were seated around a table. When the Abbot entered the room through another door, the four stood up immediately, saluted the leader, and shouted, "Atika!", the name of the movement's armed wing.

The conversation then followed the list of questions I had provided, and the Abbot had apparently prepared his answers carefully. Eloquently, and in perfect French, he restated the narrative detailing the reasons for the rebellion and its historical foundation in the experiences of colonial and post-colonial Senegal.[97] According to this account, the MFDC was founded shortly after World War II by local members of the colonial administration from the province of Casamance and by a cousin of the "queen" Alinsitowe, a priestess who had been deported by the colonial administration and later died in exile.[98] Thus linking the colonial past of the region with the current conflict, the Abbot also stressed the "ethnic particularity" of the province and its exploitation by northern Senegalese.

Since the 1960s, Senegalese entrepreneurs, with political support from the government, had not only bought land in the province for large-scale cultivation. Also, the coast line of Casamance had become the site of various vacation resorts for international tourists. These hotels appeared strangely out of place in a rural area whose population practiced rice farming, small-scale fishery, and followed a syncretistic belief with Christian and mythical elements. For the Abbot and his followers, this "Senegalese colonization" endangered the culture and livelihood of the local population. The Casamance province and its people, in their eyes, constituted a distinct "nation" that shared nothing with the predominantly Islamic and Wolof-speaking Senegalese.

Out of the imagined tradition of pre-colonial Casamance, the MFDC discourse created a project to define what a liberated state would be, once it had achieved independence from Senegal. First the Abbot invoked an international treaty between Portugal and France from 1886 that stipulated an independent status for the province which was indeed first subdued by the Portuguese. The new state to be created based on this international legal basis would then re-establish the old social and political order. According the Abbot's plans, the new Casamance would be a liberal democracy, in which education, safe nutrition, and health would be constitutional state purposes. It would be based on the traditional order of the province that, as he put it, "did not know any kind of coercion". Casamance had been, he stated, a federal system of clans, villages, and overarching levels of decision in which councils with legislative and judicial competences delegated executive powers to a King. The new society would be egalitarian and follow matrimonial rules, and it would not allow corporate ownership.

The actual interview required just over an hour, and at the end Abbot Diamacoune wanted to chat about Germany, as he recalled his travels when he was studying Catholic theology in Belgium. He concluded this little causerie by strongly advising me to do two things. "First," he said, "you should send everything you publish about us to our liaison men in Paris. We will give you the address. And secondly, tell your Foreign Minister what's going on here, how Senegal is spoiling our livelihoods!" The Abbot did not accept my objection that Mr. Kinkel, Foreign Minister of Germany at the time, would be unlikely to read what a PhD student might send to him. "I'm sure," he said," if you really want to get through to him, you will succeed."

The ideas of the Abbot and his followers may sound bizarre and contradictory, but in their syncretistic logic these ideas made perfect sense. In terms of troops, age, political success, and international attention, the MFDC certainly was and still is a small, marginal armed group, especially compared to groups such as the Hezbollah, the LTTE, or the PKK. It is unlikely the MFDC ever numbered in excess of a few hundred fighters. Nevertheless, it shows typical elements of discourses armed groups develop in order to legitimize their claims, in Africa and elsewhere. This discourse refers to local, national, and international political norms simultaneously. It is on all three levels that this discourse aims at producing belief in the group's "rightness", its legitimacy.

The most striking feature of this discourse is the persistence of the idea of statehood. Interestingly, the MFDC, unlike other armed groups, does not question the concept of statehood as such. Whereas other movements aim at changing political rules within a given state, the MFDC and other secessionist movements also follow the rules of world politics insofar as they do not strive for alternative political forms but for another, single state. In its discourse, the MFDC attempts to invoke the Western concept of territoriality, although it is inventing a political unity that has never existed in history. A state called Casamance would only have an administrative sub-unit as a precursor, thus it needed a historical narrative as foundational myth.[99]

Second, this idea of stateness is connected with the concept of a nation. Substantial effort is invested in the revision of history in order to prove that something amounting to a Casamance nation has existed for extended periods of time. In this regard, the discourse of the MFDC again follows the logic of international relations, by which the norm of "national self-determination" has been established since the end of World War I.[100] Given the multicultural history and presence of the Casamance, the effort spent on the construction of a nation has sound reasons. The more contradictory evidence there is, the more discursive work is needed in order to convince not only an international public, as in the interview with me, the Western political scientist, but also the constituency of the group itself.

A third continuity with regular politics, again clearly outward-oriented, can be identified in elements such as the balance of power and the democratic character of the Casamance envisioned as an independent state. These elements also address the local public, given that Senegal, considered to be one of the oldest democracies in Africa, has a long democratic tradition that resonates in popular opinions of what makes a "good political order". The same applies for the constitutional state purposes the Abbot mentioned. Education, health, and safe nutrition are the services found to be most debated in post-colonial settings in which the state is considered responsible for the organization of these collective goods. But the expected effect of these promises went far beyond the local and national public. It also attracted sympathizers abroad who approved of the idea of a provisional state.

Finally, the discourse of the MFDC presents a history of modernization with all its social injustices and dislocations as a process of internal colonization within the post-colonial state of Senegal and its Wolof-speaking agents. The effects of modernization – monetarization, individualization, bureaucratization, and privatization of property – social processes that have been analyzed since Marx, are seen in this discourse as the direct outcome of the malefactions of a group of people. At the same time, the use of metaphorical language exaggerates this Manichaean distinction: "The MFDC will get rid of the Senegalese snake and cut off its head as well as its tail".[101]

The social developments and the concrete political situation in which the MFDC emerged and developed, following violent repression, into an armed rebellion, are common circumstances in which these kinds of discourses develop. Even the function of the Abbot, drawing on the traditional legitimacy of descent from a royal family, and on the more modern "charisma of office" as a former Catholic priest, resembles many other cases. He is the bearer of the charismatic idea of national liberation.

Political programs of this sort not only supplement basic legitimacy insurgencies might achieve when they control territory. They are an integral part of their political struggle on three different levels. Programmatic ideas serve as mobilizing levers for the recruitment and internal structuring of armed groups. At the same time, they are used in national arenas to position the group in any given political spectrum. And finally, these programs are needed to attract external support or, at least to secure the impartiality of surrounding regimes and great powers. The effects of programs are thus not restricted to the group's internal life or to local constituencies. By taking a political stance, the politics of armed groups becomes a part of world politics. In their concrete contexts, these ideas are strongest when they develop charismatic qualities, when they become believed promises of better futures. However, these ideas undergo cycles of appreciation and depreciation.

This *mechanism of cycles of charismatic ideas* can be sketched as follows. Political systems drift into crises, and their integrative capacities decrease. Armed groups that develop out of political factions as in the mechanisms of repression and in ad hoc groups then feature as bearers of charismatic ideas, the idea of national liberation, of decolonization, of secession, ideas that promise, like revolutionary agendas, a better future.

Secular and religious ideas, likewise, are subject to life cycles. These ideas are permutations of earlier conceptions of holy lives or better political orders. Very often, these political visions have sources in which political and religious elements cannot easily be isolated, as many secular political programs have religious roots.[102] Political programs often associated with these ideas are globally present but become locally appealing only in situations when the dominant official discourse conforms less and less to everyday life experiences marked by severe socio-economic crises.

Charismatic ideas such as "the liberation", "the revolution" have a mobilizing force because they do not explicitly state what the political order they promise would ultimately consist of. They cannot fail until the movement that promotes them has real political power and is forced to administer everyday life affairs. The cycle of these charismatic ideas can only be completed when the ideas are put into action and when the unavoidable contradictions between actions and words become apparent. Then, the banality of worldly affairs inevitably affects the sacredness of the idea: offices, careers, contracts, and political compromises do not align easily with emotionally fraught expectations of salvation. Although charisma transcends time[103], its routinization is inevitable once the decisive moment of regime change has arrived.

In longer historical periods, there are instances of full cycles of such projects. The war of decolonization in Algeria, for example, began as a charismatic project, ending in a stable, almost unmovable rule by a revolutionary guard. For later generations, the legitimacy of the victorious revolutionaries was nothing more than a fairy tale, betrayed by a dire economic situation of blocked development and high rates of youth unemployment. Under these conditions, the new charismatic idea of the *Front Islamique du Salut* emerged, gained support, and led to electoral victory in 1992.[104]

An analogous cycle was completed in the case of Yugoslavia after World War II. During the war, the revolutionary tale of the Communist Partisans became the legitimizing charismatic idea. Under conditions of violent repression by the German *Wehrmacht*, it succeeded in mobilizing thousands of fighters. When the Partisans had taken over the state of Yugoslavia, this became the legitimizing narrative, taught in schoolbooks and endlessly referred to in political discourse. For following generations, especially during the years of economic decline since the early 1980s, this idea had far less appeal, if any at all. The charisma had faded.[105]

But as long as armed groups do not rule, the charismatic appeal of their political ideas consists in their character of promises. They seem to be revelations of a higher truth, and they promise redemption from ailments that have beset entire societies or political situations. The quasi-religious qualities of charisma reside in this virtual or factual belief in its relation to transcendental forces.[106] That charismatic ideas can become sources of legitimacy is dependent first on critical socio-economic conditions and second on the ability of intellectuals to formulate a program that resonates among the constituency. When this is the case, the choice of programs for armed groups is limited in two ways. First of all, they need programs that possess appeal for targeted supporters and for other external actors. For this they must draw on existing patterns of belief and imagination. The importation of an altogether alien ideology is doomed to fail. Much of the work of symbolic entrepreneurs, usually intellectuals of various types, consists thus in reformulating foreign ideas and compounding them with local contextual conceptions and imaginations.

Secondly, the choice of ideas is restricted because the doctrines of ruling regimes cannot be re-used, unless in such a way as reformist religious movements, which claim to go back to "the true message" that was revealed in the distant past but then betrayed by established institutions.[107] Usually, political opponents of incumbent regimes need alternative projects that either draw on older symbolic resources or import new ideas that they blend with local ideas and political traditions.

However, ideas need social actors to formulate them and to turn them into political projects. Groups that developed according to the pattern of the mechanism of repression often have in their midst intellectuals, and they are often formed around political agendas. An almost ideal-typical case for these groups is Abimael Guzman the renowned leader of the *Sendero Luminoso*-guerilla in Peru. Guzman, a true intellectual, was born in 1934, received his education in Peruvian universities, traveled to China after he had rejected the de-Stalinization in the Soviet Union, and became a Maoist. After his studies, he accepted a teaching position at the provincial university in Ayacucho, joined the Communist Party, and soon began a local political career (Stavans 1993). During these years, Guzman not only adopted Marxist theory but began to elucidate his personal interpretation which later became the group's official dogma. After state repression against the Communist Party began, he again traveled to China, became an even greater admirer of strict party discipline, and was trained in protracted people's warfare strategy.

Throughout the world, universities played an important role as focal points in the programmatic formation of many armed groups. From the early 20th century, universities, at first predominantly in colonial metropoles such as London and Paris, have become centers of intellectual formation for the political personnel of colonial empires. During the period after 1945, they have continued to be hubs for the international distribution of political ideas and formulas. Uganda's current president Yoweri Museveni studied political science at the University of Dar-es-Salam in Tanzania where John Garang, the leader of the Sudan People's Liberation Army joined Museveni's University Students' African Revolutionary Front.[108] The organizational parallels between Garang's group and Museveni's National Resistance Army are an outcome of a joint intellectual experience that included sojourns in the liberated zones of Mozambique in the late 1960s in order to study the practice of warfare of the *Frente de Libertação de Moçambique* against Portuguese colonial rule. Both Garang and Museveni later ruled their groups not only as military commanders but also as intellectual leaders who designed programs and conceived political strategies.

The need for intellectuals capable of formulating ideas and agendas is felt even by leaders of armed groups that come into being as ad hoc groups and have no other agenda than conquering political power. This can be seen from a statement made by Prince Yormie Johnson, leader of the breakaway faction of Charles Taylor's NPFL. When his troops captured a former vice president of Liberia, Johnson told him: "You are the first bookman I have arrested. Charles Taylor has all the other book people. I am fighter, I want you to help me put some ideas together on the economic and political side of this thing."[109]

In cases such as this breakaway faction, the choice of programs and ideas is completely pragmatic. There is little chance that these programs would develop charismatic qualities. Their main purpose is to attract external support by linking national or even personal agendas with norms and rules that dominate global discourses. As such, these ideas are proxies for the genuine support of local constituencies.

Yet these connections between single armed groups' discourses, their programs and ideas, and larger political constellations or even global settings, cannot, in many cases, be reduced to mere instrumental choices taken in order to garner external resources. Rather, they are selective affinities that emerge out of simultaneous political processes, witnessing the global spread of political ideas as part of the long history of political globalization.

## Selected affinities: the global timing of discourse

The production of political agendas of armed groups is part of global discourses, and the condition of its local production varies between pragmatic decision-making and complex intellectual concern. The spread of political ideas is thus neither the result of a plot devised by superpowers during the Cold War, nor is it completely arbitrary. Intellectual centers such as universities and religious institutions have long served as centers for the exchange of internationalized doctrines that are then locally appropriated, modified, and adapted. If there is one aspect of the life of armed groups that shows how international, if not global, these political phenomena are, it is the waves of political doctrines, their spread and recessions. Political ideas have circulated globally in the same way as other intellectual and cultural practices, being appropriated in vernacular political languages, reinterpreted, and re-imported again, as in the case of Che Guevara's and Maoist conceptions of guerilla warfare by European leftist terrorist groups.

Programmatic choices, political strategies, and projects of armed groups in Africa, Asia, Latin America, and the former Soviet Union entertain rather selective affinities with Western – or Eastern – political attitudes. The adaptation of ideas is seldom purely instrumental. Intellectuals can only understand the crises of their societies using the concepts and ideas available to them, and they will formulate them in their vernacular language. There is, however, no guarantee that these inventions will fall on fertile ground. The local adaptation of "big" political ideas can lead to very successful variations, but it can also result in sterile dogmas, largely ignored by the targeted population.

The relation between the political ideas of any single armed group and international discourses is thus complex, but a number of general patterns can be discerned. First, much information is excluded ex negativo. What can be used as a mobilizing discourse is restricted by the historical experience of the constituency. The ideology of former war enemies can only be presented with difficulty as a set of ideas the movement should strive for. Also, the ideas must match norms and customs which the local constituency embraces. Any program that is too revolutionary will sooner or later bring internal problems to armed groups. For the wars in post-socialist settings, for example, the choice of social-revolutionary discourse that would resemble the former state ideology was excluded.[110]

Furthermore, regional constellations factor into this question. The space for strategic choices is limited by the regional framing of conflicts. If regional powers are friends, a strategic positive adaptation of their legitimizing discourse is advisable. However, if they are enemies, it is forbidden to use their ideas and arguments. The wars of decolonization and social revolution in Southeast Asia were thus heavily influenced by the Maoist revolution in China, which was later seen both as a predecessor and a potential supporter by other insurgent groups.

Finally, state policies and the discursive strategies of states were important for the range of ideas and approaches armed groups could draw on. This is a highly dialectical relation as the programmatic choices of armed groups did not always simply take an opposite position in relation to foundational myths of the governments they were attacking. As can often be seen, particularly in the case of armed groups that used religious ideals and ideas, they could play on the cycle of charismatic ideas as well. In all those cases in which the idea of national liberation or religious purity was once fostered by state agencies and ruling parties, armed groups could benefit from the loss of legitimacy of governments which seemingly betrayed these ideas in the eyes of many, as the emergence of systemic opposition in Titoist Yugoslavia as well as in post-independence Algeria demonstrates.

The relation between the global tides of ideas and the programmatic directions of armed groups after 1945 thus cannot be reduced to the history of global political constellations, even if it is not independent of it. There is not a simple instrumental relation between global discourses and the political programs of armed groups. Through reading and academic debates, studies undertaken abroad, and by involvement in international political movements, these ideas have spread globally since at least the 19th century. They found admirers and opponents not only in the West, but also in Asia, Africa, and Latin America. Local actors thus do not choose freely between an array of ideas, but instead rely on worldviews and imaginations that are locally grounded and promise to resonate among their envisaged or real constituency.

In external discourses of armed groups, selective affinities between globalized political ideas and locally produced programs abound. Leaders and "bookmen" use ideas of which they are partly convinced themselves and those which might plausibly be appreciated by an external public. An example from the official discourse of armed groups shows this.

Riek Machar, a sub-leader of the Sudan People's Liberation Army, wrote after he had split with the SPLA:

"The crisis of national identity is a creation of North Sudan which defines the Sudanese identity in Arab and Islamic terms. The Northern political elites consider the Sudanese citizenship as a transition to full integration into the Arab identity. This undermines the right of the vast African majority whose identity should be fully embodied in the character of the state"

(Machar 1995)

The point about this quote is not whether it is a correct picture or interpretation of the conflict that has devastated Sudan for almost 40 years. Of primary concern here is that the norms of the addressed public, of a historical account as part of a political argument, are anticipated by the author, and they allow the narrative embedded in a normative framework to raise support or at least toleration of the group and its agenda.[111]

In terms of geopolitical concepts, the idea of the nation state has always been the most powerful. References to leftist or right-wing positions during the wars of decolonization, as Eric Hobsbawm recapitulates, were rather made due to pragmatic alliances in order to solicit support, the "globality" of the fights often being maintained by a small number of communist activists in the groups who believed in this ideology (1994: 447). Often these references worked as mutually reinforcing projections. "Revolutions" and "liberations" in the South were interpreted in the North either as an opportunity or as a threat, depending on the political standpoint, whereas these interpretations were readily confirmed in order to garner financial, ideational, or political support.[112] The fight for revolution, however, was not "ecumenical" (Hobsbawm 1994: 447). For all movements the national agenda was supreme. The ideology of the nation state overruled all other political pragmatics throughout the period.[113]

The tides of global political discourses are thus mirrored in the ups and downs of political key concepts, ideas, and claims in armed groups' political statements. This can already be deduced from the official naming of groups and long-term shifts in their usage. Whereas the term "liberation" figured highly in the era of decolonization, the attributes "revolutionary" and "democratic" became more fashionable somewhat later. While the use of religious terms is not an invention of the period following the Cold War, it has seemingly gained in importance since.

In retrospect, one can roughly distinguish four overlapping phases in the development of armed groups' discourses since the end of World War II. First is the foundational idea of the nation state and its related idea of national self-determination. Second is the idea of social revolution, characteristic, as such, for the period between the 1950s and the late 1980s. Since then, two other ideas became prominent in the public perception of matters considered at issue in ongoing wars. One is the norm of democratization and human rights, and second is the rise of religious ideas that seem recent whereas in fact they have been present for a considerable time.

As a result of its foundational function for globalized political ideas, the concept of "national" liberation survived the changes of political fashions and continues to be a norm that is globally accepted even under (neo-)liberal premises. States are the basic political structure of the world system, and this official image is so strong that no armed group would sacrifice that idea. It is so powerful because it is so widely believed. Therefore, it is no coincidence that the adjunct "national" has been a prominent reference throughout the period since 1945. The idea that a "nation" by almost natural historical necessity would strive for a separate state or need another political arrangement within a given state has thus been a constant figure within the discourses of armed groups. That it has been so prominent is also due to the fact that the concept of stateness, the "image of the state" (Migdal/ Schlichte 2005) has been deeply ingrained in any political actor's mindset since the early 20th century, if not before.

The concept of the nation has been concocted as the political idea of the nation *state* since the concept of people's sovereignty replaced monarchial and other precedent legitimizing doctrines of what modern states consist of. In the course of what historians call the "European expansion", this idea has quickly been taken up elsewhere. The struggles of Latin American revolutions were already based on the normative ground of that concept, and any other anti-colonial movement gained immediate international legitimacy when it claimed to represent a group of people excluded from official political participation under colonial rule.[114]

Post-colonial states build their legitimizing discourse around the very same idea. They teach the story of the *res publica* in schools, and politicians refer to the norm of national self-determination in myriads of speeches and interviews. The "nation" as a concept is invoked without difficulty because it serves as an image of the body politic throughout the world. Armed groups refer to that norm also by presenting themselves as the embodiment of "the people", while their sacrifices serve as proof. The transcendental links of the martyr whose death – whatever the actual circumstances might have been – are ex post interpreted as sacrifices for the cause of national liberation. Here, the legitimization by violence connects with abstract political discourse.

The second idea that had become prominent in the external discourses of armed groups added to the idea of *social emancipation*. Because colonialism in most cases was an economic as well as a political program, anti-colonial movements not only had political agendas but also aspired to transform their new states' economies. This was seen as a tool to attain more social equality. In Latin America, the emergence of social-revolutionary movements was part of broader intellectual shifts towards the political left. The "theory of dependency" that became dominant in large areas of global academic thinking regarding the problem of development in the wake of the student movement belongs to the same change in intellectual frameworks. The convergences of leftist thinking in that period formed a stage for revolutionary movements from all parts of the world. It allowed for raising international support for armed groups that superficially assumed the guise of a revolutionary movement, and for which Marxism was merely a disciplinary doctrine for their apparatuses (Hobsbawm 1994: 451). The close connection between Western governments' involvement and anti-guerilla campaigns, first and foremost those of the United States, increasingly fostered the interpretation of the global relatedness of these struggles. The same was true for the Soviet Union and other countries of the Eastern bloc that supported "liberation" movements across the world, in a growing competition of "solidarity" with the People's Republic of China.[115]

The age of the Cold War was thus a period in which political movements and especially armed groups became embedded in global power balances. Whereas in fact the dynamics of political conflicts were often causally unrelated, the Cold War as an overarching framework of interpretation allowed for molding any story into the same belief. For Western and Eastern governments alike there was no neutral or irrelevant conflict. Everything was seen as part of the same global constellation, and the symbolic strategies of armed groups searching for external support strengthened this belief.

The third global wave of political ideas that dominated international debates and resonated in armed groups' discourses was the pairing of *de-*

*mocracy and human rights*. In a basic form this discourse was present throughout the period since 1945. People's sovereignty is the foundational norm of that global political system, so any armed group had a chance of gaining international legitimacy if it could credibly claim to represent a "national" group that had no other way of expressing its political will.[116] However, with the end of so-called "real-world socialism", the norm of social emancipation has lost much of its attraction and mobilization capacity, and the global pendulum swung towards the norm of liberal democracy and the observance of human rights. The demand for democratization is to some extent only a current form of earlier emancipatory discourses. Armed groups now denounce a lack of democratic participation and the human rights abuses of their adversaries, trying to build their own legitimacy around these norms.

The fourth legitimizing discourse to which armed groups resorted has been centered on different forms of *politicized religion*. Here again, the same linkages between local productions, global and regional dynamics can be observed. The shift towards fundamentalist programs is almost always linked to two factors. One is the exclusion of "applicants" to the political class. Blocked development and waning integrative capacities of developmental states were the general conditions under which religious belief became the symbolic frame in which challenges to the foundational stories of post-colonial states were expressed. Often, these myths themselves had included religious elements, and the growing gap between these mythical promises and the dire reality in autocratic states allowed for the revitalization of these religious conceptions, as in Pakistan and numerous Arab states.[117] The other factor has been that nationalist and social-revolutionary programs seemingly failed in bringing about fundamental change. The shift from the leftist program of Fatah to the successful mobilization of Hamas among the Palestinian constituency is perhaps the most obvious example of this dynamic.

This fourth wave was also supported by and connected with regional and global developments. Since the late 1970s, for example, armed groups could take advantage of the competition between Iran and Saudi Arabia in their quest for external support. Both states pursued an active foreign policy and promoted different versions of "true" Islam (Kepel 2004: 29). During the Cold War, conservative Mujaheddin in Afghanistan and later the Taliban benefited from strong support from Saudi Arabia, but also from the United States.[118]

But politicized religion restricted itself again to national agendas, despite the mutual influences between movements and the rise of a "globalized Islam" (Roy 2003). Even in the case of the various armed groups in Afghanistan that began with external financial support, also as a part of Muslim solidarity, the overarching symbolism could not overcome centrifugal competition between leaders. By the 1990s, ethnic symbolism had overruled the religious agenda (Dorronsoro 2000: 282ff.).

## Conclusion

Armed groups face the challenge of transforming the crude form of power they achieve by violent means into legitimate rule. The task of counterbalancing the negative effects of violent actions arises on three levels. First, within armed groups the subjective belief by staff and followers in the "rightness" of the group's actions is a necessary complement to other motivating factors for joining the group and risking the consequences of armed fighting. Secondly, when armed groups want to stabilize their position in their social environment, they also need to create this belief in a social setting. This becomes an urgent need when groups achieve territorial control. The third level on which this need arises is the international arena. In order to attract external support and to avoid hostile reactions by neighboring states or international interventions, armed groups need to legitimize their actions by discourses and narratives.

In its first section, this chapter has shown that traditional legitimacy can be one source for the internal stability of armed groups. Parental ties, socially accepted forms of patrimonialism, and other established patterns of hierarchy can be conveyed to armed groups by the social habitus of leaders, staff and followers. Often, as in the case of groups that came about through the mechanism of repression, such established hierarchical forms exist in the non-violent forerunners of armed groups such as parties or religious organizations. Two tendencies have been analyzed that contribute to the erosion of traditional legitimacy. Generational conflicts within the social context of armed groups can spill over into their internal politics, with youngsters questioning the legitimacy of older order patterns. Also, successful members of armed groups, commanders or politicians, can accumulate warrior charisma. These gains can be used to challenge the positions of traditional Big Men, such as clan leaders and elders. These conflicts can increase the likelihood of the fragmentation of armed groups. However, there are also cases in which armed groups perceived the conflictive lines in their midst and proved to be learning organizations, adapting their structure to these changes.

Furthermore, two mechanisms have been sketched in this chapter by which legitimacy gaps can be filled. On the one hand, proto forms of legitimacy accrue to armed groups if they can bring unstable situations under control. This basic legitimacy is highly contingent on their ability to restore regular social life once they have conquered territory. Four elements of this basic legitimacy have been isolated that allow for further stabilizations of an armed group's power position: the supremacy of violence, the precarious order, the organizational capacity, and the participation effect.

The second mechanism sketched in this chapter is the cycle of charismatic ideas. Armed groups invoke political projects and programs which serve as legitimizing narratives for their claims. These programs allow surpassing the limited temporality of the gains of basic legitimacy. In situations of deep socio-economic crises, the core ideas of these programs can acquire charismatic qualities. Their character as promises, often gaining a quasi-religious status, promotes mobilizing of forces and allows, if not a connection of armed groups' political projects with other dynamics of international politics, at least the acceptance or neutrality of outside actors. This charismatic quality is at risk when armed groups achieve territorial control because the requirements of everyday life politics contradict unrealistic expectations.

The last section of this chapter outlined the entanglement of political programs of armed groups with international politics. These programs are not chosen freely. Their selection depends on local productions of symbols, conceptions of the political, and interpretation of political history. At the same time, these local conditions are also embedded in regional and international settings of political discourse. These regional and global constellations also enable groups to attract material support. But legitimizing discourses are thus also subordinated to the global timing of political ideas. As a result, they are also influenced by larger changes in political constellations that surround the national arenas in which armed groups engage in battle.

What could be sketched here rather than fully developed is the international embeddedness of the politics of armed groups. Even a superficial analysis of their discourses reveals immediately how deeply their political aims and ideas are enmeshed with transnational political projects. These connections are hitherto understudied but the evidence at hand already proves that the politics of legitimization are partly almost universal and simultaneously part of global history.

Furthermore, this chapter has shown that the politics of armed groups go beyond mere military activities. In fact, most of them are political actors in the full sense of the word. All of them need to mobilize through talk, symbols and discourse, they need to find supporters and to forge alliances. They are obliged to organize a minimum of administration. This means at the same time that armed figurations are not detached from mundane requirements. As the next chapter will show, the "basic needs" of armed groups, the conditions of their material reproduction, are as well embedded into local and global economic tides.

# 5. Finance and Reproduction

Since the mid-1990s, questions regarding the economic incentives to wage war have been at the center of academic discussions on organized violence. The reasons underlying this high level of activity are not easily discernable. One relevant point is certainly that the overwhelming interpretation developed in the early 1990s during the Yugoslav wars, namely to draw on ethnic differences and "culture" as explanatory variables for the outbreak and continuity of civil wars, proved to be insufficient. Many authors discovered rational motives and economic underpinnings of intrastate wars[119] as the important connections of civil wars with global markets became more apparent.

A second stimulus for this focus of the debate possibly resides in the Zeitgeist, the moral, cultural, and intellectual spirit of the times. The late 1980s witnessed the initial rise of economic explanations in the social sciences generally. Reasoning about politics in concepts that were largely taken from micro-economics became increasingly accepted because these concepts had become familiar ones in all fields of study as well as in public discourse.

The debate on the economic underpinnings of war has great merit as it has led not only to a refinement of theses on the role of economic motives and structures in the outbreak and continuity of war. Also, numerous case studies have been produced which have enriched the available knowledge of particular patterns and processes. But in concentrating the debate on war actors and their incentive structures[120], these contributions cannot account for the dynamics of armed groups that result partly from deliberate strategies and partly from changes in economies during wartime. What are these strategies, and how do economies of war affect the politics of armed groups? In answering these questions, this chapter will begin with a brief discussion of theoretical understandings and statistical findings on the economic reproduction of insurgent groups. This encompasses a criticism of rationalist reductionism that is based on a homo economicus understanding of civil wars and insurgencies. What is suggested instead is a more process-oriented understanding that can encompass much more variation, but also political contexts that have been fairly influential in the proliferation of armed groups during the last 60 years.

Three pathways of how armed groups develop economically are differentiated later in this chapter. The pathway taken depends first on the politics of armed groups, on their success in overcoming delegitimizing violence by legitimizing practices and discourse. Second is the change in their economic environment, which becomes unstable during wartime. The economic policies of armed groups are, of course, embedded in broader economic developments that have been discussed as "war economies". The economic environment of an armed group, I will argue, is not stable but changes in the course of a war. This has consequences for the economic policies of armed actors. In its second part, this chapter will therefore contain a sociological sketch of the economic changes during civil war. Using Pierre Bourdieu's terminology on different types of capital, this will allow the correlation of economic changes, in the narrow sense of the term, with other social dynamics from which a war economy cannot be separated, as they have immediate economic consequences and thereby also affect power relations within armed groups.

By means of this broader description, drawing on the distinction between an "economy in war" and a "war economy", changes in the practices and strategies of armed groups become more readily apprehended. Economic dynamics of armed groups are thus conceived as part of the changes of broader figurations. The general argument developed in that section concerns the linkage between broader economic change in war-affected societies and the reproductive modes of armed groups. Instead of considering solely how economic structures affect the architecture of armed rebellion, as is the case in the larger part of the literature on this topic, both must be seen as interrelated processes. Economies change during a war, and so do the ways in which insurgent groups manage to survive and maintain their viability. There is no single immutable law that describes this relation, but both processes interact.

This interaction, as shown in the final part of this chapter, can lead to any one of the three typically discernible outcomes for armed groups as figurations, namely statization, stagnation, or disconnection. The first is the route to state-building. Some armed groups achieve a degree of institutionalization that allows them to erect stable systems of taxation, approaching the capabilities of states or even surpassing them in their power to levy taxes. What begins as a violent appropriation becomes a regular source of funds, often betraying a certain coercive character. The strategy of these groups is to overcome the pressure of a shrinking war economy by fostering an economic basis.

The second outcome of the economic trajectory of armed groups is stagnation. When local support declines, foreign influence ceases, and no strategy to counterbalance the degradation of the economic environment is at hand, armed groups can experience reversals in their efforts, leaving them to linger for many years in a very marginal form.

The third pathway is disconnection. Armed groups that observe rather patrimonial relations internally and towards their targeted constituency can pursue an existence that has no need to form ties that go beyond mere patron-client relationships. This disconnected relation, however, is subject to regional or global political constellations and can wither away quickly when these constellations change.

As will be seen in the next chapter, these three forms of reproduction correspond to organizational forms that armed groups can achieve. However, this is not a plea for economic determinism. As will be argued in these final two chapters, there is considerable leeway for insurgents to shape their policies and resulting forms by adopting strategies that aim at the institutionalization of their power.

## Conceptions and Statistics

In the discussion of economic underpinnings of civil wars, the idea of incentive structures has certainly become the most prominent explanatory concept. In its basic form, this idea maintains that the distribution of easily accessible resources such as raw materials better explains the onset of war than the competing explanation based on motives. This latter thesis has been dominating a lot of research during the last ten years. Numerous studies have variously attempted to argue against it, to modify it, or to find further evidence that reinforces its validity. [121] Objections to this thesis have hinted at the lack of its theoretical foundations, the confusion between methodological schools and theoretical assertions, and the selective use of data. Attempts to refine the argument have made efforts either to specify the thesis for certain commodities and raw materials or to further emphasize the thesis by deducting logics of collective action in civil war (Weinstein 2005; 2007).

Such rationalist interpretations have their merits. They help to overcome a simplistic culturalist understanding of the nature of war and allow the disentanglement of many enigmatic features of civil war dynamics. There is, however, an inherent danger of overstating the rationality of war events and of ignoring historical contexts and the intrinsically political nature of economic dynamics influenced by violence. It overemphasizes regularly observable events and neglects subjective meaning. A truly satisfying explanation of social action would always encompass both elements. It must combine a thesis on observable regularities with the hermeneutic work of interpretation.[122]

There are several observations that prove the insufficiency of microeconomic theory. First is the observation that all armed groups have different sources of income, ranging from organized crime and pillage to entrepreneurial enterprises and related rents from exportations, to personal taxes and customs fees. This basic fact, often overlooked in the literature, is intriguing as it calls for an explanation of this variation. Economic contexts, I argue, have to be taken into account in order to come to terms with these differences.

Second, the reproductive form of armed groups is not preordained by existing economic structures. Evidently, armed groups develop strategies to overcome scarcity and to enlarge their sources of income. These attempts are not necessarily always successful, but on occasion they are, in the sense that these techniques not only allow a fostering of the internal relations of armed groups but also in allowing a denser relation between local populations, larger constituencies, and entire societies.

Thirdly, not only the strategies of adaptations but also the dynamics of failure are partly dependent on global circumstances. The sheer amount of subsidies armed groups amassed during the Cold War is perhaps evidence enough. The list of groups and states that were supported with financial aid or military and strategic expertise during the Cold War is virtually endless. But after 1989 and the ensuing watershed in international politics, global discourses and regional power politics had severe impacts on the economies in which armed groups move and on their strategies for survival.

The logic of these dynamics can be best understood by looking at the distinctions between ways by which domination is funded. Any political rule needs an economic basis, but relations between political associations and an economy can take on very different shapes. In economic sociology, four basic forms can be distinguished, differing in regularity and in the degree of enforcement vs. voluntariness.[123]

Table 6: *Typology of funding forms of armed groups*

|  | Irregular | Regular |
|---|---|---|
| voluntary | Donations | Self-run enterprise |
| enforced | Crime, fees | Taxes |

Source: Radtke 2009: 218

Whereas donations might be contributed in considerable amounts, they lack regularity as the willingness to give money or gifts in kind can vary for many reasons. Established taxes become more calculable over time, as is the case with individuals' entrepreneurial enterprises. Experience accumulated over time allows for more accurate estimates of the income that can be expected, and although these sources also underlie the vagaries of war, they constitute a much more reliable basis than occasional gifts and tenuous profits from corruption.

One major force that drives armed groups towards institutionalization is of very basic interest to their members. They have an understandable desire for steady incomes, either by the enduring provision of goods or by payment in currency. While plunder might satisfy short-term needs, staff members' goal will always be for more extended periods of regular income. This pressure, connected with the military necessity to enlarge the group's power base, mounts steadily beneath the tendency towards institutionalization in many armed groups.

This is an observation that dates from early analyses of processes of state formation.[124] In all historical instances of charismatic rule, with its typically unstable and irregular opportunities for income, staff members soon developed an interest in stable relationships and steady incomes. Apart from the question of how to organize succession, this interest is the single most important force at work in the "routinization of charisma" (Weber 1978, I: 249).

Armed groups attempt in different ways to fund their fight. And although, as a result of their illicit nature, no reliable data exists on the sums that are gathered in these various ways, media reports and case literature give hints as to the respective ranking of these methods.

Table 7: *Most often reported forms of funding of armed groups (1945-2005, in percent)*[125]

|  | All N=80 | Repression N=27 | Adhoc N=41 | Spin-off N=9 |
|---|---|---|---|---|
| Support from other states | 73 | 83 | 77 | 62 |
| Organized crime/taxes | 54 | 57 | 57 | 37 |
| Theft and pillage | 52 | 55 | 52 | 37 |
| Support local population | 50 | 55 | 42 | 100 |
| Illegal trade | 37 | 31 | 45 | 62 |
| Support from diaspora | 36 | 44 | 32 | 100 |
| Legal trade | 29 | 21 | 32 | 50 |
| Pillage | 27 | 27 | 32 | 33 |
| Kidnappings | 8 | 2 | 10 | 25 |
| Self-run exportation | 21 | 15 | 22 | 50 |

Source: MAG-database

By far the most remarkable observation from this overview is that support from other states is the most frequent form of funding that armed groups receive. Not only during the Cold War era, but apparently throughout the entire period under consideration, states have used insurgencies in other states as means of advancing their external policy.

While these numbers are certainly distorted due to the lack of media coverage and the varying attention accorded the particular issue, it is clear that other strategies of generating funds were at work as well. These are not restricted to practices commonly associated with internal warfare such as pillage, kidnappings, and illegal trade. Other practices that either require some degree of institutionalization or will eventually require it also rank high on that list. This applies, for example, to the practice of extortion to promise physical protection operated by organized criminal groups that can become, in effect, regular taxation.[126]

No armed group relies exclusively on one practice, and even spin-off groups acquire a certain minimum degree of popular support, albeit often from particular segments of the population.[127] Quite in opposition to theses on the path-dependency that results from armed groups "endowments" (Weinstein 2007: 7), change seems to be possible. As the case literature suggests, a number of groups that began by being financed by governments and later became spin-offs were apparently able to overcome their lack of legitimacy and stir support from at least segments of constituent populations.

Partly, this diversity of income sources mirrors the different economic settings in which armed groups operate. However, another element of the explanation for the fact that many armed groups have several sources of income lies in the dynamic of their practices. As will be shown in the remaining sections of this chapter, neither the economic basis on which armed groups live nor the policies employed to raise funds and means for their reproduction are static. In their strife, armed groups must foster and maximize their sources of income, and therefore their leaders attempt to turn irregular sources into stable and steady flows that allow long-term strategies and provide continuous income for their members.

As the findings presented above do not include an observation of changes over time, other materials must be gathered to allow for a full interpretation of the numbers given. It is only possible by the comparative discussion of case trajectories to comprehend how and why the strategies of funding of armed groups have changed. And in fact, several armed groups demonstrate a clear strategy of diversification of income origins, striving for increasingly regular and stable sources. These strategies, however, were combined with two broader developments.

First was the change of global political structures that also altered the ramifications for the funding of political violence globally. It is widely known and accepted that regional and global changes affected the financing of insurgencies throughout the period. One background of the switching and shifting in the funding of armed groups are strategies to either expand their material basis or establish alternate sources to replace state funding or channels of support that were eliminated. With the end of the Cold War, it was argued, this has quite often been the case as support from either the Soviet Union and its allies or the opposition camp, the United States and other Western states, began to diminish around 1990. In numerous cases, the Cold War compounded what was already a complicated overlapping of local and regional conflicts, which created entire sub-regional systems of war. In East Asia, in Southern Africa, and in Latin

America the dynamic of any single war cannot be understood without an awareness of these complex interrelated conflicts in neighboring countries that were often externally fueled by the provision of military and financial aid.[128] These subsidies for belligerents from both super-powers and their allies frequently became mutually reinforcing, manifesting an almost systemic character.

By the conclusion of the Cold War, a number of armed groups were in the position of finding new ways to finance their struggles. One way of doing so was to draw on regional constellations, since external support by other states has not been limited to the Cold War context of the super-powers and their allies. Every war is also embedded in a constellation of regional and sub-regional constellations. States that were most often entangled in the civil wars of neighboring states or even across regions included India, Libya, Nigeria, South Africa, Iran, Iraq, and Israel. These states either had particular ambitions to become regional powers or to maintain that status, or their political position in the international system was so precarious that they felt it pragmatic to support insurgent groups that, if successful, would become potential allies in international politics.[129]

The second general background for the funding of armed groups requires somewhat more elaboration. It consists of the dynamic that turns an economy at war into a war economy. By looking more closely into this major change, that is the imperatives and narrowing margins within armed groups operate economically, this phenomenon can be more clearly explained than by a simple path dependency argument that does not consider processes of economic change in which armed groups are involved.

## Economy in war and war economies

The outbreak of a civil war does not immediately affect the entire society of the respective country. Like international wars, civil wars have an extension in time and space, and each war has its own temporality and locality. The economy of a war-affected country is therefore in many cases only partially distorted, and some branches of business might not initially encounter any difference whatsoever.

Civil wars also take place in states and societies with very divergent economies. They extend from highly integrated industrial settings, as in parts of the former Yugoslavia, to very remote and peripheral regions such as South Sudan or Northern Uganda. War settings differ in their economic structure, in their degree of integration into the world economy, and in their vulnerability to the effects of violence.

These observations render dubious the idea as to whether it is possible to formulate general assertions about economic change in civil wars. The following observations, however, attempt to do this in order to determine the general tendencies that frame the setting for chances of the economic development of armed groups. This is not always a true war economy. Christine Messiant and Roland Marchal (1997: 15) have rightly stated that there is a difference between an "economy in war" and a "war economy". Whereas the former expression designates a change of conditions under which economic life is taking place, as for example through higher levels of taxation as states are in need of more funds for waging war, the second expression refers rather to deep structural changes within the economy due to war-caused distortions. The ultimate outcome of these changes is that violent actors become entrepreneurs themselves, so that political and economic interests are no longer separated.

With this distinction it becomes possible to explain not only the diverse sources of income that most armed groups develop. It is feasible as well to discern strategic patterns that armed groups display as they attempt to adapt their economic basis to a changing environment. The main thesis that is associated with the submission of the economy to the logic of war is that armed groups must find external linkages that allow for substituting decreasing returns in a war economy suffering from a shrinking capital stock.

The transition from an economy "at war" to a "war economy" is naturally a gradual one. The presence of violence or an approaching front might initially affect very few decisions. Only if it endures will the shadow of violence spread, thus affecting the entire economy. Three different sub-processes can be distinguished that constitute this transition. First is the shrinking of the capital stock due to the erosion of values in a war. It results in an accelerated informalization as under the hardship of war conditions social capital gains in importance to secure survival. The expansion of violent accumulation results in the de-bordering of these practices which finalizes the establishment of a war economy. All three sub-processes will be briefly described here.

Armed groups, although primarily the main actors involved, suffer from its consequences. They therefore develop strategies to counterbalance the disastrous effects of a shrinking and informalized economy while, ironically, generating the destructive effects themselves. One method is a re-formalization of the economy, based on territorial control that allows armed groups to be transformed into para-states. Another is to obtain access to resources located outside the actual war zone. This latter strategy, of course, supports the third tendency described here, the expansion and de-bordering of the war economy.[130]

*Shrinking of the capital stock*

Violence has economic effects. Immediateness as an imperative resulting from large scale violence drives an economy into a downward spiral.[131] The closer the actual fighting gets, the smaller the incentive becomes to continue to make sound economic investments. This is a result of the fact that people facing war also face a threefold decision. They can endure violence, they can flee, or they can join factions of the armed struggle. None of these decisions will lead to investments. Traders stop buying commodities as routes of transport become insecure, construction work ceases when territorial control and future ownership become uncertain, and mobile capital is transferred into safe havens.

The shadow of violence thus also falls on the temporality of economic activity in war. This general tendency, however, has very different effects depending on the concrete structure of any given economy. It also affects segments of the population differently, depending on the amount of capital they possess and its relative composition.[132] Mobile economic capital such as money, cattle, and other easily transferable goods experience an increase in value, while immobile economic capital, for example real estate, machinery, and buildings are devaluated.[133] Cultural capital, as it is embodied in education and skills, in expertise and experiences, has a tendency to lose value in times of civil war as the institutions in which it is transmitted and utilized are likely to be abandoned. Schools and universities close, research and luxury goods businesses fail. The only exceptions to this rule are forms of cultural capital that are war-relevant, like organizational skills and, of course, violence expertise. Social capital, however, the last form, increases in value. As confirmed persistently in reports and narratives concerning wars, it is precisely as all other institutions of a war-affected society drift apart that immediate social relations become ever more important for an individual's reproduction and survival.

These devaluations and appreciations appear in any civil war as similar alterations in social structures as war economies produce winners and losers.[134] The social effects of an economy at war are heterogeneous, and there are also countervailing tendencies. Refugees and internally displaced persons, of course, normally rank among the losers as flight is normally closely associated with the loss of major assets. Houses left behind can be destroyed, social relations are interrupted, and skills no longer practiced may deteriorate. Normally only a small stratum of refugees can utilize its accumulated cultural capital to achieve a regular income while displaced. Different dynamics, of course, unfold in refugee camps where the nearness of relations can generate additional social capital, leading to a new, largely informal, economy.[135]

Other groups who lose their income are state employees and wage earners. For the first group, it is the shift of state expenses to war efforts that decreases chances for promotion and often leads quickly to reductions in employment. Non-military segments of the state apparatus are steadily eliminated. This commences with regular administrations, expenses for education and health sectors, and infrastructure. State employees and wage-earners likewise suffer most severely from inflation that usually accompanies war. In the Federal Republic of Yugoslavia, during extreme phases, the exchange rate for average wages earned in Dinar fell, between 1992 and 1993, by approximately 90 percent. Inflation skyrocketed in December 1993 to 300 million percent (Reuter 1994: 479).

The devaluation of assets and skills in a war reaches ever wider circles. Carriers are brought to a halt, a massive amount of capital is destroyed, and resources are increasingly diverted from production. At the same time, economic values are consumed for the organization and exertion of violence. As a consequence, more and more people are impoverished throughout the course of a war.

However, all wars also know economic winners. Two classes can be distinguished, those who benefit from the changes while residing at a safe distance from the fighting, and those who are physically situated in the midst of a war. Winners inside the war are usually those who possess the skills and means necessary for conducting a war. Military expertise as well as applicable technical skills can be counted as such. Fighters who are paid or allowed to loot can also be seen as winners, as fleeting as this new wealth might be.

Winners within a war are also those who dispose of wealth that does not underlie the devaluation by inflation. As long as widespread dispossessions and destructions do not occur, owners of real estate and fixed capital assets and those who transfer mobile capital abroad benefit from the economic changes during war, at least in relation to their less mobile wage-earning compatriots.

The most visible winners of war economies, however, are those individuals or corporations profiting from price changes resulting from war shortages or surpluses. Companies or entire sectors that buy or market raw materials exported from war-affected countries have thus recently attracted increasing attention.[136] The export of timber, diamonds, oil, coltan, and illegal drugs create wealth at several points as the conditions of war often allow downward price pressure to extraordinarily low levels. Also, sub-centers for trade in neighboring states or in regions not directly affected by the war flourish under these conditions.[137]

Economies in war, as these observations can be summarized, change in various ways due mainly to the shadow of violence. Certain forms of capital are devaluated under the condition of immediateness, while others appreciate. Cultural capital, education, and skills lose value in the course of a war unless they are militarily important, such as the ability to organize and exert violence. On the one hand, economic capital frequently shrinks during a war as there is more consumed than produced.[138] Social capital, on the other hand, becomes more valuable because in times of scarcity and decaying institutions social ties gain in importance for the provision of even the most basic goods. The overall tendency, however, is the shrinking of capital stock in a war economy.

*Accelerated informalization*

One universal consequence of these tendencies is therefore the informalization of the economy in war. The longer conditions of violence prevail, the more the economy will be de-formalized. When wages no longer suffice to satisfy basic needs, currency will be sought via informal markets. Parental ties, access to the smallest spoils and prebends become more important than formal employment and legal status. Trade embargoes accelerate this tendency, as neighboring countries become hubs of illicit trade.[139]

The dynamics sketched above entail strategies among a war-affected population that often lead to the total informalization of the economy. *Magendo*, the Swahili expression for contraband, was the name for these strategies in Uganda in the late years of Idi Amin's rule and during the ensuing years of turmoil when the formal economic sector had almost vanished. By 1980, inflation had reduced worker salaries to 6 percent of their 1972 value (Nabuguzi 1991: 134). State employees found it necessary to supplement their income with other employment as taxi drivers, shopkeepers, or agricultural producers. Farmers who had formerly contributed to the state's income by the requirement that they sell their coffee production through the state's Coffee Marketing Board began smuggling their harvest across borders in order to get higher prices, and yet they still had to struggle for survival. The downward spiral of a shrinking state and an increasingly informalized economy ended in the impoverishment of large segments of the population and a few instances of private enrichment, with those found primarily at top political positions (Nabuguzi 1991: 140).

While informalization of an economy is not bound to ongoing wars, it enters into mutually reinforcing relations when political conflicts are resolved by organized violence. As the Bosnian experience shows, this can lead to absurd constellations. For the defense of Sarajevo, for example, the Bosnian authorities initially had to rely on the criminal underworld's expertise in violence to prevent the Serbian-dominated Jugoslavenska Narodni Armija from entering the city (Andreas 2004). Besieged by this army between April 1992 and fall 1995, Sarajevo's economic life was thrown into a condition of total informality. Sarajevo's population relied heavily on the black market for provision of food and fuel, as trade between the warring factions became crucial for survival.[140] What had taken place in Sarajevo was simply an accelerated variation of the general process of informalization, that is to say the elimination of public control over economic transactions.

The chief impact that the tendency toward informalization has on the populace is a reciprocal evaluation of social capital. When formal employment vanishes and public services are eliminated, social capital becomes the only resource which survival strategies can be based upon. Of course, these strategies themselves then reinforce informalization. A typical result of this process in African contexts has been that subsistence agriculture becomes the dominant mode of reproduction, reversing the normal relationship between cities and rural areas, since the countryside becomes the center of provision. How well one is connected to peasants who are still producing staples becomes a decisive question under such conditions.[141]

The informalization of the economy often precedes a civil war and accelerates when open violence begins. This is tantamount to the subordination of economic activity to violent appropriation. When this happens, an economy in war becomes a war economy that has its own systemic laws. Organized crime, pillaging, trade levies equivalent to extortion, forced labor, appropriation of land titles – all these spoils of war can become self-perpetuating interests in the continuation of violence. The mode of violent appropriation does not necessarily preclude the cessation of violence. It adds, however, an additional causality to the continuity of violence.[142]

This subordination of economic transfers under the politico-military logic of belligerents became particularly evident during the civil war in Lebanon between 1975 and 1989. The different militias that emerged during the war thrived not only due to their success in the global cannabis market. They also absorbed the state's capacity to tax international trade. While the Lebanese state in 1980 was still receiving about 90 per cent of tariffs, this share had fallen to 10 percent in 1986 (Picard 1996: 67). With these successes, the warring factions in Lebanon not only disconnected themselves from the economic slowdown of the country, they were able to raise more funds than actually needed.[143]

Hence, the informalization of a war economy also knows countervailing forces. To the degree that armed groups control the emerging informal economic branches, they can transform them into para-formal businesses, controlled by informal states.

*Expansion and de-bordering*

Sinking capital stock not only makes the lives of populations harder, it also creates problems for warring factions. The more time and effort required to ensure their material reproduction, the more ruthless single combatants tend to become when interacting with a population whose well-being they should consider in their own interest. This is the reason robbery and pillage factor prominently in the list of armed groups' economic activities. The resulting scarcity can become so militarily detrimental that it becomes decisive to war outcomes.[144] For war actors, it then becomes not only a wise strategy but an inevitable step to enlarge their economic bases by some form of expansion.

Jean Christophe Rufin (1999: 30) has argued that the end of the Cold War led to radicalization of economic policies of war actors as they could no longer rely on external support by allying themselves with one camp of the bipolar global constellation.[145] External support by other states, however, has not been restricted to direct transfers of money, arms and military expertise by the superpowers and their allies. The sanctuaries that numerous insurgencies had access to in neighboring states was perhaps equally important. Whether neighboring governments were either unable to hinder insurgents' activities or approved of their activities, throughout the period since 1945 this practice was essential for the reproduction of insurgent groups and continues to be so. But, as Rufin argues further, it no longer suffices to meet their needs. All groups that had previously had been sustained by superpowers now had to construct their own commercial activities. Examples for such successful strategies abound. Charles Taylor's NPFL established a complex exportation industry that encompassed timber as well as iron ore, diamonds, and rubber (cf. Prkic 2005). The expansion of that war economy into Sierra Leone is attributed by some observers to the NPFL's strategy to gain access to the diamond mines in this neighboring country. The Khmer Rouge in Cambodia, after having lost Chinese support, reportedly began to export ancient art, gems, and timber, using corrupt border police forces of adjacent states as intermediaries.[146]

The de-bordering of war economies is not only a function of strategic decisions by war actors. When capital stocks devaluate to the point at which returns cannot support subsistence, refugee movements commence out of necessity. It is probably impossible to estimate how fear of violence and flight for economic reasons relate as motives for becoming a refugee or an internally displaced person. But the expansion of a war economy through the movement of people numbering, at times, in the millions is its most evident materialization. The economy of refugee camps, then, is paradigmatic for the progression of individual, "private" survival strategies, strategies of violent actors, and external political responses to humanitarian crises.[147]

The de-bordering of war economies is likely to entail an expansion of the war zone. First, for warring factions it becomes more important to achieve territorial control over those areas in which attractive assets are to be found or generated. The same applies to transport routes these commodities require. In turn, armed groups draw increasing numbers of the population into the realm of violence. But the groups themselves also become more vulnerable as their enemies may choose to stage attacks on these sites rather than seek a decisive battle.[148]

Finally, the transformation of an economy into a war economy means a de-bordering in a moral sense, as the loss of external support can also lead to pillage becoming the sole mode of extraction for an insurgency – these practices damage insider morale and contribute, of course, to the loss of legitimacy.

## Statization, stagnation, and disconnection

In a changing economic environment, strategies of armed groups cannot be static. New opportunities emerge while others wither away. Also, armed groups tend to adapt themselves to these changes and make efforts to maximize their income by a variety of strategies. There are limits on these strategies, first set by the locally prevailing structures, and secondly by the habitus of armed groups' personnel. Despite these changes, there are sufficient instances which display the ability of insurgent movements to learn and to institutionalize their reproduction. Yet, other groups show different trajectories. They either stagnate, being unable to enlarge the register of reproductive means, or they fail as they prove unable to counterbalance losses of income. In the following, I will briefly describe these three trajectories under the headings statization, stagnation, and disconnection.

No single trajectory is predestined. As will be shown, some groups manage to overcome their dependency on other states and build stronger linkages to their constituency, as was the case with the Eritrean resistance against annexation by Ethiopia. While the first Eritrean resistance group was largely dependent on the support of Arab states, in later phases the EPLF achieved close relations to the Eritrean populace.

Others lost these bonds, degraded, and could at best end in a stagnant war situation. This is the case with the "Lord's Resistance Army" in northern Uganda. While it began as a charismatic movement composed of defeated ex-government soldiers, it forfeited its social base and degraded into a predatory group after losing support from neighboring Sudan. As with many other groups, the LRA stagnated, and the war was decided neither militarily nor did the group demonstrate any ability to tighten its organizational capacities.

The last example, exemplifying the trajectory of disconnection, proves that a successful economic strategy does not necessarily result in formal statehood. Khun Sa's violent figuration in Burma existed for years, and for a lengthy period it witnessed a degree of success as it grew and generated increasing means. But in an extremely fragmented political environment, embedded in a highly volatile regional constellation, Khun Sa eventually failed to institutionalize his power.

*Statization*

Since its inception, the "Liberation Tigers of Tamil Eelam" (LTTE) has undergone a number of organizational changes in regard to the funding of their struggle. While the organization has certainly not attracted as much external legitimacy as the EPLF, for example, it has been quite successful in establishing a highly differentiated apparatus. In 1990, seven years after the war began, the LTTE controlled its own TV-station, an ammunition plant, the operation of its own farms, taxes on tobacco and alcohol consumption in the territory it controlled, and it sent students abroad who would later serve the armed group (Hellmann-Rajanayagam 1994: 51). Since the late 1990s, the group has also maintained an air force and a commercial aviation fleet (Radtke 2009: 113).

This outcome is the result of long efforts to stabilize its financial basis. In this regard, the history of the LTTE is a prime example of the learning process of armed groups. In its early years, the group was completely dependent on external subsidies received from the Indian government. But it soon began its own business in order to stabilize its sources of income, aware that the political rent from which it drew funds could suddenly disintegrate. The first steps in that direction consisted of collective farms and taxation of luxury goods in its "liberated" areas. By streamlining the economic life of the territory it controlled, the LTTE could avoid an economic drift into a full war economy, but the income generated by these methods did not suffice to finance the needs of its increasingly sophisticated weaponry.

In the first years of the war, the economy of northern Sri Lanka regressed to mere subsistence. In order to counterbalance this slow degradation, the LTTE created a development agency intended to implement technologies that would buffer the effects of the de facto embargo that had been imposed on its territory. Producing fertilizer and beverages and serving as a capital lender for smaller enterprises, the agency proved a success. But the income generated through these commercial activities was barely enough to provide minor assistance in a situation marked by growing poverty and scarcity.

Over the years, the LTTE reached deeper into the population's financial reserves by first imposing irregular taxes and fees, and later extracting more uniform rates of taxation. A poll tax on every household in the "liberated area" was to be the first instance and then dowries were taxed, with the detrimental side-effect of rendering marriages under the already difficult circumstances of the war-affected society even more difficult.[149] As the peninsula the LTTE had conquered could only be reached overland through the Elephant-Pass, this simplified the erection of control posts for levying import and export customs.

The Sri Lankan government, fearing massive refugee movements, did not interrupt trade between the LTTE area and other regions of Sri Lanka. It also, for a considerable time, maintained operation of schools and hospitals in the areas where the LTTE was present, as it feared further escalation of violence when it completely withdrew. Whereas the LTTE thus did not need to invest its levied money into public infrastructure and institutions, it developed further means to expand its sources of income.

The first step beyond the borders of Sri Lanka was the LTTE's engagement in smuggling operations between India and Sri Lanka. As a number of its leaders stemmed from the Karajar caste, it could take advantage of older social ties to facilitate access to established maritime networks in which the city of Velvettihurai was well established, reaching up to Singapore and Malaysia. The government's response to the LTTE's involvement in smuggling was the imposition of a five-mile exclusion zone. However, this action did not impede the group's pursuit of smuggling, which led to bankruptcy among local fishermen and a dramatic protein shortage in Northern Sri Lanka.

While during the 1980s rumors abounded that the LTTE was increasingly involved in drug trafficking, its most important source of funding came about with the massive move of refugees in the 1990s. The LTTE became the master example for transnational funding of armed groups by the taxation of a diaspora. The first steps in developing the techniques of taxing the diaspora apparently originated by chance rather than on the basis of a deliberate decision, as one LTTE staff member elaborates.

> "At that time we were not very much interested in the expatriate Tamil community, [...], but we thought it [London] to be a very good international center. Because [...] in the '60s/'70s almost all the liberation organizations had their [...] office in London. [...] Whether it was Palestinian, or Eritrean or whoever [...], everybody is there. So we have been connected. That was the reason, mainly, why we were interested [...]. Only after 1983 the expatriate community role came in [...]. Even before that, okay, we collected, but not in a big way as such. That money was only enough for us to maintain our office, our traveling. At that time we were traveling here and there and sometimes [...] to Colombo [...] to put some pamphlets there."
>
> (Quote from an interview by Katrin Radtke with a LTTE-official, Colombo, February 2003 (Radtke 2009: 130))

A similar process has taken place in the case of the Eritrean liberation movement, whose trajectory will be delineated in chaper six. Here too, the group has set up a policy to change its sources of funding. In both cases one can observe a robust institutionalization of sources of income, as both groups either deliberately or by iteration modified their material sources. Beginning with attacks and robbery, employing irregular forms of taxation or organized criminal activity, both eventually had state-like forms of taxation that could even bridge long distances and nebulous political situations.

However, two important differences exist between these two cases. Contrary to the LTTE, the "Eritrean People's Liberation Front" (EPLF) developed from another group that had previously established political relations with foreign governments that would support its cause. One has to include the experiences and structuration of the EPLF's forerunner to comprehend the full range of institutional developments that took place in this war of 30 years duration.

Secondly, the EPFL did not suffer international criminalization. Quite contrary to the fate of the LTTE, the cause of Eritrea's independence was viewed neutrally, if not with a degree of sympathy, at least by European leftist groups. The LTTE suffered from the loss of international legitimacy largely due to its use of suicide attacks and other violent practices that delegitimized the group in the Western perception (Radtke 2009: 116).

The LTTE's and the EPLF's abilities to establish regular incomes do not represent the only instances in which this has occurred. Other groups were as apt or even more capable of establishing such dense, even if predicatably conflictive relations towards their targeted constituency. Hamas, to a large extent financing itself by zakat, tax-like donations, of the Palestinian population, has even stronger ties to its constituency.

Much more successful, for example, was the *Ushtria Çlirimtare E Kosoves* (UÇK), the Kosovo Liberation Army. This group rather commenced as an exile project, soon aligning militaries who had quit the Yugoslav People's Army, the underground opposition against Serbian domination, and exiled Kosovars. The channels that existed among the Kosovar diaspora, primarily in Germany and Switzerland, and their families who remained in Kosovo, had been politically streamlined before the conflict turned violent in the late 1990s. The UÇK later established its own system of informal banking that allowed a quick and effective transfer of about 500 million US Dollars that reportedly represented funds transferred from exiled Kosovars, as well as profits gained in drug trafficking.[150]

The mechanism of statization, however, can also take a quite different trajectory. The LTTE in Sri Lanka, the EPLF in Eritrea, and the UÇK gained momentum partly due to political repression by the respective regimes in power. In the case of the Chetniks, active in the early 1990s in the former Yugoslavia, institutionalization took place without the establishment of regular self-organized funding. This spin-off group rather benefited from its early association with an occasionally violent but as yet somewhat formalized political system. The Chetniks were led by Vojislav Šešelj, on trial since 2003 at the International Criminal Court of Justice in Scheveningen. Šešelj was one of the key competitors to Slobodan Milosevic in the 1990s. Born in 1941 in Bosnia, Šešelj obtained a doctoral degree from the University of Sarajevo where he taught political science until 1984. In that year, he was sentenced to eight years in prison for producing a "counterrevolutionary manuscript" in which Bosnia and Montenegro are considered "artificial nations" that should be included into a greater Serbian republic (Judah 2000: 187). After almost two years in prison, Šešelj was released and joined the oppositional circles in Belgrade. In 1990, he co-founded, with Vuk Drašković, who would become the Foreign Minister of Serbia in 2003, the "Serbian Renewal Movement". But the alliance split after its two leaders accused each other of the embezzlement of funds gathered from exiled Serbian nationalists.[151]

This political success is astonishing since Šešelj's followers were irregular war participants in the early 1990s. By May 1991, his so-called Chetnik units participated in the war in Slavonia, later taking part in the siege of Vukovar. While Šešelj at times had 10,000 men under his command, former officers of the Yugoslav People's Army speak of 3,000 to 5,000 troops who were known among the military for their lack of discipline and excessive consumption of alcohol.[152]

During the 1990s, the Milosevic regime arrested Šešelj several times, but in 1998 he joined the government as vice president and supported Milosevic throughout the Kosovo War. In February 2003, Šešelj left Belgrade voluntarily to defend himself in The Hague. Before he left, thousands listened everyday to his speeches on Belgrade's Square of the Republic, and since 2003 his Serbian Radical Party has been the most successful political party in parliamentary elections, with taking more than 25 percent of votes.

Šešelj's group began with the tacit agreement if not actual support of government agencies. His party and militia were funded either partly or in whole by Serbian diaspora communities but were given approval to engage in battles by the Yugoslav government. Šešelj's continuous political success, however, is largely to be explained by the dynamics of violence itself. The stereotyping that resulted from violence in World War II rendered a nationalist attitude legitimate that could then only be fostered by the experiences of Šešelj's Serbian constituency during the 1990s.

In this case, the modes of funding did not determine the course of organizational development, as important as material support for the groups had been. In both cases, charismatic legitimacy of "heroic" politicians, and the legitimizing shadow of violence were seemingly transformed into modes of organization which brought different forms of material reproduction. In Šešelj's case it is the spoils of professional politics.[153] Quite in accordance with Weber's distinction between "living for politics" and "living from politics" (2000: 318), Šešelj turned from being a dissident intellectual into a violent political entrepreneur, and later into a regular politician, despite his international indictment by the ICCJ for war crimes.

For the statization of armed groups to take place, several steps are apparently necessary. It is necessary that armed groups that are not yet accepted political forces, like those that develop along the mechanism of repression outlined in chapter two, build basic legitimacy soon after they control an area. Whether they achieve further legitimization depends on either charisma that accrues to its leadership or the legitimacy it can build as an administrative body. For groups lacking sufficient legitimacy, their co-optation by an existing state structure, as in the case of Šešelj's Chetniks, can be an alternative route to institutionalization without the creation of independent sources of income.

Other groups might have a comparative advantage as legitimacy accrues to them simply from repression exerted by other actors. As the trajectory of the LTTE demonstrates, even fear and pressure might be an element in the relation between the armed group and its targeted constituency. But in order to attain para-stateness, including the ability to switch between sources of funding and to establish stable incomes, a successful routinization of the group's operation must be achieved. But regular and stable sources of income in the form of taxes from a self-created tax base not only require a functioning apparatus but also a minimum of legitimacy.

This mechanism of the regularization of an armed group's funds is an early indication that the "material basis" of insurgencies is actually a political economy. The economic success of armed groups depends on their capacity to build up legitimacy. All three groups outlined here achieved, by a blended strategy of force, moral pressure, and political discourse, a certain degree of legitimacy in their targeted communities. That the regularization of income could be reached was also due to these political battles. Differences in the international framing of the respective conflicts, however, account for the diversity of their overall success.

## Stagnation

When the victorious insurgency of the NRA in Uganda pursued fleeing soldiers of the old regime into their home districts in Uganda's North, they encountered a reconfiguration of the leaderless fleeing soldiers. The Holy Spirit Movement (HSM) of Alice Lakwena, a spiritual association that emerged amidst huge refugee movements, marauding soldiers, and violent excesses. Its main resource was that it offered rituals for the reinsertion of combatants into the Acholi moral community, and it imposed a rigid code of behavior on its members who were thereby disciplined.[154]

The HSM was surprisingly successful and repelled the forces of the new government under Museveni, coming within 20 miles of the capital in the summer of 1987. But its 12,000 troops were defeated, the charisma of

Alice Lakwena faltered, and the movement decayed. Some HSM members were temporarily integrated into the national army, while Alice Lakwena fled to Kenya. Some combatants, however, joined the group associated with Joseph Kony, Alice's nephew who claimed to have equivalent spiritual powers.[155] Kony launched a follow-up group, the Lord's Resistance Army (LRA) from Southern Sudan. Kony did not enjoy the powerful charisma of his aunt and found it necessary to rely on support from the Sudanese government, which paid for the Ugandan aid to the SPLM/A, which had been fighting to topple the regime in Khartoum since 1983.[156]

The LRA soon declined and had less than 300 troops when the constellation of forces changed again, and the Sudanese army regained control of stretches of its border with Uganda, using the messianist group as a tool to destabilize its neighbor. Bolstered by this external aid and equipped with advanced military hardware, the LRA rose to 2,000 troops, (Prunier 2004: 366). But after that time the LRA did not reach a higher degree of institutionalization and was unable to gain control of any territory. The war institutionalized as the Ugandan government forced the population of the northern districts Kitgum and Gulu to settle in "protected villages". This policy had the effect that the LRA was disconnected from its social base and resorted to forced recruitment and a hit-and-run strategy of night attacks on villages. As a consequence, it lost its legitimacy within the Acholi-community and was forced to live under precarious circumstances while depending on international aid.[157] At this time, no agreement could be reached, and the LRA also proved unable to enlarge its economic and social base. Under military pressure and dependent on its relations with forces in another war it could not control, the civil war in Sudan, it did not develop forms of steady income, also lacking a political agenda that foresaw distributional benefits for their ethnic constituency. The LRA degenerated, lost its communal support, and has been stagnating for more than 15 years.

The case of the LRA indicates that armed groups might share the fate of the social space in which they move. Not all groups are able enough or have sufficient opportunities to develop a stable economic basis while the economy in their environment decays. The move towards violent predatory practices rather leads to rapid delegitimization and exacerbates the situation further.

The degradation of the HSM into the LRA can certainly be partly attributed to the segmentary political tradition of the Acholi community from which most of its followers came. With such a historical tradition, it is very difficult to construct a centralized and hierarchical organization, as Christopher Clapham (1998: 11) in his comparative analysis of African guerillas has indicated. Also, the lack of easily exploitable resources contributed to the group's fragility. Under such conditions, the routinization of charisma is almost certain to fail.[158] Rare are such cases like the Sudan People's Liberation Army (SPLA) who could both overcome the obstacle of a fragmented population and a lack of resources by mobilizing neighboring regimes and benefiting from external humanitarian aid (cf. Johnson 1998).

But even with huge financial assets, success is not guaranteed if armed groups do not reach a balance between delegitimizing violence and legitimizing politics. The Partiya Karkerên Kurdistan was able, for a considerable time, to amass funds from migrant Kurdish workers in Europe. It also taxed trade across the eastern Turkish border. Between 150 and 500 million US Dollars had been the annual budget of the PKK, according to external estimates.[159] Not only weakened by the arrest of its leader in 1999, but also due to delegitimizing violent behavior against dissidents and internal disciplinary violence, the PKK failed in utilizing these assets to achieve a legitimate basis. Its stagnation throughout the 1990s was thus rather due to intense military pressure by the Turkish army, including the use of counter-insurgency militias and the loss of legitimacy.

Although it is likely impossible to find a single causal law explaining why armed groups fail, the cases of groups with stagnating economic bases unambiguously display a lack of legitimacy in more than one regard. They are either unable to change their own organization into a clear-cut form as their structures remain contested, or, as in the case of the LRA, they also lack popular support, as their predatory practices destroy any chance of a good standing among their constituents.

As these case stories indicate, many armed groups seem to be unable to alter their economic basis. Organizational learning, as sketched in the mechanism of statization, does not necessarily set in. When the delegitimizing effects of violence prevail, even repressive violence by a strong military adversary, as in the case of the PKK, does not outweigh these effects. The road to taxation then is blocked.

The last mechanism about the political economy of armed figurations, will display that even a favorable resource base is no guarantee for political success of armed actors. Prebends and rents from international markets might suffice to create basic legitimacy. But very often the only result are patrimonial ties between armed groups and a local population. The figuration, the web of interdependencies, does then not expand beyond the group's boundaries. Consequently, the fate of such a group remains volatile, it is subject even to light political changes.

*Disconnection*

Khun Sa, born in Burma in 1934, can be seen as the typical war child. He grew up and spent most of his life in the Western triangle of Burma, surrounded by China, Laos, and Thailand. Since World War II this area has been plagued by continuing political violence. British colonization, the Chinese revolution, Japanese occupation, the Korean War, and the wars of Indochina have had the effect that this part of Burma has been affected by insurgencies since 1948.

By the age of 16, Khun Sa organized his first militia, serving remnants of the Kuomintang near the Chinese border who had been mobilized by the CIA for a clandestine invasion of China, as a second front in the Korean war (McCoy 1999: 134). A few years later, Khun Sa aligned with the Burmese government in order to force the Kuomintang from the country, using state support to strengthen his militia. In the early 1960s, Khun Sa joined other militias from the Shan-region over whom the Burmese government wanted to exercise stricter control. After breaking with his new allies and realigning with the government, he became one of the most active drug traffickers in the region. By virtue of his good relations with generals in Northern Thailand who were also benefiting from the drug trade, he was out of the reach of any state's army. As a consequence of this protected situation, Khun Sa was successful in achieving a quasi-monopolist position which in turn allowed him to manipulate drug prices. In the late 1980s, when South Asia's share of the New York City heroin market jumped to 80 percent, Khun Sa controlled half of the world's opium supply (McCoy 1999: 141). He thus became one of the main targets of the US anti-drug policy worldwide.[160]

During almost three decades, Khun Sa survived as a drug producing and trafficking warlord, due to the strategic shifts of alliances and the enormous income he could generate in a booming global heroin market. His attempts, however, to create a sound political basis came too late. His export-based economy remained with strictly basic legitimacy and did not survive changes in the regional power constellation.

In the 1990s, Khun Sa's fate coincided with the political struggle regarding control of his home Shan region. This part of Burma was fragmented into small princedoms in pre-colonial times. British colonialism did not alter this arrangement but rather preserved the political structures with its 34 principalities as the Shan federation that should later determine by referendum whether or not it was a part of Burma. Burmese governments impeded this, thus giving rise to ethno-nationalist separatism. While Khun Sa sought to gain a rather political profile, given the international legal persecution, first and foremost by the United States, the Shan National Congress, in 1993, elected him as leader of their secessionist movement, believing that only he had sufficient military capacity to achieve their political aims. Khun Sa's army of 20,000, however, soon retreated to the borders of the country, since the Burmese regime resented this political move by Khun Sa. Before his army was to be utterly defeated, Khun Sa surrendered and stepped down from political office and began a life as a private businessman in Burma (Lintner 1999: 412).

The trajectory of Khun Sa is only partly the story of an armed group, but it shows how marvelously adept irregular actors are in their ability to transform disparate means of power for their survival. During the 45 years of his de facto politically sovereign position, Khun Sa could draw on a fragmented local and regional political situation as well as an influx of money generated on the global market. His acceptance as supreme political leader by the Shan National congress proves that this externality of income did not spoil the basic legitimacy he had already gained. Not only commanding an army of 20,000 men, Khun Sa also linked remote areas to world markets, and in his para-state, shops were full of imported goods. Furthermore, he had built a hospital, schools, and a functioning market (Elliot 1993).

The story of Khun Sa is thus proof of the transformability of armed groups that develop without any political legitimacy, often with external support. In the course of the war, or based on pragmatic decisions, these figurations can become patrimonial entities that more or less mimic their official counterparts, recognized by international law. That Khun Sa's para-state faltered under changed international and regional conditions[161] and eventually vanished should not be interpreted as proof of a lack of institutional capacity. Rather, it demonstrates the transformability of the acquired funds. The power that his Shan Army had constructed did not vanish, but rather was transformed into assets.

Such assets, as in the case of Khun Sa, might suffice to build basic legitimacy. Life under such rule, however, is still marked by a degree of arbitrariness and uncertainty. Such rule is not openly violent. The limits of these types of patrimonial systems are that they do not create actual interdependencies between armed groups and their social surrounding, consisting of mutual obligations. The figurations resulting from these rent-economies are rather loosely institutionalized criminal activities in which protection is exchanged for political and economic obedience.[162] Armed groups remain disconnected, and their economic basis equalizes between random booms and busts on international markets.

## Conclusion

In this chapter, it has been argued that the debate on "war economies" has neglected a number of aspects that are crucial to an understanding of the organizational trajectories of armed groups. The first neglected aspect is the insertion of civil wars into international and regional political constellations that permits armed groups to mobilize external support. Political embeddings are not restricted to the era of the Cold War but equally encompass current regional and global constellations. In a number of instances, as in the region of the Great Lakes in Eastern and Central Africa or in the Middle East, these constellations show almost systemic features.

The second aspect neglected in the literature but promoted here is the dynamic character of economies affected by large-scale organized violence. The shadow of violence is cast on the economy as well. Built on the distinction between an "economy at war" and a "war economy", it was shown that opportunities and constraints for violent actors are not constant. Armed figurations adapt – or fail to adapt – to a shrinking capital stock, to informalization, and to de-bordering tendencies of war economies.

Three pathways have been outlined, then, in order to map the fates of economic strategies armed groups pursue in connection with their political and military strategies. As could be shown, even rich endowments cannot prevent armed groups' failure if they do not exercise control over the delegitimizing effects of violence. If they succeed, they can transform an informalized war economy into a statized (verstaatlicht) economy, be it in the form of formal independent statehood, or as informal states that merely lack the status of international recognition. Two other pathways were distinguished, stagnation and disconnection. While the latter is typical for patrimonial forms of rule, normally based on rents, the former can result from a variety of constellations that include political, military, and economic stalemates.

As these basic depictions illustrate, there is no economic determinism at work in the politics of armed groups. The ways in which non-state war actors fund their efforts to turn violent power into legitimate rule vary, and they change over time, adapting to circumstances, not always strategically but rather in an iterative manner.

However, the processes by which the funding of armed groups can develop are limited in at least three regards. First, armed groups cannot break out of historical patterns of world market integration. Apart from those changes connected with the de-bordering tendencies of war economies such as refugee movements and collusion with illicit markets, armed groups can only thrive on structures that had been set by political rulers in the respective contexts prior to war.

Secondly, the strategies of armed groups to develop their economic bases are limited by the habitus of their leaders and staff members. Depending on political visions, experiences in management, and concepts of what is meant by "economic", very different forms of funding can be developed or remain excluded.

Thirdly, the means of funding are circumscribed by regional politics and world historical timing. Global and regional political constellations both allow and restrict the opportunities of political actors, whether violent or not. Changing circumstances may alter the possibility of strategies abruptly and may lead to disastrous or wondrous outlooks.

As will be seen in the following chapter, the political economy of armed groups corresponds with its institutional capacity. However, it is not possible to determine one overriding causality here: While economic assets and their availability are, of course, important conditions for the institutionalization of armed figurations, they are neither fixed nor determining the group's fate. What an explantion of armed groups' dynamics has to look at is the complexity of conditions that play into the processes of formation.

# 6. Hierarchy and Organization

The main observations regarding hierarchies and forms of organization within insurgent groups can be summarized as follows. The hierarchical structure of armed groups that can overcome threats of decay and fragmentation oscillates between patrimonialization and formalization. Both work as forms of institutionalization. Whether armed groups adopt one way or the other, and whether they decay early or remain unsuccessful depends largely on the structures of their social origin and on their enemies' capacity. Generally, armed groups seldom exceed the degree of formalization of their social origins.[163] Structures of the original context spill over into the armed group, and they often cause conflicts, since the forms of hierarchy and legitimacy within armed groups depend on their composition. Many conflicts within groups result from the divergence of internal segments of which the competition between young, urban intellectuals against established authorities represents a typical instance. But armed groups can grow and adapt with their enemies. When an opponent is efficiently structured, this requires that a group improve its own internal functioning as well. However, not all groups can live up to the standards set by their opponents.

In this chapter routes to decay and institutionalization as well as contradictory external forces and cleavages inside armed groups will be outlined. Multiple requirements pull armed groups in all directions and threaten their unity and coherence. Most, if not all, groups seem aware of these dangers and therefore, although not always consciously, apply a wide range of strategies and techniques.

The first need for centralizing forces and command is created by military requirements.[164] Whenever armed groups engage in battle against superior forces that can draw on established structures in the way state armies regularly do, the military pressure is high. A decentralist structure might suffice in order to survive, but any sustainable progress in the war is possible only when forces are co-coordinated and when scarce resources are allocated effectively. It is only when opponents themselves lose cohesion and organizational capacity that the need to centralize structures is less urgent.

But the ultimate aim of this ideal-typical armed group is to transform power into legitimate rule, into domination. To obtain this status, armed groups must first streamline their internal structure. While in the stage of fighting an irregular war against state armies, decentralist structures and flexibility might be advantageous, as soon as armed groups gain territorial control the need to enlarge and centralize the organization becomes urgent.

This is related to simple functions that any growing organization confronts. When domination in everyday life is administration, as Max Weber reminds us[165], then this means that armed groups must develop state-like capacities. Ordinary life problems such as conflicts involving village neighbors, the taxation of an economy, and the provision of goods not only for the fighting forces but also for the administrative staff must be organized. This requires a functional differentiation of the group, which in turn enlarges the problems of creating stable and effective structures.

Many armed groups succeed in creating such structures while others fail. Explaining the difference is not an easy task, especially as most internal political dynamics of armed groups are shrouded by the imperative of secrecy. The ensuing lack of documentation hinders analysis of the internal politics of armed groups enormously. When such impediments to complex empirically-oriented argumentation occur, one alternative is to utilize established theory in order to construct at least a hypothetical set that can be checked against the material at hand. This is also the method of this chapter. I intend to construct two mechanisms which explicate the ways by which armed groups institutionalize. The mechanism of patrimonialization leads to forms of domination in which control of power within an armed group is still personal. It is normed, but most decisions hinge on the will of one or at most a few persons. This situation changes when the mechanism of formalization sets in. Power is then institutionalized into positional forms. While, of course, the quality of incumbents continues to play a role, the actual functioning of the group and many decisions are controlled and directed by procedures that work independently of specific individuals.

Before these two mechanisms are elucidated, the empirical variety one encounters in the study of armed groups will be illustrated by two case sketches on Hezbollah and the Tuareg rebellion in Mali. From both cases one can see that structures set limits on the form figurations can assume. These two cases will demonstrate that the possible structuration of armed groups depends first and foremost on the social structure of their origin. It is within this structured frame that other dynamics can unfold or are prevented from taking place. This applies, for example, to the centrifugal effects on the coherence of these groups. One such tendency is the delegitimization through violence, while another is the dynamics that are triggered by the production of warrior charisma. Finally, growth and differentiation render the centrality of armed groups more difficult to maintain.

However, there are a number of counter-techniques at work simultaneously that strengthen the interdependencies within an armed group. Three of them are discussed here: subjectivation, closure of social space, and shuffling. All of them tend to transform these relations into domination. Techniques of disciplinization rank highly among them, but they also encompass the calculated provocation of state repression or the restriction of other social ties, the use of short-term incentives, and the restructuring of internal political relations.

In a manner similar to states overtaken by armies and military organizations, armed groups are also in danger of losing their capacity for political action when military logics become predominant. As has been argued even for phases in the life of modern democracies, the "military ascendancy" (Mills 1956: chap. 9), very often takes place within armed groups as well. The shadow of violence then prevents politically advisable decisions and becomes an obstacle for the transformation of the armed group into a regular political actor. This argument, developed in the final part of the chapter, constitutes a bridge to the last chapter of the book, dealing with the relations between states, violent rebellion, and the international system.

## Ways to rule and roads to decay

Hezbollah, the radical Shi'ite Muslim organization in Lebanon, is an almost extreme case of institutionalization. It emerged during Lebanon's civil war (1975-1990), but fully developed later when the frustration of Shi'ites with post-war politics was unprecedented. "A member of parliament gets about 300,000 US Dollars in four years," explains Hassein Hajj Hassan, a representative of this religious party in Lebanon's parliament. "How can they afford apartments that cost between 7 and 10 millions US Dollars?" he asked, alluding to the visibility of political corruption among the political class in post-war Lebanon, which has been one constant source of Hezbollah's attractiveness. Meanwhile, this former war faction has become much more than a violent opposition group. Hezbollah has a state sense and literally forms a state within a state. Its guards, in blue uniforms, regulate traffic in the southern suburbs of Beirut. Its modern and well-equipped hospitals and schools are free, while state hospitals charge patients in advance.

"People sympathize with parties which defend their interests," explains Hajj Hassan. "We are probably a bit better organized than the others." After the brief war during summer 2006, Hezbollah distributed cash among the refugees. A family that had lost everything due to the bombings could immediately receive 10,000 or 12,000 US Dollars to pay for living quarters. That a large part of these sums stem from Iran is not a secret. The Hezbollah Member of Parliament stated, "The other political parties in Lebanon get their money from Arab states or from elsewhere. All the parties have created their own TV station. Who is paying for that?" (quotes from Johannés 2007: 22).

Hezbollah came about by two processes. First, the invasion by Israeli forces during the civil war in southern Lebanon and the ensuing practices of this occupation had led to a growing feeling of insecurity among its mainly Shi'ite population (Hanf 1990: 359f.) Second, Iran's attempt to export its Islamic revolutionary model used the linkages between Iranian and Lebanese Shi'ite clerics who had studied together in Najaf and Karbala in southern Iraq.

Since the early 1980s, Iran had sent Revolutionary Guards to Lebanon, and frustrated members of another Shi'ite militia had gathered around them. They formed the first kernel of Hezbollah. Over time, many other young men from rural areas and smaller cities also joined the group, while Hezbollah benefited as well from many sympathizers in virtually all strata of Shi'ite communities in Lebanon.

Its structure is hierarchical and fuzzy at the same time. While the leadership of the group is apparently strictly organized along functional and hierarchical principles, its followers are not easily distinguishable from the general Shi'ite population (Ranstorp 1994). Functioning as a political party in Lebanon, as a social movement in villages and towns, and as an armed group simultaneously, Hezbollah's structure is complex and not without contradictions. At the top of its leadership is a High Council in which the general secretary plays a decisive role despite its formally homogenous structure (Hamzeh 2004: 47). Beneath this leading organ, five functionally differentiated administrative units operate in the roles of an executive committee, a political office, a parliamentary council, a legal council, and a "jihad council". The political office then controls a number of sub-units, among which five semi-autonomous foundations regulate the social work through which Hezbollah attracts so much popular support.

The group, thus, not only has a role in the Parliament of Lebanon, it also, at times, has had two ministers in the government of the country while still keeping thousands of fighters under arms. It operates a TV channel and a radio station and delivers a number of services that the Lebanese state was unable to provide after the civil war ended, such as schools and hospitals. Hezbollah is an employer and a welfare organization as well (Harik 2004: chap. 6).

The structure of its military arm is less known. However, even after the Iranian training officers had left Lebanon in the early 1990s, Hezbollah maintained training grounds throughout the country and secured its functioning by relying on an ad hoc mobilization system that can operate without barracks and easily detectable installations (Hamzeh 2004: 71). At least some of the fighters reportedly receive a regular income of between 150 and 200 US Dollars, while many others are only temporarily mobilized and return to their civil occupations after military operations.

To lead such an organization certainly requires numerous qualities. Its current leader, Hassan Nasrallah, acquired most of these qualities within the organization as one of its foundational members. He was elected as general secretary from the High Council after the former incumbent had been killed by an Israeli helicopter attack in 1992. Beyond this formal legitimization, Nasrallah's position also relies on his status as an erudite Islamic cleric who devoted a number of years to the study of the Quran and Shia writings. His credibility was further increased when his oldest son was killed in an encounter with Israeli forces in 1997. Being the factual commander in chief of Hezbollah's armed forces, he also acquired the charisma of the successful warrior when Israel's troops retreated from South Lebanon in 2000 and again when Israel was unable to defeat Hezbollah in the short war during summer 2006.

Among the sample of armed groups that has been investigated for this book, Hezbollah is certainly one of the politically most successful. As its strategic use of violent attacks in the summer of 2006 demonstrated, it could maintain a central command but is at the same time a competent political actor in parliamentary and other politics in Lebanon. It is firmly institutionalized and functionally differentiated. In extending its power deeply into the social realm by offering a wide variety of services to its constituency, it could also be seen as a social movement with a political party as its nucleus. Its biggest success, however, is certainly its recognition as a regular political actor both by other parties in Lebanon as by foreign states, if not de jure at least de facto.

Several circumstances account for this successful institutionalization. It is in part due to a regional constellation that has not been altered dramatically since the civil war in Lebanon was ended with the Taif Accord. Hezbollah was not disarmed as other militias by Syria but was instead used as a buffer and as a trump card to maintain pressure on Israel (Harik 2004: 45). Another component of the explanation of this trajectory can be found in the legitimacy that Hezbollah has acquired. It fulfilled the functions that were necessary to attract the unspecified support described in the foregoing chapter as "basic legitimacy". But also, due to the ongoing violent confrontation with Israel and the relative military success of avoiding defeat, it has gained even more legitimacy in the eyes of a population caught between dire economic outlooks and a political stalemate.

Other groups share this trajectory. They form under conditions of political repression with support from other states or agencies but eventually gain independence from these sources. The position of Hamas, for example, derives from a similar set of conditions (cf. Mishal/ Sela 2005). The transformation of the PLO into a ruling body is even more advanced than in the case of Hezbollah. The creation of the Palestinian National Authority (PNA) after the Oslo Accords in 1993 allowed stricter centralization within the organization than it had previously as an exiled body (cf. Ghanem 2001: chap. 6). The FSLN, which took power in Nicaragua in 1979, and the FLMN in El Salvador, which became a regular political actor, can also be seen as such success stories of armed groups. Not only did they survive in a war against state armies that were heavily supported by the United States, they also maintained their followers for protracted periods of time. The FMLN could not win the war militarily but was intermittently in control of as much as 25 percent of El Salvador's territory and participated successfully in elections on all levels after the conclusion of the war. In the case of the Sandinistas, the centralization was again even more pronounced after overtaking state power.[166]

While these groups are products of preceding wars, formed around focal points with external subsidies, and transformed into regular political actors at least on a national scale, other armed groups show rather opposite trajectories. This, for example, was the case with the Tuareg rebellion that shook the northern parts of the West African state Mali in the early 1990s.[167]

The *Mouvement populaire pour la liberation de l'Azawad* (MPLA) began this insurgency in late 1990. It was led by Iyad Ag Ghali who, in the same way as other Tuaregs, reportedly fought for Muammar Ghaddafi's Islamic Legion in Syria and Lebanon. Ag Ghaly and other fighters found themselves estranged from the Tuareg society after Libya dissolved the legion. After the first attacks by his troops on military and police outposts in the desert zone of northern Mali, the government reacted with harsh repression against the civilian Tuareg population in the region. More than 2,000 people were killed, and thousands fled across the borders. Following pressure by the government of Algeria in January 1991, a treaty was signed between the MPA and the Malian government. This Accord de Tamanrasset, however, immediately led to a splintering of the MPA. The first splinter group was the *Front populaire pour la liberation de l'Azawad* (FPLA). Shortly thereafter, the *Armée revolutionaire de liberation de l'Azawad* (ARLA) was created and pursued armed attacks on government installations, also killing the second-in-command of the MPA. Finally, a fourth armed section emerged, the *Front islamique arabe de l'Azawad* (FIAA), in which primarily Arab-speaking Kounta were represented. When the French and Algerian governments undertook efforts to include these new factions in another settlement that was concluded in 1992, the *Front national pour la liberation de l'Azawad* (FNLA) broke away from the ARLA.

The leaders of the MPLA for a long time denied that any factionalizing had taken place and attributed the continuing attacks following the signing of the treaties to the work of "bandits" (Klute 1995: 59). Later they declared that the factionalization was the result of political differences and problems between the leadership and sub-commanders. In fact, however, long historical cleavages between different strata of the semi-feudal Tuareg society played a much more important role in this process. While the FIAA indeed represented another nomadic group, the other three factions splintered from the MPLA because Ag Ghali and his entourage monopolized the positions which were the spoils of war insofar as the Malian government granted rights and functions to the rebellion's leaders in the treaty. They felt historically entitled to these spoils of war as they all stemmed from the old aristocracy of one confederation within the Tuareg community.

The practice of raids as a form of warfare very much resembled the traditional pattern of the Tuareg and did not converge with the impetus of centralized and simultaneously differentiated organization. Certainly, the need for coordinated action in this case was also hindered by the concrete circumstances of war. The units of the MPLA moved independently and often were not in contact. The sheer size of the area in which the confrontations took place and the characteristics of the southern Sahara effectively impeded the maintenance of a smoothly functioning organization.[168] In this particular case, especially difficult circumstances made factionalization likely to occur.

But the rifts between the groups were first and foremost related to earlier historical periods. The Kounta had been employed by the conquering French colonial troops around 1900 to subdue other segments of the nomadic population. During that period, they had used their borrowed firepower to levy tributes from other confederations, thus turning upside down the entire balance of tributes and rights between different segments of the nomadic and sedentary populations in this area of the Sahara. Brief but costly rebellions by different groups against French colonial rule occurred at intervals until 1920, and again after the "peaceful" interlude of colonial administration.[169]

In their responses the colonial authorities played on older hostilities between the confederations in order to mobilize local auxiliary troops when they quashed these local uprisings. And again, the young state Mali experienced a first revolt of Tuareg warriors in the early 1960s. All these events were collectively memorized and structured the mutual perception of the loosely connected confederations that remained largely unaffected by the politics of the Malian state.

The Tuareg rebellion in 1990 that had begun under the banner of "temust" – the Tuareg nation – soon failed as a result of these long-standing stereotypes and allegiances between different parental and tribal ties. The young "ishomar"[170] who had started the rebellion after being driven out of

Algeria's and Libya's labor markets had believed in a new egalitarian and more democratic concept of society. Quickly, however, the rebellion was monopolized by a group of aristocratic descent from one particular confederation. As a reaction, the movement splintered along old fracture lines of the Tuareg society. It was not astonishing to see that a later peace accord could be reached only by traditional diplomacy between these confederations and more traditional leaders.[171]

While the rebellion indeed changed the political institutions in Mali and Niger insofar as more autonomy rights were ceded in both cases to the northern provinces, the actual rebellion had failed. The project of the young "ishomar" to form a nation and to overcome the largely traditional structure of their constituencies did not come true. The older elite, who had denounced the rebellion in the beginning as banditry, benefited much more from the peace arrangements after bringing themselves into the situation as brokers. Meanwhile, the unending violence, the continuing army retaliations, and the general insecurity had distracted popular support from the rebellion.

Many armed groups have similar records. The Front de Libération Nationale du Tchad (Frolinat), an alliance that attempted to topple the government in Chad, could not stabilize for an extended period of time as it was lacking the right person as a leader. Even after it had conquered state power in 1979, following 13 years of war, it fragmented further. Only when Idriss Déby became the leader of this heterogeneous alliance of Northerners was he eventually able, in 1990, to lead an already fragmented alliance to state power. Déby combined descent from a traditionally noble lineage with formal education and military training in France, and furthermore, he had combat experience. He needed all these qualities to bridge the gaps between different factions, at least for a certain period of time. Frolinat, though, remained an extremely unstable figuration, lacking internal interdependencies. Most members of this former alliance have meanwhile fought against their ex-allies in one way or another since the group's inception.[172]

Failed attempts of institutionalization can be observed in further cases. The *Front pour la restauration de l'Unité et de la Démocratie* (FRUD) in Djibouti also was unable to keep its four factions together when a first settlement was negotiated in 1994, three years after the war had begun. A faction separated from the group and continued its insurgency until 2001 when it could also be accommodated in the next peace accord. Meanwhile, the dominating ethnic group in Djibouti had segmented, and various militias developed and complicated the situation.[173] Apparently, the refugee movements from the wars in neighboring Somalia and Ethiopia had rendered the political management of alliances impossible.

Hezbollah and the Tuareg rebellion, the two groups used here to begin the reflection, stand as symptomatic cases for the variance of sizes and trajectories of armed groups for which no single overriding law can likely be detected. Too many differences would have been taken into account, and too numerous are the initial and intermittent conditions that shape the trajectories of armed groups. The two groups begun with here differ not only in size but also in many other regards, and their trajectories seem diametrically opposed. They display different degrees of centrality, of hierarchy, and they function according to different principles. Hezbollah became a regular political actor within post-war Lebanon, although it retained its violence competence. Deeply embedded in elements of Lebanese society, its reach into the social space had been fostered by further warfare across the border with Israel. Led by a charismatic speaker who combines eloquence, Islamic learning, and organizational skills, it evolved into a highly efficient, functionally differentiated, political and military actor.

The Tuareg groups in Mali, on the contrary, failed this test. They did not become a full-fledged organization. In fact, after having fought the Malian army for two months without being defeated, they did not survive the second challenge, namely to remain cohesive after a negotiated settlement. The movement fragmented quickly along intrinsic lines of traditional loyalty and over the question of how political opportunities would be shared. However, some parts were politically successful as well, since they also eventually participated in the political rearrangement of the Northern regions.

While examining this highly diverse picture, commonalities should not be overlooked. Both movements benefited from violence expertise that was organized by external actors, that is by other states. In both contexts, earlier violent incidents had created a web of meanings and narratives that allowed the legitimization of violent rebellion. And finally, in both cases larger processes of social change had delegitimized the inherited political order.

How can these differences between insurgent groups be accounted for? A number of structural causes are discernible from the cases mentioned. Divisions within societies from which armed groups emerge will reappear in the group. Insurgents cannot invent society anew, but depend instead, to a considerable extent, on existing concepts of power and allegiance. Seemingly, those groups who can look back on an older tradition of political opposition have better chances than the ones characterized as ad hoc groups in chapter four. The theoretical explanation for this can be found in Elias' idea of interdependencies, and thus in the idea of figuration itself. When political contexts from which armed groups develop show a longer tradition of resistance and a higher degree of interdependencies, then insurgent movements drawing on these interdependencies have better chances by far of success.[174]

## Centrifugal forces and centripetal techniques

The reasons armed groups fail are manifold and are not susceptible to be theorized in a satisfying manner. There are nevertheless a few discernible dynamics that render the failure of armed groups more likely. Before these forces are presented, a few remarks will summarize the limits within which these processes of institutional development take place.

As mentioned above, the structuration of armed groups always happens within limits. First are the general social, political, and economic conditions under which the groups' development is taking place. These conditions create boundaries for what is possible as an organizational form and not only as a matter of choice. Leaders, staff, and followers do not come "unstructured" but with a particular socialization that has shaped their social habitus, their patterns of perception and evaluation.[175] Within the figurations that constitute armed groups, therefore, many patterns are established and pursued that transcend deliberation and decision. They come about as a result of routines and habits inherent to the actors in armed groups.

Second, the general constellation of forces shapes what is feasible. This applies not only to the military situation. Each war is also embedded into a regional and global political situation. Neighboring states will observe developments, often prepared to intervene when deemed necessary. During the Cold War, the competition between superpowers created multiple constraints and opportunities for armed actors. More recently, a highly moralized observation of war events creates further boundaries to political and military action. The delegitimizing effects of violence can spill over into what is referred to as the international public sphere, to the detriment of international acceptance of an armed actor.

Third, the general rules of politics apply to insurgencies as well. Observing customs and fulfilling a minimum of the staff's material interest are among those rules. Commanders in insurgencies cannot decree anything recklessly without endangering their unit's coherence. Many actions are taboo as they are morally coded, and these codes cannot easily be abolished.

It is under these general conditions and structural givens that the politics of armed groups unfold. While the forestanding cases have shown the degree of institutionalization to which this can lead, the following section of this chapter will generalize on the one hand those forces that contradict the hierarchization of armed groups and, on the other hand, those techniques employed by insurgencies in order to counterbalance centrifugal tendencies.

Both, centrifugal forces and centripetal techniques, are related to the shadow of violence. Organizational failure in the context of war is a question of life and death, and therefore armed groups tend to be "greedy institutions" (Coser 1974). Forced by the existentiality of military confrontations and the threats of state repression, they tend to cut their activists' other social ties and connections or subdue and integrate the respective social institutions.[176] Armed groups favor undivided loyalty. They attempt to reduce claims of competing roles and status positions on those they wish to encompass within their boundaries. In their struggle to maximize military and political power they also attempt to move their internal relations from a mere power relation into relations of domination. The pressure to eliminate competing loyalties seems to be a function of the enemy's capacities. When the states attacked possess strong intelligence and a far-reaching security apparatus, armed groups feel increased pressure to develop equivalent organizational forms that allow resistance to that pressure.[177]

As will be shown in this section, the ensuing process of institutionalization is endangered by several dynamics that are partly "regular" insofar as they affect any organization and that are partly related to warfare, to the exertion of violence. Three centrifugal forces that endanger the cohesion and institutionalization of armed groups can be identified, namely delegitimizing violence, struggles at the top, and differentiation. And at least three centripetal counter-techniques – subjectivation, closure of social space, and shuffling – are empirically observable methods by which armed groups attempt to contain the effects of these centrifugal forces. Centrifugal forces such as these seem to increase in strength extraproportionally with the growth of an armed group, while the centripetal techniques referred to are apparently most effective when an armed group's size has not yet exceeded a certain threshold. These forces will be sketched here only briefly as they can be found in diverging mixtures in basically any good case description. I will only use a few examples in which they become most evident.

*Delegitimizing violence*

The effects of violence as described in chapter three affect armed groups as well as their opponents and their social environment. Being afflicted by physical force, but also exerting it casts the shadow of violence not only on individuals but also on the organizational forms of insurgencies. Guilt, honor, and shame are associated with it, and armed actors, whether organized by states or not, endure traumatic experiences.

The delegitimizing effects of force become apparent when state repression becomes violent, but they also appear when armed groups surpass the boundaries of custom in their constituency or any other group. Terrorist practices, the expulsion of people from their homes, theft, plunder, rape, corporal punishment, and executions are practices that occur in the contexts of most, if not all, wars. They do not, as Stathis Kalyvas (2003) has convincingly shown, always follow the major dividing line of confrontation but often take place in its shadow, as crime during war often remains undiscovered and unpunished. In order to have a delegitimizing effect, it suffices that these acts are attributed to an insurgent group. Shame and guilt result from these acts anyway, as they took place under conditions that had been created by waging war.

Violence delegitimizes even more when it becomes established knowledge that armed groups themselves are perpetrators of deeds that violate the insider morality of their members or of their potential constituencies. Cases like the Sendero Luminoso (SL) in Peru, but also the Fuerzas Armadas Revolutionaria de Colombia (FARC) have lost huge portions of their initial legitimacy among the peasants they claimed to liberate, simply by increasing the pressure on these communities excessively.[178]

The exertion of violence by an armed group can also have delegitimizing effects on its members. Numerous accounts witness the feelings of alienation induced by traumatic experiences that estrange combatants from their group and delegitimizes programs, leaders, and the insurgency altogether.[179] One source of this alienation is indiscriminate violence against the civilian population, while another, of course, is the forms of violence exerted within the group as part of the technique of subjectivation.

*Struggles at the top*

Successful commanders who gain symbolic capital from military deeds are potentially able to defeat leaders holding higher rank. There are able to do so because warrior charisma is a form of legitimacy that changes their relations within the figuration into relations of domination.[180]

In many armed groups, this military ascendancy is a regular outcome of war events. In groups that were formed by the mechanism of repression such as the MFDC in Senegal, briefly outlined in chapter four, leaders stem first from the political class. Often they are intellectuals or party officials or held offices in state administrations. Their leading position during wartime is often challenged when the charisma of successful warfare accrues to a member of an armed group. In the case of the MFDC, referred to in the previous chapter, this was Sidi Badji, a veteran of the French colonial army with combat experience in Indochina and Algeria. During the first round of negotiations, the MFDC split along the lines of loyalty to the former military and to the former Abbé respectively. While the latter was the intellectual politician, the former accumulated warrior charisma during the insurgency and did not trust the Abbé to strike a deal that would not endanger himself.[181]

The production of warrior charisma can even lead to outright competition between leaders, as was the case between different emirs in the second civil war in Algeria (cf. Martinez 1998: 321).[182] Often, warrior charisma creates such strong positions that commanders can ignore official decisions without resistance. An instance of this is the rise of Shamil Bassajev of Chetchnya. His predecessor, Aslan Machadev, had nominated the more intellectual Sheikh Abdul-Halim Sadulajev. After Machadev had been killed in March 2005, Sheikh Sadulajev was confirmed in that position by several leaders of the insurgency. However, ruthless strategies and his long survival while closely pursued by Russian intelligence and militaries rendered Bassajev the much more popular and renowned leader of the Chechen insurgency.[183] His impressive warrior charisma allowed for that ascendancy, but it was simultaneously a risk for the insurgency. After his death in 2006, the Chechen insurgency collapsed entirely. As warrior charisma is the specific form of symbolic capital that is produced in violent conflicts, military events have an enormous impact on the relations within armed groups, far beyond the immediate military confrontation.

*Differentiation*

Part of the success of armed groups is their growth. However, growth usually includes differentiation, both vertically and horizontally. Structures can no longer be operated on a person-to-person basis, and more and more people with divergent backgrounds might join so that shared descent and common socialization are no longer of assistance as regulating patterns. Even more pressing becomes the urge for functional differentiation. Armed groups that control territory, for example, not only need to continue organizing force, they also find it necessary to establish a basic administration or they risk losing popular support.

All these additional tasks require strong ties within the armed group as conflicts of interest begin to emerge between units and branches as in any other growing and differentiating institution. Only when these conflicts can be channeled through legitimate procedures and decision-making bodies will the group remain intact. Both formalization and patrimonialization offer such venues. Formal regulations give hindsight rules for decisions, and patrimonial rule is also calculable, although within certain limits. Empirically, however, one will always find mixtures of both elements as no formalization can foresee all eventualities, and offices and positions are often appropriated for patrimonial practices.

In a number of armed groups, conflicts emerge due to growing heterogeneity among staff members who at the same time fulfill different functions. The classical case is the encounter between older political elites and younger, often intellectual leftists who introduce ideas of social change and emancipation within the constituency. The manner in which the Tuareg rebellion in northern Mali failed because of such a contradiction has been sketched earlier in this chapter. Similar generational conflicts occurred in Kurdish groups such as the KDP-Iran and the KDP-Iraq. In Iraq, the Kurdish Democratic Party not only allied with the regime of Saddam Hussein for some time in order to eliminate the competing Patriotic Union of Kurdistan, but also had an inherent contradiction between a patrimonial clan logic and nationalist modernist doctrine that favored other forms of rule. In Iran, the Kurdish party was first dominated by land-owning oligarchs and traditional urban elites. After its first successes, the group gained increasingly numerous supporters, and as a consequence younger members who preferred a party logic to the traditional pattern of clan politics took control. The KDP-Iran, however, was crushed with ruthless violence by Iranian governments.[184]

In the Burmese Communist Party that fought between 1948 and 1989, violent confrontations between factions developed and resulted in several splinterings. A part of conflicts within the group were the competitions between local leaders and members who returned from lengthy exile in China. The fragmentation followed loyalties along these lines. Eventually, none of these factions had an impact on the political constellation in Burma.[185] In that extensive history, all varieties of failure occurred. Some factions vanished, others were defeated, and some surrendered and joined the ruling junta.

The danger of differentiation, in sum, consists of the fact that armed groups need to address broader constituencies in order to enlarge their power base. But this enlargement also introduces the differences among the constituency into the group itself. Growth, therefore, is not just a problem in terms of functional differentiation but also in a more direct political sense. The larger the base gets, the more difficult it becomes to maintain coherency. In this regard, as in many others, armed groups do not differ from many other organizations. They do differ from civilian groups, however, when it comes to the techniques they employ in order to counterbalance centrifugal forces.

*Centripetal techniques: Subjectivation*

It has been widely stressed that the formation of fighters, their training in military practices, and their political education have been crucial for the success of insurgencies.[186] It is a question of theoretical viewpoints, if not of political positions, how to evaluate this finding. Observers sympathetic with the cause of an insurgency might view it as the creation of political consciousness or awareness. Critics of such methods might see it as part of the practices of greedy institutions.

The ambiguity of these practices that many armed groups employ can best be accounted for with the concept of asujetissement which Michel Foucault (1995) developed in his study of modern techniques of punishment. Roughly to be translated as subjectivation, this concept designates the double-edged process of turning single persons into active and reflective individuals while at the same time "subjecting" them in a relationship of domination. Techniques of subjectivation are thus aiming at inserting individuals into the logic of an institution. They function as disciplinization, but they may encompass discussion, deliberation, and persuasion as well. In this perspective, training, education, and any hierarchic discourse can be used for this purpose. The main purpose of the technique of subjectivation is to implant the functional requirements of the armed group into the minds of its trained members.[187] Armed groups often use these techniques, which are as old as institutionalized political rule, systematically and in a highly differentiated manner. The case of the EPLF elucidated in this chapter will demonstrate that the formation of staff by an armed group can be highly differentiated, depending on the function for which staff-members are scheduled.

This technique involves the use of force within armed groups and has therefore to be carefully weighed against the delegitimizing effects these very same measures can entail. Much violence within groups, essentially all that which is labeled as "disciplinary", serves this end. It is known that at least one third of armed groups use disciplinary force within their ranks.[188]

Within the National Resistance Army in Uganda, for example, a ten-point program was employed that regulated the ethos of its fighters, predominantly stressing relations with civilians and, secondly, the inner structure of the NRA. The program prescribed ways of participation, declared the formation of cliques as forbidden, thus delegitimizing alternative forms of power formation beyond the centralized institutions. Undisciplined fighters were court-martialed and executed, so the fear of capital and corporal punishment complemented the rudimentary code of conduct (Schubert 2001: 287).

In spin-off groups, military elements are used more often than political education as means of subjectivation. Arkan's Tigers, a militia described in chapter two, were based on a rigid hierarchical structure that included corporal and capital punishment for members in cases of disobedience. Members not only had to swear an oath of allegiance to Arkan, they were trained in a military camp in Erdut and were subjected to rigid command structures.[189]

In Angola, UNITA used settlements for the formation of its fighters that became the subjects of even broader schemes. Arma, inchada e lapis, weapon, hoe, and pencil, were the tools of the fighter, according to the political textbook. The UNITA leadership also encouraged their fighters to marry and settle as families in its camps. These total institutions were then surveyed by UNITA's own judiciary.[190]

As these instances show, political education and training not only serve the purpose of mobilization and legitimization. They coalesce with disciplinary force and allow for the transformation of power into domination. Political education combined with disciplinary force will contain the centrifugal forces that come about with the growth and differentiation of armed groups.

*Closure of social space*

In order to achieve their goals and acting under the existential threat of being killed in combat or through violent state repression, armed groups tend to monopolize power relations. Their tendency to subdue, dissolve, or integrate any other form of social organization stems from this existential need. Armed groups are "greedy institutions" since anything in their reach can either be used for the group's purposes or it will become a resource for its enemy. Insurgent movements therefore apply practices that close the social space in which their adherents live, as this also allows counterbalancing centrifugal forces and easy alternatives. Any social relation adherents have outside the figuration could become an escape route and is thus a potential threat to the group's integrity.

There are two main ways in which the closure of social space is accomplished. One is the usurpation of structures that already exist, and another consists of the destruction of alternative forms of organization. The first becomes very apparent in the politics armed groups use in diaspora communities.[191] The Liberation Tigers of Tamil Eelan (LTTE) succeeded in monopolizing the social space of the Tamil diaspora in Canada by two mechanisms. First, it could use a mixture of moral argumentation, incentives, and coercion to coax the community of migrants who had come to Canada before the war to join its so-called front organizations. These exile organizations did charity work and served as local self-help systems, but they became increasingly controlled by the LTTE and were used for the channeling of funds raised in the diaspora community. The second mechanism was the influx of war refugees to Canada in the course of the war. This new wave of migrants were either closely related to the LTTE and its cause, or they shared the traumas of war, were much more concerned about events in Sri Lanka, and therefore more easily mobilized (Radtke 2009: 192-207). Similar developments took place in the Eritrean exile community (Radtke 2009: chap. 8) or among Turkish Kurds in Germany (Mertens 2000). The appeal to ethnic solidarity, incentives in the form of maintaining rights after the country is "liberated", and negative sanctions if support is not forthcoming are the main tactics employed by armed groups to bring social institutions under their control.

Similar techniques can be seen in the second main field in which practices of closure take place, namely the local political surroundings of armed groups. The LTTE as well as the EPLF are also prime examples for the strategy of either destroying political alternatives or integrating them into existing structures. This is partly accomplished by violent suppression and partly through persuasion and negotiation. Attempts at closing the social space by destroying existing organizations, however, has legitimacy costs that should be carefully weighed.

The Sendero Luminoso of Peru failed largely as a result of rigidly enforcing its policy to violently suppress any form of social or political organization that was unwilling to subject itself to the strategy of the Maoist guerilla (Rénique 1998). Both the LTTE and the EPLF employed violence in forcing out competing representative organizations, but without losing a significant amount of their legitimacy. They buffered the negative effects when they created front organizations for women, peasants, and youth through which they could distribute additional benefits.

## Shuffling

Leading circles of armed groups also employ a technique that serves the end of reconfiguring power relations by changing staff members and positions or by creating new councils and departments.[192] While it is not always clear in any particular instance to what extent these shuffles are of a rather symbolic nature and to what extent they address an actual change in relative power within an armed group, this issue is of secondary importance. The function of this technique is to visibly demonstrate to all a group's supporters that change and learning is possible, thus enhancing the legitimacy of the group's internal order.

Again, the National Resistance Army in Uganda is a showcase for this technique. When it began in 1981 it had no more than 35 members. Within months, the group was several hundred men strong and continued to attract supporters. In the same year, as conflicts began to occur within the group, it became necessary to adapt its internal structures. While the initial commanders came mostly from the southwestern parts of Uganda and had the same ethnic background as Yoweri Museveni, the new recruits were local Baganda. Furthermore, older commanders competed with urban, intellectual newcomers for positions in the group. The NRA organized a "representative meeting" and restructured itself with a new National Resistance Army Council at the top that included all commanders and the leaders of administrative divisions. Elections in the areas that the NRA began to control served the same function of control through integration.[193]

Shuffling does not need to be practiced in quasi-legal procedures such as the case of the NRA. It is also operational for charismatic leaders who rather promote such decisions as the outcome of personal wisdom while, in fact, they adapt staff positions to changed power structures within the figuration. The adaptation and invention of new formal structures is thus often part of the practices of armed groups' leaders who both in formal and patrimonial settings build up charisma by this apparent wisdom.

The role of charisma in the regular politics of armed groups perhaps best comes to the fore in the analysis of caudillo politics, the specific style of raising political support that is said to be typical of Latin American politicians.[194] The caudillo can be a violent actor, but his success also depends on his ability to gain the acclamation of his followers by his rhetorical skills. That is why stages and balconies play such an important role in politics. The orator stirs emotions, unites the feelings, and attempts to be not only the homo faber but also the homo magus (Cassirer 1944).

With techniques that closely resemble religious practices, leaders preach and speak in order to create relationships with their followers that are not only rational and cognitive but have effects over a broad band of dimensions. Public speeches or speeches at party congresses function to create a kind of belonging that is symbolically framed and includes emotions and expectations as well as shared memories of sufferings and grief. What is taking place during moments of public speeches is the acclamation, an anonymous but powerful installation of the leader even without elections that produces an image, a visible order, a location of obedience and domination. These acts of acclamation shall create legitimacy that is necessary to overcome centrifugal forces. It is legitimizing policies such as shuffling from the top, which would otherwise seem to be arbitrary practices and threaten the overall legitimacy of the group's structure.

*Leaders, staff, and followers and the institutionalization of power*

These basic theses about the politics of armed groups shed some light on what is happening in these figurations that seem to be, for many observers, rather opaque. And while detailed material concerning the inner dynamics of armed groups is certainly scarce, further differentiations are possible through the combination of aggregated statistics and comparative case studies.

From a statistical overview, one can see that in fact many armed groups succeed in developing remarkable organizational capacity, but in different forms. A centralized and functioning organization is not yet a guarantee of final victory, nor even of survival. But certain mechanisms seem to exist which compel armed groups to foster their internal functioning and also to transform their military organization into domination, even if the outcome of this institutionalization is not homogeneous and remains contested during a war.

*Table 8:* Organizational features of armed groups (1945-2005)[195]
(N=80)

| Organizational feature | percentage |
|---|---|
| Territorial control | 77.5 |
| Institutionalization* | 58.8 |
| Schism | 51.3 |
| Successful transformation** | 40 |
| Hierarchical and bureaucratic elements*** | 38.4 |
| Disintegration through military action | 30 |
| Disintegration through fragmentation | 23.8 |
| Outright patrimonialization | 22.5 |

Source: MAG data base
\* Thresholds for institutionalization are rather low as any form or regular organizational feature was taken as indicator.
\*\* Note that a number of armed groups included fight in wars not yet finished as of the end of 2005.
\*\*\* Indicators for bureaucratic features are congresses, regular business activities, and internal elections.

As this brief overview shows, many armed groups are successful in so far as they achieve some degree of territorial control, of which a number produce complex forms of inner structures.[196] Quite a number of groups fragment or dissolve due to military defeat. Yet, the most remarkable finding of this overview is that many armed groups are in fact able to develop patterns of institutionalization in the sense of recurring rules for decision-making and chains of command. Also, a great number apparently show elements of hierarchical and even bureaucratic organization. At the same time, though, there is a danger of fragmentation, of decay, and also the threat of defeat by the enemy's military force.

While this overview does not tell us anything about the actual patterns and dissolutions in these figurations, two theoretical ideas will guide the following investigation of organizational dynamics in armed groups. First is again the distinction between three different types of members of insurgencies, that is between leaders, staff, and followers. The second idea relates to the process of changing sporadic power into positional power. The organizational task of armed groups can thus be conceived as the problem of a change of internal relations from being based on spontaneous or norming power into positional power.

Whether such figurations institutionalize, that is whether the power relations within become relations of domination, hinges on the kind of relationship existing first between leaders and staff, and second between staff and followers.[197] The respective passage in Weber's analysis of political associations reads as follows:

> "The members of the administrative staff may be bound to obedience to their superior (or superiors) by custom, by affectual ties, by a purely material complex of interests, or by ideal (wertrationale) motives. The quality of these motives largely determines the type of domination. Purely material interest and calculations of advantages as the basis of solidarity between the chief and his administrative staff result, in this as in other connections, in a relatively unstable situation. Normally, other elements, affectual and ideal, supplement such interest. In certain exceptional cases, the former alone may be decisive. In everyday life these relationships, like others, are governed by custom and material calculation of advantage. But custom, personal advantage, purely affectual or ideal motives of solidarity, do not form a sufficiently reliable basis for a given domination. In addition there is normally a further element, the belief in legitimacy."
>
> (Weber 1978, I: 213)

Figurations can thus only obtain stability when their constitutive power relations become legitimized, which means when they institutionalize. There are several ways in which this institutionalization can begin. First, armed groups do not emerge in a social vacuum. As has been stressed previously, the structures in which they develop are extended into the groups themselves. Forms of authority that dominate the context are likely to be reflected in an armed group.[198] This is true not only because former state functionaries, politicians, and militaries become leaders or high-ranking staff members in these groups but also because followers bring their respective expectations. In some instances, large segments of armed groups stem from the same institutional background, for example clans, political parties, or state armies. The local rules of political games within these institutions are not set aside but structure the expectations in the habitus of all those involved. For insurgent groups' leaders, there is therefore always something on which to build.

From the work of another sociologist, further clues on the ruses of the institutionalization of power can be gained. Heinrich Popitz distinguishes three transitional stages of power: sporadic, norming, and positionalized (1992: 233-260). Whereas the first is restricted to "here and now" relations, the second has the form of "whenever-then" relations. Sporadic power that is bound to situations and to the actual presence of related persons can be transcended through repetition. When the means of power are permanently at hand, when coercion can be used repetitively, and furthermore, when deliverables become regular, sporadic power is likely to evolve into norming power. Another precondition for this to happen is, of course, that the more powerful are able to prevent the less powerful from desertion or from abandoning the group cause.[199]

Any power tends to become norming. Sporadic power that has assumed regularity offers starting points for this. When repetition becomes regularity, this regularity can become a rule. Side-payments and special benefits, but predominantly coercion and habituation, render this step more likely. To turn this "whenever-then" rule into domination thus can draw on other dynamics. When relations become calculable, they tend to intertwine with others, and thus are less often called into question. The positionalization of power, this final step, is then not far away. It is in the interest of the more powerful to enjoy the economies of scale of this organization by delegating functions, and the less powerful tend to accept this when sanctions and benefits have proven to be reliable. Rituals and other practices of symbolism usually accompany this process. These processes often develop unnoticed by participants, but for armed groups it is clear that the task of turning relations with new recruits, for example, into stable relations of domination is an intended, deliberate technique.

The institutionalization of power can thus be understood as increasing de-personalization, as increasing formalization, and as increasing integration of power relations. In that sense, a figuration becomes denser, interdependencies overlap, and relations between relations emerge. Why some groups bureaucratize and reach complex systems of organization while others fragment or decay will be explained below by two mechanisms that draw on these ideas.[200] The first is the mechanism of patrimonialization. Here, power is normed but not yet positionalized. While this is already a form of institutionalization, the second mechanism, formalization, goes even further. It displays features of depersonalization in procedures and elements of bureaucratic rule. There are a number of prerequisites for these mechanisms to begin operation. Again, they are not automatic. They can be stopped by numerous intervening events, but also if armed groups, their leaders, staff, and followers are unable to overcome obstacles on their way to institutionalization. Neither of these mechanisms carries any guarantee of success. Insights into these dynamics, however, allow a better understanding of the dynamics that are at work within armed groups.

## The mechanism of patrimonialization

Patrimonialization means that resources and chains of command and control are centralized, usually on one person, and that the organizational functioning relies heavily on personal relations of domination.[201] Patrimonial figurations are stable as long as a sufficient flow of resources can be distributed through the networks of relations that are structured like an inverted tree. At the top, the "Big Man"[202] is controlling the inflow of resources, and beneath him are heads of clientelist networks who serve as sub-centers for the further transport of these means. Thus, on these lower levels, sub-chiefs maintain analogous relations to their followers. Like the roots of a tree, these clientelist tentacles reach into the social space.

Patrimonial relations are not single-tracked, however. In exchange for the means of subsistence such as offices, money, land titles, or other prebends, the Big Man expects political loyalty and, in the case of armed groups, obedience to commands. Usually, patrimonial relations are symbolically framed. Shared languages, common descent or institutional socialization, or other communal relationships bind Big Men, sub-chiefs, and followers together.[203] However, the degree to which these symbolic ties will bridge moments or periods of crisis differs enormously. Power in patrimonial figurations is not yet fully positionalized as it does not function independently from the person holding a position. But power in these figurations is normed, it is no longer sporadic.

General Abdurrashid Dostum, a commander of the Northern Alliance in Afghanistan and chief of staff of the Afghan army since the elections in 2004, is an almost typical example.[204] Dostum was born in 1954 as the son of poor peasants from the region of Shibergan in Northern Afghanistan. He attended only primary school and then became a guard in the local gas works. In the 1970s he entered one of the militias that the Afghan government was forming in order to enlarge its military capacity against the Mujaheddin. In 1980, Dostum benefited from a military education in the Soviet Republic of Kazakhstan. Five years later he became a general in the Afghan army and commanded a force of 50,000 men which was responsible for securing the transit route from the Soviet Republic of Uzbekistan to Kabul. When the Soviet Union eventually terminated all its support for the regime in Kabul, the Communist Party as well as the government forces fragmented, and Dostum's militia became a warring party on its own. Renamed *Jumbish-i-Milli-I Islami* (National Islamic Movement), these forces entered Kabul in April 1992.

Only a few months later, after a conflict with allied Mujaheddin, the forces of Dostum were again driven out of the city. Dostum created his own para-state in Northern Afghanistan, having Mazar-I Sharif as its capital. Due to royalties from the exportation of natural gas and to good agricultural conditions, Dostum's patrimonium flourished. His mini-state printed its own currency and soon had its own airline.

Shielded by mountains from large parts of Afghanistan's other warring factions, with Russian and allegedly also through Turkish and Uzbek support, the proto-state survived until 1997 when it finally fell under the control of the Taliban. It was only when Dostum became an ally of the United States in 2001, in return for a payment of 250,000 US Dollars a month according to some sources, that he could recapture territory (Adamec 2005: 106). He first became vice minister for defense and then vice president in the transitional government under Hamid Karzai. But after the elections of 2004, he resigned from political office and took the position of chief of staff of the Afghan army's high command, thereby becoming the patrimonial lord of this newly created coercive apparatus.

There was probably not one single warring faction in the more than 20 years of Afghanistan's civil war with which Dostum did not have an alliance for some period of time, while fighting the same group either before or afterwards, including the Taliban. And as unstable as his external relations were, his own forces were equally volatile at times. His second-in-command, Abdul Ali Malik Pahlawan, defected in 1997 and joined the Taliban, but he broke with them shortly afterwards. Also, Dostum's forces were often criticized for human rights violations, plundering, and other criminal activities. His political personnel, however, gained the reputation of being extremely disciplined and responsive to the requirements of parliamentary work after 2001.

The organization of violence was, of course, central to the political trajectory the group has taken. And the fact that since 2001 Dostum has maintained a command of at least parts of the present national armed forces is indicative of the continuous importance of violence expertise and capacity in Afghan politics. Simultaneously, however, it is analytically unsatisfying to denounce Dostum as a warlord who is simply relying on violence in order to enrich himself. It is obvious that he has political ambitions that go far beyond such an agenda. His efforts to enhance his reputation can also be seen in his undertaking a pilgrimage to Mecca, in his numerous travels abroad to prove his importance as a valuable interlocutor, and in his declared mission to become the protector of national minorities in Afghanistan.

How this political project developed will probably never be established with absolute certainty. It is simply not possible to analyze a posteriori whether Dostum had these ambitions from the beginning or whether they developed as a result of his militia's logic. There are a number of reasons to assume that the latter had a causally much more important effect. These reasons can be deduced from general logics of organizations. Dostum, being a successful warrior, attracted followers. These were structured in army ranks[205] and fought for their survival in an environment marked by uncertainties and within unstable alliances. In the same way as any other personnel in an emerging organization, the men following Dostum developed an interest in stable relations and their personal safety, especially after the withdrawal of the Soviet Union from the war in Afghanistan and the ensuing decay of the Afghan army. The political agenda that Dostum established during these times could thus be seen as an outcome of circumstances and simple collective interest in the survival of the group.

It is also apparent that Dostum had a need to legitimize his position by further means in order to maintain his forces' cohesiveness and to unite his troops in an arena filled with constantly shifting alliances. The creation of his party, the *Jumbish-i-Milli-I Islami*, can be interpreted as such a step, as dubious as its success might have been.[206] To survive the vagaries of war in Afghanistan over such long a period of time is itself an achievement. But at the same time, the loose institutionalization of his Jumbish-i-Milli-I Islami was not without frictions. Defection of sub-leaders has occurred, and the degree of disciplinization of troops is low. Dostum is eager to have personal control of decisive resources, consisting in earlier times of taxes on long-distance trade and levies on opium exportation, now coming from the latter and the spoils of positions within the Afghan national army.

Dostum's trajectory is emblematic for the mechanism of patrimonialization that can be summarized as follows. Its first stage is the crisis of a political system that is already beset and structured by patrimonial practices. In armed groups that develop in these contexts, patrimonial patterns are therefore already entrenched and dispose of almost "natural" legitimacy. A necessary precondition for patrimonialization to occur is a centralization of the chains of command and the channels of resource distribution. This can be the work of an aspirant for the Big Man position who then usurps the position of a boss, encompassing all functions. This usurpation and centralization is the second step, and it is usually connected with violence within the group.

The centrality of the figuration can then only be maintained when the new Big Man attracts legitimacy on various levels. The distribution of benefits helps to foster it, turning the sporadic power between the Big Man and the staff into norming power as described in the section above. This includes his success as a warrior, albeit in the function of a general commander, remote from actual battlefields. As pointed out already, military success is one source of charismatic legitimacy. An additional source can be his public appearance, serving as opportunities to display his mastery of public speeches or political mise-en-scenes. Furthermore, the Big Man needs to glorify a traditional attire or mark his rule with symbols of traditional legitimacy. This accumulation of symbolic capital then allows a further streamlining of the figuration centered on him.

---

Patrimonial situation → war → armed group formation → hierarchization → usurpation → traditional legitimization → fostered centralization

---

All three mechanisms of formation can apparently lead to patrimonial figurations. Many factors play a role here. Rent-like income structures, of course, is one of them. This can be royalties on the exportation of raw material, subsidies by neighboring states, or military and financial aid by superpowers, as was often the case during the decades of the Cold War. Dostum's current patrimonial position could also be seen as a rent, taken from an externally financed state that is monetarily supported in a likewise globally constructed confrontation, namely by the "war on terror".

The second most important factor that renders patrimonialization more likely is the inherited pattern of politics. In contexts in which patrimonial practices in politics had been the rule before a war, they most likely become common practice during the war and also in its aftermath. Striking examples of this pattern can be found not only in Liberia and Sierra Leone, but also in Haiti, in the Philippines, in Nicaragua, and in the DR Congo. As the example of the EPLF will show, there is, however, no necessity that patrimonialism be continued indefinitely.

Neither is the mechanism of formalization, for which Eritrea's EPLF is a case in point, a predictable outcome of specifiable preconditions. There are only structures and strategies that make this outcome more probable. Quite a number of armed groups, as will be shown, have managed to build such formal institutions in which the role of personal rule has decreased considerably. In fact, there is scarcely any group that does without a certain element of personal rule. Formal structures, positionalized power, are thus always a single element of the internal hierarchy. Their role, however, as will be seen, is not to be underestimated.

## The mechanism of formalization

It is an open and contested question whether Eritrea was ever part of Ethiopia. After a brief British military administration from 1941 to 1953, it was federated with Ethiopia. This larger neighbor simply integrated it without international protest as a regular province in 1962. The armed struggle of Eritreans against Ethiopia had already begun a year earlier.

The EPLF became one of the must successful armed groups in the period since 1945.[207] It fought for almost 30 years against Ethiopian state forces, an army that had once defeated Italy's attempt at colonization. After 1945, Ethiopia was first heavily supported with arms and financial aid by the United States and after the fall of Emperor Mengistu Haile-Selassi in 1975, by the Soviet Union. During the nearly 30 years of war, the EPLF mobilized up to 80,000 troops from a population of 2.5 million people, and more the 65,000 died in combat. However, in 1991, the EPLF in an alliance with other insurgencies in Ethiopia, defeated the Ethiopian army, and two years later Eritrea declared its independence, with the EPLF cadres forming its government.

Two conditions created a favorable setting for this success. First, the EPLF had joined with Ethiopian anti-government groups that were also militarily successful. The second condition was world historical timing.[208] In 1991, other events kept the machinery of international diplomacy busy, and the EPLF was not the only armed movement that was at the brink of becoming a state pursuing full sovereignty.

It is generally attributed to the education of its fighters and its formalization that the EPLF, within a highly fragmented society, developed into an effective armed group that could counter an army of at times more than 200,000 men. Also, it was able to keep its organization streamlined. The EPLF was able to turn its social environment, the Eritrean society, into its social base[209], and it molded its recruits into a highly obedient and disciplined force. Indeed, central to its approach was the programmatic decision that all members of the Front would undergo a compulsory six-month training period, including political education and literacy programs. This enabled the EPLF to change the general narrative of Eritrean history and also to create a shared belief regarding its mission. Nationalist discourse was used to bridge the divide between Orthodox Coptic Christian and Sunni Muslim segments of the population that had not only been a social divide but also represented a language barrier.

In the first phase of the war, armed resistance was not yet united. The *Eritrean Liberation Front* (ELF), in its rebellion, mimicked the system of the Algerian *Front national de libération* (FLN) by dividing its field of actions into combat zones. Although different layers of commanding councils existed, they could not prevent the local leaders of combat zones from becoming patrimonial lords who did not act in a coordinated fashion and thus slipped from central control (Radtke 2009: 78). Only two years later, new fighters, who had been trained in Cuba, China, Syria, and Iraq, invented a system of reorganization with the Arab name *eslah* (improvement) that simplified the internal structure by decreasing the number of zones.

This reorganization, though, was not long-lasting. The new councils fragmented after violent purges within the ELF that resulted in the death of 300 guerillas. Three fragments then reunited in 1973 and founded the EPLF, in which all social communities were represented. Benefiting from the political crisis in Addis Ababa, the EPLF could establish a command center in Eritrea, and the repressive warfare by Ethiopia's new military regime led to further support among the population. The newly formed EPLF councils introduced functional departments within the organization and violently suppressed remnants of other ELF fragments that did not join the new alliance. When the regime in Addis Ababa had defeated Somalia in the Ogaden war of 1977, it turned its troops north and brought the Eritrean resistance to the brink of defeat as well. The remainders of the

ELF fled across the border to Sudan, while the EPLF also made a strategic retreat but took over control of the zones left by the rival ELF fragments.

Throughout the years, negotiations between the segments of the EPLF persisted and turned into a highly centralized organizational structure that combined elements of democratic centralism and free elections. Deliberation was allowed, but once decisions were made deviations were severely punished. The cadres trained in China, Syria, and Cuba formed a resolute leadership and selected personnel for parallel institutions such as a clandestine party, political cadres, and an internal security organization.

Members for the core of the secret party were selected from the most loyal fighters who had joined the new alliance before 1975 and who then in turn recruited younger members. Little is known about the exact mission and work of the secret party, but it is assumed that it combined propaganda regarding the "mass line" with security intelligence for the leadership. Political cadres were selected by literacy, commitment, and work ethic and then trained at a separate school in organizational techniques and political education. These cadres became political commissars in military units, in the mass organizations of the EPLF, and in refugee camps. The functioning of the internal security organization, finally, is less known, but apparently it served as a military police and worked to prevent Ethiopian infiltration.

A further functional layer of the EPLF was formed by its mass organizations. Women, students, workers and finally also the Eritrean diaspora were mobilized for this end, and this broad engagement allowed the leadership of the EPLF to reach deeply into the Eritrean society at home and abroad. Inspired by the Maoist model, these structures were introduced into any village under control of the EPLF. The armed group took on state-like form and functions, granted majority votes to poor peasants, and distributed basic medical and veterinary services to pastoralists. However, the EPLF was cautious in changing political and social structures too quickly, especially in rural areas. In cities, though, it established "people's assemblies" via its mass organizations that dealt with judicial cases, collective work, checked price controls, and collected taxes.

When the EPLF eventually took over the new independent state of Eritrea, it thus already had a long-standing experience of government. During its fight, it had not only institutionalized its own structures from power relations into domination. With its mixed policy of enforcement, moral persuasion, politicization, and political favors, it was capable enough to alter its power over a population, if not into legitimate rule, at least into toleration and endurance.

The most remarkable outcome of this organizational trajectory remains the degree of political structuring within the EPLF as an armed group. In 1977, during its first congress, it adopted the principles of democratic centralism with the concept of a strong leadership and a broad basis. The 315 members of this first congress had been elected by fighters and the mass organizations. The second congress took place in 1987 and was attended by more than 1,000 delegates who elected a central committee of 71 members. This organ proved impractical for routine decisions and became a mere ratification board for the political bureau in which 13 members directed the EPLF. They functioned like ministers for the eleven departments of the organization that closely resembled typical governmental segmentations.[210]

Huge doubts are justified as to how free and regular participation in these elections had been and whether democratic centralism is democratic at all. The interesting point in this development is rather the degree to which the political life within an armed group became formalized. As the earlier phases in the history of Eritrean armed resistance against Ethiopian annexation shows, formalization has not been a deliberate policy from the outset. Instead, it was born out of a perceived necessity to invent means for keeping a heterogeneous group together that otherwise would have been decimated by a powerful enemy. To some extent, the formalization of the EPLF can therefore be interpreted as the outcome of the search for legitimacy within the group. But it was also a functional requirement in the military and political struggle.

At the same time, it is obvious that a group of the size of the EPLF, having thousands of fighters under arms and performing outreach services in many directions, can no longer operate on the basis of a single person's decisions. The sheer size, but also the degree of functional differentiation, create the need for internal bureaucratization and therefore for formalization. Another indicator for formalization taking place is the creation of a second tier of internal control. When leaders start to mistrust the structures it actively created, it does so because they fear that the actual working of the organization, its formality, is beginning to escape their control.

The mechanism of formalization is essentially a process of depersonalization. Power becomes positional. Decisions are taken by persons or groups of persons, but the increasingly long chain of interactions simultaneously enforces the establishment of rules and procedures that exceed the control of any single individual. Also, longer chains of interactions create the need for other techniques of legitimization. Mere patrimonial practices no longer suffice as positive social work can be attributed to incumbents of lower positions, thus threatening the image of a caring and competent leadership. In a surprising similarity to state armies, armed groups that reach a certain size begin to streamline their organization. Membership becomes readily discernible, if not to outsiders at least to insiders. Defection and treason are severely punished, and fighters undergo professional training in which types of subjectivity are formed that complement the group's project. The production of these fighters and functionaries then allows further growth and functional differentiation within the boundaries of a formalized organization.

---

Growth → specialization and complexity → longer chains of interaction → streamlining and disciplinization → growth and formalization

---

The EPLF is not the only armed group that has gone through such a transformation. To some extent, all armed groups that have become members of state agencies or incumbents of state offices have undergone similar processes. The complex structure of Hezbollah that shows strong features of formalization has been sketched in an earlier part of this chapter. Likewise, Hamas and the PLO, participating in regular politics in the Palestinian Administration, show elements of formalization.

## Conclusion

In this chapter, it has been argued that in all armed groups there is a functional necessity for hierarchy and centralized command. While for certain phases of armed action a decentralized structure might be advantageous, armed groups can no longer do without central control and coordination when their size reaches a certain threshold. A second impetus to establish vertical structures arises from the needs of coordinated administration when armed groups begin to control territory.

This need translates into the task of transforming loose relations into institutionalized power relations within armed. Based on the distinction between situational, norming, and positional power, two processes of such an institutionalization within armed groups have been ideal-typically distinguished, namely patrimonialization and formalization.

Patrimonialization consists of a traditional legitimization of positions that have been usurped by "Big Men", using distributional positions to maintain clientelist relations with their staff and followers. Formalization, however, is rather enforced by the growth and functional differentiation of armed groups and is empirically visible in formal procedures and bureaucratization.

The ways in which internal structures of armed groups develop are influenced by a variety of factors. First and foremost is the social context from which the armed group emerges, second is its internal composition. Structures and features from these contexts appear again within armed groups. Joint socialization in institutions, however, can have a positive effect by creating particularly strong ties between members.

But even when armed groups have been structured as patrimonial or formal figurations, they remain unstable. Delegitimizing violence, differentiation, and struggles at the top work as centrifugal forces to the detriment of an armed group's cohesion. These threats are usually countered by an assortment of techniques, of which subjectivation, shuffling, and the closure of social space have been highlighted here.

The mechanisms and techniques sketched in this chapter do not constitute the definitive road to success for any armed group. However, they allow a better understanding of a variety of otherwise enigmatic features and practices of armed groups. Quite contrary to assumptions that have been promoted in the recent literature, the fate of armed groups is thus not preordained by their economic basis. The politics of armed groups, overshadowed by violence, allow for changes, albeit within limits.

# 7. Conclusions: Armed Groups as State-Builders

In summer 1992, a small war broke out in the Republic of Moldova, which had recently declared its independence during the collapse of the Soviet Union. The conflict began as a result of the new government's plans to declare Moldovan the national language, while at the same time another party agitated for unification with Romania. This precipitated violent resistance by an unlikely alliance of business and security agencies dominated by ethnic Russians concentrated on the eastern bank of the Dniester River that flows through Moldova. The fighting, however, was short-lived, and after two weeks Russian troops had secured the front line, thus determining the outcome of a violent contestation. Over the next few years, the left bank entity developed its own institutions, attempting to garner international recognition as Pridnestrovskaia Moldavskaia Respublika (PMR) or Transdniestria, as the area is commonly called.

The PMR government, led by a former manager of a state enterprise, created its own parliament, organized elections, and lived reasonably well from the transit trade and heavy industry that remained from Soviet times. The only quality that this new figuration lacked in order to become another successor state of the Soviet Union was international recognition. Not even Russia, with which PMR has maintained an ambiguous relation ever since, has formally acknowledged its status as a state.[211]

The forces fighting for the separate and independent status of Transdniestria from Moldova were a curious mixture of Russian volunteers, Ukrainian Cossacks, as well as local soldiers and policemen who were loyal to the elite of business managers and security officials conducting the resistance. This quirky amalgamation, of course, differed significantly from the form regular armed forces typically display, but the results of this short confrontation are remarkable. With its own currency, a national flag, a parliament, an internal security agency, and all the other attributes of statehood, PMR is a just one example of how internal warfare leads not to the decay of statehood but to a political reordering. From this loosely connected fighting figuration developed a stable political unit that had gained full territorial control, could run complex business relations, and which could also maintain control of a territory despite considerable pressure from both the Moldovan government and powerful international organizations such as the European Union.[212]

The story of PMR, the rise of Eritrea as an independent state, the successful insurgency of the National Resistance Movement in Uganda, the transformation of the FMPLN in El Salvador from a leftist guerilla group into a regular political party – all these changes indicate that armed groups are not necessarily only destructive forces that solely negate order. In 50 percent of 81 internal wars that were concluded between 1945 and 1992, insurgents either won the war or were integrated as regular actors in a settlement of the conflict (Gantzel/ Schwinghammer 2000: 152). In these cases, the politics of armed groups can also be seen as part of a violent reconfiguration of political orders. The institutionalization that occurs within armed groups then becomes a contribution to state-building. Quite a number of armed groups, therefore, can be seen as outright state-builders.

These counter-intuitive insights will be discussed in this conclusion first by summarizing the main mechanism of the politics of armed groups. I will briefly connect these findings with more theoretical considerations of concepts such as power, domination, violence, and legitimacy that are central for the argument of this book. Also, the methodic and theoretical approach will be reconsidered. What are its limits and merits, and what alternatives do we possess for the scientific study of insurgencies?

A second step will then place the findings on the politics of armed groups into a broader historical context. A short typological summary of internal wars and their results in the period after World War II will be used in order to assess the role of insurgencies for the structuring of world politics. A brief comparative reexamination of the process of state formation and the role of violence within that process will reveal that this interpretation of armed groups can refer to a long history of similar processes.

This conclusion will end with a summarization of related observations on a structural dimension of internal wars that has often been stressed in recent debates, the insertion of the politics of armed groups into international politics. The counterpart to the politics of armed groups is the politics which resist them, currently framed either as the "war on terror" or the politics against "state failure". And although this subject would require at minimum an additional book-length study, a couple of prospective remarks can be concluded from the material and theses developed in this book.

## The politics of armed groups

The focus of the investigations in this book has been placed on the dynamics of power and domination within and around armed groups. The primary challenge for armed groups, it was argued, is to overcome the delegitimizing effects of violence. The relation between violence and legitimacy is thus central in order to understand the politics of insurgencies. Armed figurations can only succeed if they achieve a degree of institutionalization, namely by transforming the mere action power of violence into legitimate forms, into domination, within these figurations. They also need legitimacy in relations with their immediate social environment and the international community.

Using this perspective of political sociology, this book aims to overcome the reductionism of rationalist approaches that develop explanations of the different fates of groups by relying on preconceived models of means-end rationality without taking into account central political concepts such as power, domination, violence, and legitimacy. The variety of factors and circumstances that shape the possibilities and limits of armed actors, it was also argued, is much too expansive to be cast into a formula capable of explaining each and every change in the fate of any armed group. Instead, the heuristic aim pursued here was to identify fundamental mechanisms that can account for at least a considerable number of such differences in the results of the politics of armed groups.

Conditions necessary for the success of insurgencies, however, can be formulated. The ultimate condition for armed groups to be successful, defined as becoming part of regular political systems, is their institutionalization. Two ideal-typical forms of such an institutionalization have been described in the last chapter. Armed groups can either become more or less formal institutions, or, alternatively, develop according to the mechanism of patrimonialization, operating much more by principles of personalism and arbitrary rule.

The success of armed groups is related to mechanisms and interdependencies that have been presented in the previous chapters of this book. A brief summarization of the mechanisms that shape and mold armed groups might be helpful in order to relate the individual theses to a comprehensive theorization:

In chapter two, the stories of Arkan's Tigers, the National Patriotic Front of Liberia (NPFL), and the Moro Islamic Liberation Front (MILF) served as examples for the design of three different mechanisms for the formation of armed groups. Groups like the MILF are formed chiefly as a result of state repression mechanism emerging from an oppositional milieu during economic crises. The NPFL followed the ad hoc mechanism characterized by the deliberate attempt of excluded members of political classes to struggle to reclaim the spoils of government, largely without any further political objective. Arkan's Tigers were described as a prime example of the spin-off mechanism that is based on state agencies' decisions to bolster armed forces in critical political and military situations by creating informal subsidiary forces which then often develop a life of their own.

Groups that come about by these mechanisms develop in different ways, although formation processes do not create path-dependencies. The way in which their formation transpires merely renders certain further developments more or less likely. For the explanation of these likelihoods, chapter three is central. The shadow of violence is cast not only on the fighting members but on entire groups as the use of violence creates trauma and interrupts social relations. Through a superficial overview of the practices of violence differentiated by the methods and means by which armed groups have been formed, rough trajectories can be sketched. For example, groups created by the mechanism of repression apparently tend to be less violent towards their social environment, while spin-off groups do rather the opposite, often in tacit or open alliance with state forces. Accordingly, both groups have divergent problems resulting from the use of violence: While repressive groups and ad hoc groups have fewer problems building forms of legitimacy among the population, spin-off groups face great difficulties in creating such bonds.

Violence, it was argued in chapter three, has a delegitimizing effect in that it produces traumatic experiences that are not easily overcome and that are also unforeseen. While armed groups are neither consistently aware of these effects nor do they necessarily consider them as cause for concern, most evidently attempt to counterbalance the effects of violence by politics that will create legitimacy on three distinguishable levels. These politics are the subject of chapter four. Internally, insurgencies can draw strength from various sources among which personal loyalty, often based on traditional legitimacy, is paramount in many groups. The charisma of ideas and of promising programs aims at gaining legitimacy on the other two levels as well: Also, social contexts and certain elements of the international community will be convinced by discourses on the validity of armed groups' intentions.

At this point at the latest, the international relations of armed groups enter the picture. The connections between global discourses and political divides in the international system on the one hand and the political agendas or rhetoric of armed groups on the other hand are partly pragmatic and partly a relation of selected affinities. A prerequisite in order for these discourses to be effective, it was argued, is that insurgents – and state armies alike – achieve an end of open violence so that basic legitimacy can accrue to them.

As examples of their trajectories throughout the book have shown, the legitimacy of armed groups remains contested. It is subject to reversals in the military situation, to the possibility of derailing violence by its fighters, and also to the volte-faces of international politics. In regard to the latter, however, armed groups have demonstrated an astonishing ability to adapt their discourses to changes within the current global political sphere.

In chapter five it was shown the extent to which the issue of legitimacy also affects the economic bases of armed groups. Here again, the benefits of institutionalization became visible. Groups like the LTTE in Sri Lanka not only achieved territorial control but also were able, by using a mixture of coercion and moral persuasion, to collect taxes from diaspora communities. But not all armed groups can draw on similar support. Many others stagnate for lengthy periods of time when the combination of military shortcomings, unfriendly regional surroundings, and dire economic conditions block institutionalization and a regularization of revenues. The Lord's Resistance Army in Uganda was described as an example for this pathway.

If favorable conditions are not present locally, armed groups can rely only on sources of income that keep them even further aloof from their social surroundings. The de facto army of Khun Sa in Burma was a case in point, as it gained sufficient means from its involvement in the global drug economy. Such rents that can be gained on international markets then unburden groups from the task of seeking close relationships with populations under their control. The single most frequent source of material resources for armed groups, support supplied by other states, creates similar problems. It not only creates dependencies that many armed groups attempt to overcome by developing alternate forms of funding. Furthermore, these transfers can lead to estrangements vis-à-vis local populations with detrimental effects on the insurgency's legitimacy.

In chapter six, the final explication of the institutionalization of armed groups was based on theories concerning the transition from power to domination. Apart from discourse and practices, the steps that foster existing power relations and transform them into domination have been identified. The transition from sporadic power to norming power and, finally, its positionalization could be seen in the trajectories of Rashid Dostum's *Jumbish-i-Milli-I Islami* in Afghanistan and in the Eritrean People's Liberation Front. While the latter achieved independent statehood, the former continues to control parts of the country in a patrimonial manner. Both groups institutionalized, albeit to different degrees, and both can be considered "successful" in terms of conquering at least parts of state offices.

Two general observations on the politics of armed groups deserve to be particularly highlighted at the conclusion of this summary. Firstly, there are only limited path dependencies in the trajectories of armed groups. Structures simultaneously impede and allow certain organizational forms, but they do not preordain the manner in which an insurgency develops. While the "shadow of violence", the complex relation between physical violence and legitimacy, is central to all organizational aspects of armed groups, many trajectories indicate that there is considerable maneuverability for the shaping of the group's fate.

Secondly, the politics of armed groups are not the diametric opposite of state politics. Transitions from state politics into insurgency, as well as instances of the reverse course of events, abound. States fund insurgencies, they delegate violence that gains its own momentum, and states co-opt armed groups' structures. Armed groups include violence expertise that has been produced by states, they exploit interstate rivalries, and they convert, if they are successful, into states or become part of regular politics within the global political system.

In this book, I followed a Weberian conception of power and examined the ways in which armed groups institutionalize the power of violence and the methods they employ to transform violence into legitimate domination.[213] Armed groups as figurations consist of such power relations, but they are also inserted into broader networks of further interdependencies, as, for example, with other states, armed groups in neighboring countries, and diasporas. To view power from this perspective and to see it as an asymmetrical mutual dependency seems much more cogent than attempts based on utilitarian rationalism. Power is relational. It is not "owned", and it is not immutable, but rather depends on the embeddings of a relation into other relations. That is the very idea of figurations Norbert Elias has promoted and that proved able to serve as an alternative framework for the analysis of armed groups' politics.[214]

The alternative to this understanding consists of a conceptualization of power that imagines it as a substance that actors can possess and use as a positive force. Realist theories of international relations, for example, understand the power of nations in terms of economic wealth or military capacity. Both are then measured in numerical codes and expressions such as the monetarized value of gross domestic products or the numbers of troops and tanks. This understanding of power is also dominant in rational-choice based studies on the politics of insurgency that conceive power as endowments or capital if there is at all a conception of it.

The issue with this understanding of "having power" is that it fails to take into account the relativity of power stemming from the fact that matters other than the sheer amount of material means are clearly involved as well. Tanks might be ineffectual against terrorists, and huge national economies may force another government to open its market, but the same wealthy economy might not aid in the solutionIto problems of food shortages in other regions. The understanding of power as a substance cannot account for the relativity of power means, and therefore it is also unable to develop a comprehensive theory of the dynamics of these relations. What has been suggested here instead is a return to core categories of politics in lieu of meager micro-economic language.

The approach suggested and applied here is perhaps not yet a full-fledged theory. The reasons for this incompleteness reside partly in the lack of reliable and comprehensive material. Our means to observe power relations in armed groups are very limited. No armed group has documented the proceedings of either its councils' or leaders' discussions, nor will their private reasoning ever be revealed. Even the limited number of available biographical and autobiographical accounts offer little assistance in this regard, as these texts normally serve primarily to rectify single persons' positions in an unresolved and conflicting set of interpretations. They represent a significant aspect of the strategy of legitimization and, therefore, require a particularly critical assessment. The same caveat applies to all other sources which in a historiographical sense are used as material for the analysis of figurations. Leaflets, pamphlets, speeches, and interviews are indispensable for the hermeneutical task of probing the meaning and self-understanding of armed groups. However, they are never to be taken at face value, as they are without exception essentially an element of political strategies or individual rationalizations.

The analysis of the figurations and of their trajectory will therefore always be a perplexing activity that requires considerable reasoning and critical discussion of sources. Of course, the "accounts", the systematic reconstructions of events, are formidable sources for inferences on the inner working of armed groups. Their reaction to external threats, to military events, but also to events abroad or in neighboring countries, is telling in itself. The painstaking reconstruction of the chain of events is nevertheless only one tool and requires enhancement by other means, as it will never be complete. Conclusions based on these indirect observations will therefore always be contested.

However, for the analysis of armed groups there is no alternative than to begin with case material and combine it with the entire methodological panoply of social scientific research. Case studies are as indispensable as general histories of social and political contexts, since both are needed not only to reconstruct the trajectories of figurations. Additionally, they shed light on the situational backgrounds in which armed groups such as their opponents operate. It is solely through the historical and anthropological literature that the horizons of understanding emerge. They allow scholars to ascertain how actors possibly perceive themselves and their situations, and this, as Weber reminds us, must be part of any truly sociological explanation.

Furthermore, as could be seen in numerous instances in this book, it is only through the study of contexts that main specificities become explicable. This is an indispensable analytical step, as the social forms of organization that characterize the context in which armed groups emerge are very often reflected in the internal structures of these groups as well. In societies, for example, that are governed by patrimonial practices, political challengers will very likely also include patrimonial elements in their internal regime. It is thus only by considering the historicity of contexts that it becomes possible to develop ideas about the main currents of insurgent politics.

Theses that come about through this systematic reading, however, need to be checked and specified by comparative case studies and also by assessing their reach with large-N studies. Yet none of these "distant" methods can replace what is inadequately labeled as "field research". Interviews with actors and bystanders, and the interpretation of discourse are the only means to reveal the subjective meanings and interpretations of events and actions by the actors themselves. The intentions of actors cannot be anticipated or deduced from presupposed theoretical understandings as, for example, lists of preferences. There is no replacement for a close study of discourse, although problems of reliability will never be overcome. The bundle of methods called "field research" is indispensable especially when dealing with topics such as legitimacy that basically is a subjective belief. Even the most superficial and dishonest conversation with war veterans or bystanders, for example, may reveal perceived legitimacy deficits, since merely what is included in a conversation, what is omitted, and how it is phrased is informative in itself. The heuristics of the study of insurgencies, therefore, must always combine hermeneutic understanding and causal explanation. And it will still fail to present a "true" picture, as all reconstruction is colored by later events, needs of interpretation, or the rationalization of memories.

The ultimate challenge then is to keep all these findings and interpretations together using a reflective theoretical viewpoint. Without such a perspective, there is no agent for bringing observations together. Here, Weberian sociology and other writings in the field of political sociology proved capable of delivering a sufficiently integrative understanding with which a number of regularities could be identified. And while the extent to which "facts" are constructed or really observable[215] is an ongoing debate in social sciences generally, the struggle seemingly remains inconclusive which among various theoretical paradigms is closer to "the truth". But an alternative way of judging competing theoretical attempts is to see how credible their results can be shown to appear within the framework of broader questions.

Any theory on the politics of armed groups might thus be evaluated by asking the following question. What is the range of its connectivity to other political phenomena? Does it help us to understand the relations between other events then occurring, and what does it tell us about larger questions, for example the role of the politics of armed groups within their political surrounding? Here, this will be accomplished by discussing findings on the politics of armed groups in relation to two broader processes. One is the question of state-building, and the second is the insertion of the politics of armed groups into the larger picture of world politics. In an effort to resolve these questions, this book will conclude by returning to rather structural considerations that were also the basis of the formation of armed groups sketched in chapter two.

## Armed groups as state-builders in historical perspective

Despite the image that the current debate on intrastate wars has created, there is little evidence that insurgencies during the past 60 years have caused a massive destatization of the world.[216] While all insurgencies, by their nature, question the legitimacy of incumbent regimes, many, if not the majority, have over time led to a fostering of social control by state or state-like agencies. The politics of armed groups can thus be considered part of the politics within and around statehood as the structuring principle of world politics.

War violence oscillates around the state as a political form. While war violence destroys institutions and breaks biographies into scattered pieces (cf. Nordstrom 2004) and dissolves social contexts, at the same time it creates new contexts and new social relations. The politics of armed groups are simultaneously destructive and creative. Often, but not always, this long-term effect is reduced to a mere circulation of elites and new patterns of exclusion. From a structural perspective, this can be seen in a rough typology of internal wars waged after 1945. Violent politics shape the form and the viability of state rule, but they do not mean the end of state-centered politics altogether as the thesis concerning "failed states" purports. There is little reason to believe that the politics of armed groups will directly threaten the structure of international politics. This perhaps challenging thesis might appear less unusual when placed in a broader historical context. Before doing this, a rough typological summary of the results of internal warfare in the period since the end of the World War II adds more evidence to this claim.[217]

Post-colonial states in particular have become central points of economic distribution and political accommodation, while at the same time, as the addressee of international politics, they were also at the center of struggles regarding resources and political participation in the heterogeneous societies they were intended to administer. This link has made internal warfare very prominent through the period after 1945 to the present. *Wars of decolonization* are the first type of internal wars in which the effects of armed groups' politics can be examined. Starting in the 1940s and ending in the mid-1970s, numerous internal wars were part of the historical upheaval, the dissolution of colonial empires.[218] While altogether, this sea change was surprisingly peaceful, in a number of cases the contradictions between colonial powers, settler communities, and autochthon populations escalated into open civil war. Anti-colonial armed groups became state builders in French Indochina, Algeria, Kenya, Cameroon, and Southern Africa. In most cases, the mechanism of repression was at the root of the formation of groups that became violent organizations which, often with considerable external support, later turned colonies into new states.

The result of these wars was always independent statehood conserving, at least formally, many elements of the former colonial states. First and foremost, the ways in which these states and their economies were integrated into the world market constituted de facto path-dependencies for future political structures. When independence was achieved by violent means, those armed groups turned into statesmen and armies, creating a military backlog that made further violence more likely. The shadow of violence loomed for an even longer period than the war endured, as the experience and hardship of warfare made the new state leaders and their clientele less prone to concede power to opposition groups.[219] While many of these wars were thus superseded by subsequent ones, statehood, once achieved, typically remained. The new leaders internalized the idea of the state in a manner equal to that in which the colonial servants had done.

Similar effects can be seen in a second type, *internal wars in developmental states*. Here again, the repression mechanism was a major source for the formation of violent resistance that crystallized in opposition to policies which would have meant a further encroachment of the state into social life, to the detriment of other agencies of social control. States, perceiving themselves as agents of modernization and social change, were often merely creating the resistance which they then responded to with violent means.[220] The courses of these wars were as varied as the fates of the armed groups waging them. In some cases it was possible to reintegrate the violent challengers into the state via patronage (cf. Martinez 1998). In other cases, armed groups were severely defeated or kept in check for long periods. In some instances the challengers were granted statutes of autonomy. Wars in developmental states have thus often led to new institutional arrangements but did not weaken states. However, where governments' reactions were violent, in the continuing shadow of violence, the ongoing delegitimization of incumbent regimes was a consequence as well.

A third type, *social-revolutionary wars*, has become an exception during the last 10 years but has still existed as in the case of Maoist insurgency in Nepal and a number of revolutionary movements still active in India proves.[221] These wars had rather indirect effects on political institutions, but once again, armed groups could also be seen as vectors of state-building. Initially, most of these armed groups failed in their attempts to topple a regime in power and overcome existing social and political orders. But where they were successful, they became regular political actors, who by their participation in regular politics not only returned their followers to an erstwhile illegitimate system but also incorporated the internal structures they had created into a part of these states. Nicaragua's Sandinistas and the FMLN of El Salvador, as outlined at the very beginning of this book, are both cases in point. One significant result of these wars, therefore, was rather an increase in the social control of societies by the state writ large.

A last type is *wars in neo-patrimonial states*. Here, political rule is largely dependent on the distribution of resources via clientelist networks. The civil war in Liberia is a prime example for this as, typically, armed groups in neo-patrimonial states are formed following the ad hoc mechanism sketched in chapter two, when elements of the political class feel dissatisfied at times of shrinking quantities of resources channeled through the state's agencies.[222] Wars of this type, especially, have recently been discussed as proofs for "failed" or "failing states", although it is not clear whether the causal relations of such de-institutionalizations should not instead be seen in changes of the political economic bases of these states (Wade 2005). While it is impossible to ascertain whether the waning of previously often loosely structured political institutions can be attributed to the effects of warfare, it is clear from the post-war politics that, even in these states, little has changed in terms of political structures. The principles of neo-patrimonial rule still prevail, and the precarious economic basis of these states has, for the most part, remained unaltered. Furthermore, even weakly institutionalized neo-patrimonial states cannot escape the political structure of the international system. War actors during the war and afterward do not question the principle of statehood as such, but rather fight for their own place in the formal sphere of politics.

In long-term historical comparison, the global political order since 1945 appears astonishingly stable. In earlier periods, the decay of states in long-enduring wars, the dissolution of empires into single states, and even the violent incorporation of a state by an aggressive neighbor do not seem to be particularly rare phenomena. The history of the modern state system is replete with these events. But after the stabilization of the state system, internal wars and insurgencies have been unable to change this enduring institutionalization of politics.[223] Between 1945 and 1990, not a single state has vanished as a result of an armed insurrection, nor has a state suffered violent annexation. Compared to other periods of world history, territorial changes have been a rare exception since World War II. After the end of the decolonization period, almost all such changes were related to the dissolution of the former state-socialist societies Yugoslavia and the Soviet Union.[224] While the latter cannot be attributed to warfare, the decay of the Federal Republic of Yugoslavia is clearly a consequence of war. However, even it did not lead to less statehood. With the exception of Bosnia-Herzegovina, these wars have resulted in strong states with largely homogenized ethnic populations, in the manner of the classical project of nation-building that came about in a violent way.

Apparently, the politics of armed groups are rather part of the long story of war-related state-building than of the opposite, that is, the de-institutionalization of politics on the globe. Reflecting on the internal history of other states, this becomes even more plausible. All regions of the world have experienced phases in which violent internal confrontation resulted in new political orders. This applies to the frontier zone in US history as well as to the dissolution of the Holy Roman Empire of the German Nation. The alleged emergence of "new wars" might in fact rather be the continuation of a long violent history of the formation of domination.

To accept that violent contestation is often at the root of a new political configuration is not to depreciate the human suffering related to warfare, be it international or internal. It merely means to acknowledge that processes of state formation historically involve much more violence than idealized images and narratives of existing states would have us believe. In this regard, the politics of armed groups differ from the tales of modern states insofar as they have not yet had the opportunity to create their own myths hiding the violent history of political rule.

The coding of insurgent politics as being part of "state failure" and stressing only its anomic face can perhaps be explained with growing expectations that are based on the West's recent history, while forgetting its violent past. Armed groups that have recently conquered state power by violent means face a quite different international environment than their antecessors in the epochs before the 20th century. The normative framework of today differs from the evaluation of politics one or two hundred years ago. While our contemporary moral order is based on the recent peaceful experiences in Western societies, it should not be forgotten that neither was the road to this institutional setting void of violent conflicts.[225] The building of powerful yet democratically controlled institutions that are also effective in delivering collective benefits such as security, welfare, education, and public health required at least two centuries in European and North American history. Now, the result is taken as yardstick for gauging political dynamics elsewhere. And if there is one agreement among historians, it is that the formation of modern states was not an intended outcome. Rather, it is the result of several interrelated dynamics that no one ever preconceived. Meanwhile, the violent history of modern statehood has been forgotten.

Any modern-day state leader who would attempt to create a strong state by employing the means that Prussia's Frederick the Great used to push his sandy agrarian province into the first ranks of European powers would be likely to find that he was soon facing the International Court of Justice. Those practices included recruitment by force, enforced settlements, the invasion of neighboring countries with the intention of seizing its economically promising areas, and the incarceration of opponents and intellectuals, sometimes even those who were formerly befriended, as in the case of Voltaire. All these practices were part of the creation of modern Prussia and later of Germany, but also of other Western states. Nowadays, such policies would rightly be considered to be those of a rogue state.[226]

The politics of armed groups thus stand in a long tradition of organized violence and state formation. The historical linkage between external threats and warfare and the formation of states no longer applies to the degree that it did throughout centuries of history. And while in many instances military threats still exist, infringing on state policies in regions of

Central Africa, South Asia, and the Middle East, the use of force for the enlargement of territories or productive populations is no longer politically feasible since such actions are internationally condemned.

This is only the most visible aspect of a general change in circumstances under which the formation of states is taking place today. Wars and state formation are happening in a fundamentally changed global environment, and as a consequence, a number of strategies which earlier states used to banish internal opponents are unavailable to contemporary state leaders. The violent subjugation of internal rivals, for example, which was still taking place in Iraq, Persia, and Afghanistan in the first half of the 20th century without raising international attention, would nowadays, for good reasons, give rise to international protest and very likely a variety of sanctions, including humanitarian interventions.

In order to assess the politics of armed groups in this broader historical context, it is helpful to look a bit closer into older mechanisms of state building. The centralization of state forces, the famous monopolization of violence, was itself a violent process. In the depiction of modern Western states is just often forgotten that the formation of states in Europe and North America as well was a process of violent expropriation. This is the first insight of Max Weber's historical reconstruction of state formation in Europe, confirmed in case after case by other studies. The construction of kingdoms in early modern Europe was first of all the expropriation of multiple competing local power holders. Knights, lords, bishops, and free cities were subdued by violent means, threats, or political chicanery.

In his magisterial study on the "King's mechanism", Norbert Elias has shown that in the case of France this process took centuries, but it ultimately led to a configuration of forces that was centralized around the royal court, in which the feudal lords became dependent on the King's decisions related to offices and prebends.[227] This reconfiguration led to the absolutist state but was a violent process itself, as well. The monopolization of the use of force was engendered by countless battles between royal armies and local feudal power holders, by struggles between ecclesiastical lords and kingdoms, and by long enduring rivalries among smaller political units. This internal monopolization cannot be separated from another structuring process that began simultaneously, but lasted much longer. That is the famous linkage between the internal structuring of power and external threats.[228]

The monopolization of the use of force, however, did not bring about modern statehood in and of itself. Further processes were concomitant. Norbert Elias and Max Weber have already stressed the enormous role of the disciplinization of individuals who were transformed into obedient subjects by the work of state institutions such as armies, schools, and universities. The spread of discourses and narratives that legitimized state rule was thus supplemented by practices that converted peasants and unruly classes into law-abiding subjects of state institutions. It is to the credit of Michel Foucault (1995) that he demonstrated the function of these institutions as "state makers" in the sense of disciplinary machines.

Three dynamics, the emergence of the monopoly of the use of force, the simultaneous construction of the monopoly of taxation, and the long and meticulous work of disciplinization through state institutions were all part of the construction of absolutist states in early modern Europe. Later processes supplemented these monopolizations. The modern nation-state has its social origins in social and economic differentiations that altered the forms, aims, and scope of political rule. After the bourgeois revolutions, states were expected to deliver more and more services, from barring world market competitors and protecting internal markets to constructing an effectively functioning infrastructure and providing answers to the social questions that arose with industrialization. The modern nation-state is therefore the historical result of a long chain of social conflicts and the slightly varied national trajectories of political constellations. But it has always rested on similar major social processes.

The structural changes of political rule in other parts of the world are not identical with the development of the state in modern Europe. The period of colonization and European imperialism has, quite to the contrary, led to the global generalization of a concept of statehood that is heavily influenced by an idealized image of what defines a modern state.[229]

The politics of armed groups appear, in this historical perspective, rather as a violent appropriation of the idea of statehood, taking place under different global conditions than similar, mostly nationally framed but equally violent processes that took place in Europe or North America. At its root, this violent appropriation might, as in the Western experience, be a social differentiation that molds new institutions. Whether the result of this will be modern statehood as we tend to imagine it, however, remains an open question. It is neither determined by automatisms of modernization, nor does it depend on strategic planning.

## The politics of armed groups and world politics

While there is thus sufficient evidence to suggest that the politics of armed groups can be interpreted as being part of processes of state formation,[230] these processes are not confined to local or national arenas. They are, as has been shown in different regards throughout this book, part of global politics. There are multiple connections between the actual fighting, the discourses, and the organization of armed groups on the one hand, and the fashions, the discourses, and the organization of security policy in countries remote from the actual theaters of war on the other hand. In this section, I will briefly summarize which stages of international embeddedness have subsequently marked the politics of armed groups and how these politics had repercussions for the form and content of politics elsewhere. The main observation I derive from this overview is that a growing internationalization of warfare has taken place, which in its latest stage, the age of humanitarian intervention, leads towards an internationalization of domination. Which political forms will emerge from this constellation in the medium and long term is the question I will discuss at the end of this section.

### *Internationalized wars*

Internal wars after 1945 were not isolated events.[231] They were not only embedded into regional politics and international politics on military and security issues. The relations reach much further. They equally concern the spread of political norms and imagineries, forms of organization, or the organization of international relations as such. As can be seen in numerous cases, internal wars have often had severe repercussions even in countries that were only marginally involved. While it is not possible to give a detailed account of these connections, some basic characteristics can be outlined here, following the same rough typology used in the section above.

Wars of decolonization had been international since their very beginning. While both sides, the colonized and the colonizers, were marked by a wide variety of factions and fault lines, the overarching interpretation of these wars was the dichotomy between these two. Wars of decolonization were waged in order to abolish "foreign rule", the duration of the presence of these "foreigners" notwithstanding. The resistance of colonial powers was not based on economic rationales, but on ideas of world order and one's own place in it. The fact that colonial powers such as France and Portugal already adhered much more to the maintenance of empires which had become dysfunctional is telling in this regard. And the arithmetic of power among the allies of World War II determined to a large extent what was possible and what became intolerable.

The fate of French colonialism in what was then called Indochina is perhaps particularly illuminating in this regard, but it is far from atypical. From a US perspective, the restoration of the French colonial empire after 1945 was already anachronistic. However, following the conceptions of its own "domino" theory, the United States supported the illiberal project for the sake of global power politics. While French Indochina had been invaded by Japan during World War II, its nascent nationalism did not cease when the area was again overtaken by French administration afterwards. France, however, severely weakened economically by the warfare and economic exploitation during German occupation, could not alone afford to bear the cost of the continuation of colonial rule. In Vietnam, when anti-colonial resistance turned violent, France relied on troops recruited in other colonies to serve as soldiers in Indochina, while the United States funded most of the French war chest. The defeat of the French troops at the battle of Diên Biên Phu was also a signal to all other anti-colonialist movements in France's empire that it was militarily possible to defeat the once overwhelming power.[232]

Forms of military organization on both sides, as well as the import of Western political norms such as people's sovereignty and civil liberties, witness the deeply global character of wars of decolonization. Also, the political projects of anti-colonial movements were appropriations of this joint, even though conflictive, history. The boundaries of new states followed the lines drawn by colonial powers, and the idea of the developmental state, born in colonial times, had a continuing effect, albeit in the varied guises of market-led and socialist modernization.

In later years, with the rise of the student movement in the West, decolonization movements were able to attract considerable public support not only in the camp of socialist states but also in Western countries. Once again, shifts in public discourse elsewhere altered the political environment in which these armed groups operated.[233]

In this regard, social-revolutionary wars stood in a line of continuity. In those cases where social-revolutionary movements developed within the context of decolonization, as in Southern Africa or Indochina, the sympathy of progressive governments was presently increasing. The South West Africa People's Organization (SWAPO), for example, was supported by a broad network of Lutheran churches, but also maintained quasi-diplomatic delegations in most Western capitals (cf. Vigne 1987).

Social-revolutionary wars were quickly enmeshed with the dynamics of the Cold War, as both superpowers attempted to instrumentalize opponents as proxy war belligerents. At least partially, this involvement had its roots in the strategies of armed groups to attain international legitimacy. The civil war in Greece (1946-1949), for example, was already interpreted in that manner, although it was not until the war in Korea (1950-1953) that the Cold War became the master narrative for the explanation of most, if not all, violent political conflicts across the globe, often covering a decidedly more complex social and political reality. But despite all due differentiations between these diverse arenas and constellations, during the period between 1950 and 1990 almost all civil wars were globally connected by networks constituted by "international solidarity" or military "aid".[234]

The internationality of these wars, their global character, however, was manifest not only in these networks and references. Already, the fundamental coding of social and political relations that armed groups addressed in their discourse reveal the extent to which this was clearly the outcome of a joint history. Latin American guerillas as well as independence movements in Southern Africa and Maoist guerillas in India referred to ideas that had been formulated in Western Europe, materialized in the Russian and Chinese revolution, and were since appropriated and reformulated throughout the world.

A similar joint history and appropriation can be detected in the wars in developmental states. The global spread of the idea of modern statehood was also, when considered locally, an appropriation that was molded differently in many regards.[235] It is therefore not merely accidental that the practices with which these developmental states attempted to modernize "their" societies were frequently authoritarian and repressive. Enforced resettlements, huge developmental projects, the establishment of market-oriented production, and the creation of bureaucracies intended to control these social and economic changes resemble, in many regards, the "governmentality" that was characteristic of Western states since Early Modern times.[236] The unspoken tradition of the very idea of development (Crewe/ Harrison 1998: chap. 2) has been at work in all these states, supported by an industry of international institutions, NGOs, and a global discourse about progress in its various guises (cf. Ferguson 1987).

But the discourses and practices of armed groups that challenged regimes undertaking such projects were also marked by influences that surpassed local or national contexts. The immense number of regionally based organizations being formed under ethnic labels framed their discourses in a language drawing on ideas of nationhood and self-determination that have spread globally since the 19th century. Even fundamentalist religious groups incorporated modern organizational forms, elements of older political dogmas, and tactics adapted from other armed groups. As noted in chapter 4, with the wars in Afghanistan and Iraq, the use of Islam as a symbolic resource for cross-border mobilization has again become common.[237]

There is no doubt that since the era of the Cold War the politics of armed groups have become a constitutive part of international politics. Causal and semantic relations worked in both directions. Support of armed insurrections in this period was never strictly confined to neighboring regimes or cross-border assistance from other armed groups. Throughout the period since 1945, the politics of armed groups have equally become the subject of transactions in the upper echelons of world diplomacy, of huge military engagements, and of interventions that often expanded into systems of war involving entire sub-regions. The effects of the violent and peaceful politics of insurgents at times even lead to severe crises in remote arenas for which the constitutional change in France 1958, unthinkable without the ongoing war in Algeria, and the end of military rule in Portugal in 1974, triggered by the military stalemate in colonial Angola and Mozambique, are the most evident examples. Evenly well-known are the effects that war-engagements of the US in Vietnam and the Soviet Union in Afghanistan had on their internal political life respectively.

On the level of discourses, the speeches and writings of insurgents have been part of one global discursive field in which armed groups themselves not only participated, but they also shaped self-perceptions and reactions by various international actors, ranging from single governments to churches, NGOs, and major international institutions like the United Nations. Reactions were never unanimous. The "world historical timing" that has been a decisive variable for successful state-building in earlier phases of history is still of great significance for the odds of armed groups gaining such a high degree of international legitimacy that their struggle to turn firepower into political domination cannot be blocked from outside. In the remaining pages of this conclusion, I will therefore touch upon recent shifts in the global discourse on armed groups and insurrections and the possible outcome of this new framing.

### Another wave of internationalizing internal warfare

If the European experience of state formation, with its huge costs in human lives, broken biographies, and use of force and suppression is no longer repeatable, is the formation of states still possible at all? If so, how can this process be supported by external actors, so willing to assist, and what would be appropriate strategies?

The changes in the normative framework that occurred during the 20th century certainly have consequences for insurgents. The politics of armed groups are currently framed in political discussions in the Western public as one aspect of a broader problem identified as the issue of "transnational terrorism" and "failed states". According to this perception, which has found its way into the security doctrines of the European Union as well as of the United States, the weakness of administrative capacities and political control is at the same time the main obstacle to the old project of development, but it is also seen as the major security challenge of the early 21st century.[238]

Internal wars, according to this position, indicate the loss of "state authority". Armed groups appear in this image as part of the problem. Greed-driven warlords threaten the integrity of states and force entire subregions into chaos and anarchy. The idea that anomie rules within these groups and is introduced by them in conflict-ridden societies is paramount within this narrative, creating the need for foreign intervention and the continuous presence of international agencies that attempt to foster precarious political constellations and resolve the underlying conflicts. This intervention would also be necessary as it prevents unruly world zones from becoming safe havens for terrorist networks that act transnationally.[239]

Transnational terrorism, "state failure", and intrastate wars have amounted to "legitimate problematique", to use an expression of Pierre Bourdieu, equating all these phenomena with each other. Although considerable difference exists between the political lessons and practices that

Western states and international institutions have deduced from this new image of global dangers, a number of general observations about the relation between this new framing and the politics of armed groups can be outlined. The simplification of conflating intrastate violence with transnational terrorism leads to erroneous and detrimental decisions. It renders the emergence of spin-off violence more likely and overlooks potential local arrangements (cf. Eckert 2008).

It is dangerous to subsume all types of violent intrastate conflicts under the label of terrorism since this simplification leads to inaccurate political conclusions. The term terrorism signifies a particular strategy of political violence. Using surprise attacks on military and civilian targets, this strategy aims at spectacular effects. Terrorism is, as many scholars have stressed, a strategy of communication. Of course, other practices of violence can also be seen as acts of communication, as they also want to deter, to frighten, and to impede certain actions. They demonstrate strength to opponents and followers simultaneously, they help mobilize new supporters, and by the "charisma of the deed" indicate to members that what had before seemed impossible to achieve is indeed possible. All forms of political violence, after all, have power effects that are based on its physical effects, the trauma it causes, but also on warrior charisma as explained in chapter three. Sociologically, terrorist acts as such do not represent a particular type of actors. Terrorist practices appear in many intrastate wars, and they appear in situations that are not war-like. Bomb attacks on civilians and politicians were practiced by the Basque ETA in Spain and the leftist RAF in Germany, and they were part of the register of violent practices of the Titoist Partisans against the German Wehrmacht during World War II, as well as the Chechnyan separatist in the 1990s. To speak of a "war on terror" is misleading in a double sense. This expression does not address a precise type of actors, nor can particular tactics be defeated. Because this is such an unclear expression, it is prone to promote suspicions and stereotyping of entire religious communities and groups of people.

But transnational terrorism only emerges when different agendas coalesce. In local armed conflicts, when stalemates occur, such networks become an additional resource to draw on. Al Qaeda had become involved in Bosnia for that reason, and it was also solely due to the threatened position of Chechnyan secessionists that they accepted the assistance of Arabs, who, as foreigners, lacked legitimacy.[240] The same is true for the Taliban in Afghanistan and the MILF fraction of Abu Sayyaf.

For the Western public, these connections then appear as a single context. And in analogy to the simplifications of the Cold War, when all local conflicts were interpreted as "proxy wars", a broad diversity of conflicts, contexts, and actors are coded as being part of one binary opposition. This image threatens to become a constitutive element of world views from several perspectives. Patterns and mechanisms that characterized Cold War politics are repeated, including the escalation of accusations, the armament of clients, and a rise in the proliferation of violence expertise. Also in a similar manner to the Cold War period is the distinction between those conceiving strategies, those who bear the economic burden, and those who actually exert violence and are afflicted by it.

The discourse of the "war on terror" thus threatens to repeat the unintended outcomes of the Cold War, a global degradation into continued political violence caused by the armament of repressive regimes and a further distribution of military expertise and hardware. The "sorcerer's apprentice" syndrome, described briefly in chapter two as one mechanism of the formation of armed groups, is then increasingly likely to occur again and again. Spin-off groups that emerge from the delegation of state violence are more likely to occur as asymmetric warfare remains unchecked by international pressure, and states feel compelled to employ paramilitary units to fight their internal challengers.[241]

Similar caveats should apply to the discourse on "failed states". The discursive shifts that underlie this new interpretation are not yet entirely evident. However, as has been shown by numerous commentators, the rise of the term "failed state" and the merger of developmental and security discourse is functional for a variety of political actors, both in the regions concerned and for Western agencies utilizing this framework for the legitimization of their continuing existence and expansion. Armies, secret services, and developmental agencies rank prominently among these.[242] If one accepts the writings of regional scholars and critical authors in the field of international relations as serious, the merger of the developmental discourse with security doctrines is possibly based less on actual recent changes in the political structures in the world than on a discursive shift that has gained its own momentum. Policy planning units, military doctrines, journalists, and aid agencies all agree on an unspecific image of what constitutes the overriding political problem of the world, and their mutual references turn this discourse into a self-sustaining language game.

It is still unclear what effects the ensuing interventionism will have on the project of state-building as pursued by these agencies. The complex interactions that interventions maintain with local political structures do not yet present a clearly delineated picture. The answer to this question of interventionism must first take into account that there is apparently no universal strategy upon which all international actors agree. There is no global consensus regarding the conditions under which international interventions are mandatory, under which regime they should be led, or when their mission would be fulfilled. Instead, a plethora of agencies is engaged in all those countries that are currently discussed as "failed states", "fragile states", or "weak states".

The question of what type of political order will result from these multi-faceted interventions and engagements in their interactions with the politics of armed groups depends first on concrete local constellations of social and political forces. Depending on the degree and form of social differentiation, the outcomes might differ enormously.

One reason why we do not know much about such results is that the engagement of such external actors as NGOs and international agencies is uneven and poorly documented. There is no reliable account of the number of single projects, the amount of money spent, or the personnel employed. Instead of a consistent and diligent collective effort for the construction of political institutions, the situation in Afghanistan, Kosovo, the DR Congo, and other long-standing interventions gives the impression of anarchic competition between various institutions that admittedly pursue the same goal – namely the construction of an efficient state that is democratically controlled – but that unwittingly produce something else entirely that rather resembles a Babylon of policies, institutions, and discourses.

It is indeed highly questionable whether out of these constellations something will emerge that even remotely resembles the model of a modern Western state. In Uganda, for example, where after 20 years of civil strife and internal warfare the international community and a bewildering number of NGOs has been active since 1986, the outcome is a form of internationalized domination that places the actual state into limbo. The regime itself is a former armed group, it came to power by an insurgency. Great Britain and other states, together with international financial institutions, subsidize the central budget by more than 30 percent with grants and loans, while NGOs, as well as churches and other charitable institutions, organize basic health care and supplement a defunct judiciary. German development organizations are active in maintaining national parks, sewage networks, and road building. Danish aid agencies support local administration and make efforts to build a functioning legal system. The coordination of aid, frequently requested and certainly needed, is often reduced to negotiations concerning salary ceilings. If this is the outlook for the governance of those regions currently labeled as "failed" or "fragile" states, their future will be a highly internationalized patchwork of competencies and claims.[243]

It could be, however, that beneath this apparent chaos of institutions, processes may occur that result in the functional equivalents of state formation. The amount of bureaucratic knowledge that international institutions, national agencies, and non-governmental organizations have acquired might provide the basis for forms of rule which post-colonial states cannot reach without assistance. Also, the processes of individualization brought about by market forces could erode existing loyalties to older systems of patronage. That forms of subjectivation take place even in times of civil war, which are thus part of the processes of state formation, has been shown in chapter six of this book. In fact, many of the cruel practices of armed groups fighting in contemporary civil wars bear numerous similarities to the practices of European armies, so important in the formation of European states.

Other questions, though, remain unanswered. It is not clear, in current attempts at state-building, which groups could serve as a functional equivalent to the bourgeois classes in Europe who forced states to become democratic and to deliver services rather than using their resources for military adventures. Is the moral and legal pressure of the anonymous "international community" strong enough to enforce the same process, given the inclination of state officials to bend the policies imposed by external actors?[244] But, on the other hand, even those practices denounced as corruption and clientelism could be a means of strengthening the ties between central power holders and their local followers. The feudalization of Europe and the corruption of its administration in Early Modern times allowed central states to at last bridge power gaps between cities and rural areas. The twisted routes leading to state formation have seemingly taken on a different guise now than in those earlier times. The outcomes of the politics of armed groups – and of the politics with armed groups – are not predictable. But perhaps, once again, the unintended outcomes of uncoordinated action will prevail over single plans and long strategic discussion.

# 8. Notes

1 The list reads as follows: Sudan and Lebanon (Jago Salmon, 2003) Eritrea and Sri Lanka (Katrin Radtke, 2003), Nicaragua and El Salvador (Astrid Nissen, 2003), Serbia and Uganda (Klaus Schlichte, 2003, 2004, 2005), Moldova and Cyprus (Daria Isachenko, 2005, 2006), DR Congo (Alexander Veit, 2005, 2006), Angola (Teresa Koloma Beck, 2005/2006). Earlier research by the author on small-scale rebellion in Senegal, Mali, and Liberia was carried out in 1994 and 1997 respectively.

2 This thesis was first introduced by van Creveld (1991), who was later followed by Kaldor (1998) and Münkler (2002b). Kalyvas (2001) was among the first critics of this discourse. Other scholars followed this criticism, cf. Marchal (2003), and Schlichte (2006). On the debate surrounding this question in Germany see also Brzoska (2002).

3 For this account of the FMLN's trajectory I am drawing on the work of Astrid Nissen (2003), see also Grenier (1999) and McClintock (1998).

4 The most frequently quoted author of this position is certainly Robert Kaplan (1996). The German writer Hans Magnus Enzensberger (1993) developed a similar apocalyptic vision.

5 Only recently, such attempts were undertaken from the rationalist camps, as in the work of Weinstein (2005; 2007). While benefiting enormously from a fresh approach to ethnographic methodology, his framework is still mired in micro-economic categories. I will return to that important contribution in later chapters.

6 Norbert Elias brought the term figuration into sociological discussions. He understood it to mean the ensemble of changing patterns of relations between interdependent individuals (1991: 76f.). Conceptually, Elias' aim was to find a third way between the alternatives of methodological individualism and abstract structuralism. Using the term figuration he wanted to show that societies consist of numerous ensembles of social relationships that are related to each other, with each of these ensembles consisting of interdependent individuals. On the concept and its application in several of Elias' writings see Mennell (1998: 250f.).

7 This transition to de-personalized forms of political authority is the subject of other major studies on the emergence of kingdoms, cf. Kantorowicz (1997).

8 They consist of mutual dependencies, exactly as Hegel depicted it in his famous dialectic of lordship and bondage in his "Phenomenology of the Spirit". A command must be responded with obedience, a wish with fulfillment. And as powerful as a master might be, to some extent he is always dependent on the role his servant plays. These relations are always open to renegotiation, and therefore Elias described figurations as "fluctuating power balances" (1991: 142).

9 On Weber's understanding of these fundamental definitions see his own elucidations (1978, I: 53 et passim) and Breuer (1994).
10 For this ongoing project and its publication see Gantzel/Schwinghammer (2000) and www.akuf.de. The group does not use a quantitative threshold for the definition of war, both for theoretical reasons and because data on civil war is unreliable and incomplete. The operational definition is based on the works of Istvan Kende (1978) and conceives war as a violent mass-conflict that involves state forces on at least one side. Warring factions need to show a minimum of strategic action, and violent events must take place continuously.
11 These are Ellis (1999) work on Liberia, Geffray (1990) on Mozambique, McKenna (1993) on the Philippines, Dorronsoro (2000) on Afghanistan, Schubert (2001) on Uganda, and Stern (1998) on Peru. Extremely helpful are also the following comparative works: Reno (1998), Clapham (1998), Jean/Rufin (1996), Marchal/Messiant (1997), McClintock (1998), and Wickham-Crowley (1992). Apart from databases on war, such as the one in Hamburg, the most comprehensive compendium on contemporary armed groups has been produced by Balencie/de la Grange (1999).
12 This school of thought is represented, for example, in the "Journal of Conflict Resolution" or the "Journal of Peace Research". For a methodological criticism of this strand of research cf. Dessler (1991). A classical example of this type of study is Fearon/Laitin (2003).
13 On this school of thought consult the works of Weinstein (2005, 2007), also Kalyvas (2006), Fearon/Laitin (2003), Barbara Walters (1997, 2003). For a recent assessment of this school see King (2004).
14 Collective judgments like these are necessarily unjust. In the following chapters I will introduce a number of exceptions. Hopefully this book is able to show how single works and streams of research can be linked in a mutually benefiting way.
15 A fair and telling account of this process is now given by Hashim (2006) who distinguishes regrouped army units from insurgents without former military background, acting out of "nationalism, honor, revenge and pride" (2006: 99).
16 Two factors have been highlighted by this research, namely material interest and coercion. This explanation is certainly not covering all relevant forms of motivation that are empirically never pure. Interviews with war veterans always reveal a complex mix of motives and even participation not even based on real decision. The more recent literature is discussed in Gates (2001). Humphreys/Weinstein (2006) deal with the consequences of recruitment based on material incentives for practices of violence. Richards (1996) has challenged the presupposition of mere material interest, implying that the logics of exclusion matter much more. McKenna (1999) stressed the role of immediate security needs.
17 On this notion cf. the first paragraph of Weber's "basic sociological terms" (1978, I: 4). By this notion, Weber attempted to bridge the still sensible gap between causal explanation and interpretation of meaning by introducing hermeneutic elements into modern sociology. This rests on the assumption that subjective meaning is inter-subjectively comprehensible and accessible. "One need not have been Ceasar in order to understand Ceasar" (1987, I: 5). Believing in the fundamental feasibility of understanding motivation by observers, he insisted on the need to include in a valid explanation the interpretation of meaning. Both observable regularities and hermeneutic steps of interpretation are, ac-

cording to Weber, indispensable parts of such an explanation. Otherwise, social sciences would either consist of abstract reasoning or would exaggerate intuition. Discourse is as important as economic statistics.
18 "But custom, personal advantage, purely affectual or ideal motives of solidarity, do not form a sufficiently reliable basis for a given domination. In addition there is normally a further element, the belief in legitimacy" (Weber 1978, I: 213).
19 As useful as Weber's contribution for this basic typology of political figurations is, it has limits and shortcomings like any other theory. Weber, for example, falls short of an explanation for the dynamics of forms of domination that could cover all historical changes. There is certainly a number of elements for such a theory in his writings as, for example, on the routinization (Veralltäglichung) of charisma, but the whole range of political change is not covered by these scattered remarks. Here and in the ensuing chapters, I will therefore add other theoretical elements to his sociology of domination as outlined in chapter two. My interpretation of Weber follows Stefan Breuer (1994).
20 As mentioned above (cf. introduction) the database from which this information is taken had started with 50 rough sketches of armed groups in order to identify important aspects of actors (leader, staff, follower), organizational aspects (form, agenda, lifestory), and practices (funding, violence). The most frequently occurring qualities were then systematically investigated in a sample of 80 cases. Although this enlarged sample roughly followed the regional distribution of internal warfare after 1945, preference was given for pragmatic reasons to well-documented cases. For more detail on the database cf. Malthaner (2007).
21 This argument has been prominently presented first in the debate on economic agendas in civil wars, cf. Berdal/Malone (2000). In a larger research project instigated by the World Bank the "greed" thesis was first elaborated and later attenuated, cf. Collier (2000; 2003). A fundamental criticism of this reductionist argument has been formulated by more case-oriented scholars, cf. Marchal/Messiant (2001).
22 Source: MAG-database.
23 The following account largely follows the impressive study of Thomas M. McKenna (1999), see also Gomez (2005) and Sidel (1999) on political structures in the Philippines.
24 It is impossible to list all the groups whose emergence rather follows the pattern of the mechanism of repression than the two others. Cases include the National Democratic Front of Bodoland (George 1994), the Sudan Liberation Army in Darfur (Prunier 2005), the Maoist guerilla in Nepal (Ramirez 2004), the Tigray People's Liberation Movement in Ethiopia (Young 1997) and a number of groups in Latin America. The FSLN in Nicaragua and the FMLN in El Salvador are classic examples for this cf. McClintock (1998).
25 An extensive account of the formation of the NPFL is given in Ellis (1998), a much shorter version can be found in Reno (1998: 91–95), stressing much more his economic connections. On the later development of this business network cf. Prkic (2005).
26 Certainly one reason for this support was the marital politics in West Africa. Adolphus Tolbert, a son of the former president of Liberia who was toppled by the putsch in 1980, was married to an adopted daughter of the president of Cote d'Ivoire, Houphouët-Boigny. The Ivorian president henceforth despised Doe as a brutal, uncivilized soldier. Blaise Compaoré, president of Burkina Faso, was another son-in-law of Boigny (Reno 1998: 81). On the relevance of parental structures in African politics see also Constantin (1986).

27 The formation of armed groups in such an international space is nothing unusual. The experience of being exiled, apparently, is strongly connected with the emergence of armed groups. Examples abound and evidence is also given by the high percentage of time spent in exile as part of the biographies both of leaders and staff. Hypotheses why this is so important might be built on lack of integration in host countries, on formal education and politicization abroad, or on social ties growing stronger between fellow countrymen living in a culturally distinctive environment. The formation of first kernels in exile is however not connected to ad hoc groups. The first steps in the formation of Eritrean resistance also took place in Sudan (Markakis 1987: 107). See chapter six for more detail of this highly formalized group.
28 In anthropological terminology, these armed groups start out as "bands" (cf. Walter 1969: 57). A counter-example to Taylor and much more successful case is Uganda's current president Yoweri Museveni, who controlled external political connections at the beginning of the NRA's rebellion and could also credibly present himself as the military leader of the rebellion; cf. his own biographical account (Museveni 1997).
29 The history of the RUF is recounted in Abdullah/Muana (1998), the story of Kabila's AFDL is told in Nzongola-Ntalaya (2002: 225f.) and Kennes (2003: 218–221).
30 This interpretation is also bolstered by findings based on larger data sets, cf. Laitin (2001).
31 On the interpretation of the strategy of the NRA cf. Museveni (1997), Schubert (2001, 2006), Kasfir (2005), and Weinstein (2007).
32 Source: interviews in Belgrade, March 2003. Cf. also the documentation of the veterans of Belgrade's quarter Rakovica (Sekulić 2001).
33 In comparative regard, it is one of the particularities of the wars in Yugoslavia that the country had compulsory military service and regular military training so that almost the entire adult male population had intensive military education. The strong militarist tradition relates to the Partisan's war victory as the foundational myth of Yugoslavia and with the security situation of Yugoslavia during the Cold War as it was perceived after the Soviet invasion of Czechoslovakia in 1968 (cf. Remington 1997).
34 Source: interview with former SDG member March 2003, Belgrade.
35 Source: interviews with war veterans in Belgrade, October 2005. Another coup of diversification was Arkan's marriage to the extremely popular turbofolk-singer Ceca, transmitted by television throughout the country in January 1995. The costs of the wedding celebration allegedly amounted to 150,000 Euro and were paid by his business partner Giovianni di Stefano, who was also being sought on criminal charges in various European countries (Anastasijević 1996).
36 The trajectories of militia leaders in Serbia vary however, as they do in other cases. Cf. Salmon (2006), Schlichte (2009).
37 On the role that the "Hajduck" image played for the politics of militias during the wars of Yugoslavia cf. Allcock (2000: 390ff.). The more general reading on social bandits is Hobsbawm (1959).
38 For empirical evidence of the reported violent practices of spin-off groups cf. chapter three.
39 I am drawing here again on the comparative study of Jago Salmon on the People's Defence Forces in Sudan and the Lebanese Forces in Lebanon, cf. Salmon (2006: 96f.)

40 Spin-off groups thus resemble the "sorcerer's apprentice" in Goethe's poem, trying in vain to control the forces once unleashed: "spirits that I've cited, my command ignore" (Goethe 1957).
41 The spin-off groups included in the sample are the SLA in Lebanon, cf. Endres (2004); Interahamwe in Ruanda, cf. Prunier (1998); the HVO in Croatia, cf. Burg/Shoup (1999); Mchedrioni and the National Guard in Georgia, cf. Gordadze (2003) and Fairbanks (1995); the SUA in Burma, cf. McCoy (1999); Dostum's militia in Afghanistan, cf. Giustozzi (2003); on the SDG and the Chetniks in Serbia cf. Schlichte (2009).
42 Source: interviews with ex-JNA officers in Belgrade March 2003, October 2005.
43 Cossack volunteers formed voluntarily as nationalist paramilitaries in Soviet Russia during the years of its demise. Their only actual campaign apart from their involvement in the defense of the Parliament in Moscow in October 1993 was their participation in the short war in Moldova, apart from rumors that they joined the secessionist movement of Abchasia.
44 On this conception, which goes back to a Weberian understanding of "the political", see the last chapter of this book. An excellent discussion of the changes in the meaning of "the political" can be found in Palonen (1993).
45 For most social theories that are centered on modern societies, violence is not mentioned or it is marginalized as an anomaly that has been overcome by the achievements of modern institutions. It appears in the form of a problem solved by modern statehood and the ensuing monopolization of violence (cf. Joas 2000; Reemtsma 2006). It was only recently that civil wars have brought the subject back into theoretical debates, cf. Bauman (1991), von Trotha (1999), Scheper-Hughes (2004), and Münkler (1992; 2002a). The task remains to come to terms with the issue of violence in social and political theory and can build on excellent work such as Hannah Arendt (1970), Eugene Walter (1969) and René Girard (1977). Regarding contemporary debate on the theory of violence cf. Reemtsma (2006; 2008) who states that it has become almost a tradition that each study on violence presents itself as a "foreword" or "first step" in the endeavor to create such a theory. However, there seems to be no major progress in theory-building over the last 30 years. On the one hand, there is a broad stream of literature that sees violence as means similar to any other and looks for causal relations by factor variations. On the other hand, there are rather phenomenological approaches that delve into single events or lengthy descriptions of certain forms of violence (cf. von Trotha 1999; Sofsky 1996; 1997; Pewzner 2005).
46 The thesis of barbaric violence has been promoted first by the journalist Robert Kaplan in his widely quoted article, "The coming anarchy" (1994). It is also found in Kaldor (1999: 18), Herfried Münkler (2002b: 142ff.) although neither author has presented more than anecdotal evidence for this claim. That the thesis of a "brutalization of warfare" in the late 20th century in comparison to earlier periods does not withstand close analysis is shown by Kalyvas (2001) and Brzoska (2004).
47 An alternative explanation has been offered by Weinstein (2007), built upon "endowments" of insurgent groups. According to this argument, what is here called derailed violence can be explained by the short-term incentives that groups with few social ties to its members have to offer in order to recruit enough fighters. Ranking highly among these short-term incentives is material reward, which in turn encourages defection and assaults. While it was impossible to accurately assess this explanation, it has the ability to

overcome the simple "greed" vs. "grievance" debate, but seems to neglect the dynamic character of the economic basis of armed groups, cf. chapter 5.

48 This very restricted definition has the advantage of excluding many phenomena that would render the analysis of the social meaning of violence even more difficult. Surely, this definition has its limitations. It does not include the threat of violence which could instead be discussed as coercion. However, immediateness and horror are somehow "around" when coercion is applied. The main reason for this definition is that there seems to be a major difference both in the legitimization and in the outcome, and on the individual psyche as well as on the social level whether violence is only threatened or indeed exerted. The definition used here also excludes the notorious confusion created by terms such as "structural" or "symbolic" violence as it has been suggested by Galtung (1969) or used in Pierre Bourdieu's work. Speaking in the language preferred here, such an understanding would confuse violence with other forms of power and domination. For the most recent debate on the concept of violence cf. Reemtsma (2008).

49 The evidence for this main effect of violence is overwhelming. What has been acknowledged as a medical fact over the last decades as "post-traumatic stress disorder" (PTSD) is nothing other than the belated recognition of the disastrous psycho-physical effects physical violence entails. For an impressive example dealing with this topic cf. Merridale (2005: chap. 8) on the trauma in the Soviet Red Army during World War II.

50 The historical change of forms in these orders of violence is still understudied as Elias (1983b) reminded us, cf. despite the attempt by Chesnais (1981) to aggregate findings on the history of violence. The important question of how to write this story would encounter a number of problems. This task would consist of constructing a perspective that allows taking into account how violence is organized and how organized violence functions, fails, or succeeds, while at the same time, other forms and incidences of violence are not ignored. A true genealogy of violence, then, would encompass the history of organizations as well as of individuals, inclusive of their feelings and minds.

51 On the genesis of this term in Elias' thinking cf. Menell (1998: 217).

52 In modern societies, it is argued, only those forms of violence seem legitimate that serve to restrain other forms of violence. All those practices that do not have that aim but instead serve other ends tend to be seen as pathological. But as Reemtsma (2006: 6) has convincingly argued, this is a modern moral framing. There was no scandal in using violence before Thomas Hobbes' writings became a standard position. Modern societies continuously struggle with that image of violence as the catastrophes of the 20th century still require explanations that the hint of "pathologies" cannot replace.

53 In Weber's words, "What is prohibited in relation to one's brothers is permitted in relation to strangers" (1978, I: 614). On the complex mechanisms that lead to the production of such strangers cf. Appadurai (2006: chap. 3).

54 An incisive recent summary, both of the sociology and psychology of mass violence, can be found in Chirot/McCauley (2006).

55 It is noteworthy that despite this political rationalization, even modern armies cannot do without elements that appear anachronistic to outsiders, such as ceremonies, oaths, and chants, cf. Euskirchen (2005).

56 This is the old insight that can be found in Weber (1978, I: 388). "Any cultural trait, no matter how superficial, can serve as a starting point for the familiar tendency to mono-

polistic closure", and how these rules change over time. This observation has later been more finely differentiated by Frederik Barth (1969) and Rogers Brubaker (2004).

57 For illuminative evidence cf. Dorronsoro (2000: 136) on Afghanistan. Quantitative findings have meanwhile confirmed this observation, cf. Weinstein/Humphrey (2006).

58 A complete history of moral codes that simultaneously allow and restrict the use of violence both within communities and towards non-members has not been written, although material abounds. The literature extends from the emergence and functioning of knights as local monopolies of violence (cf. Bloch 1994: 435 et passim), through the different trajectories of state-building in Europe (cf. Elias 1982), up to the debate concerning the ways democratic states behave towards each other and towards differently structured political organizations (Oneal/Russett 1997).

59 This is said, for example, of the work of Lewis (1965) on Somaliland.

60 Rawadsch: this traditional law, was still seen as legitimate reference for violent action in the 1960s. It is centered on such a concept of honor, according to which males must defend the honor not only of their households. They can also be drawn on as support for feuds of their clan or wider groups. This could include violent actions that were forbidden according to state law, but following the rules of this moral code led to higher social esteem than wealth or any other social achievement (Orywal 1996: 66).

61 Cf. the work of Ali Mazrui (1977) for colonial and post-colonial Africa, and of Rouquié (1987) and of Waldmann (1978) for Latin America.

62 The defeated usually develop their mythological version of their fate, often presenting themselves as morally superior to their adversary (Schivelbusch 2003: 31). Weber highlights the same point. "Shared political fates, i.e. predominantly shared political conflicts about life and death, tie communities of memories that are more stable than bonds of shared languages, cultures or descent" (1978, II: 903).

63 Cf. the inversionary discourse model of David Apter (1997) according to which one could distinguish "logocentric" wars from cases in which power and resources are central. In how far discursive strategies are part of the power dynamics in and around violent figurations will be shown in the following chapter.

64 There is recent social psychological research on ways in which violence is "inherited" between generations, cf. Elbert et al. (2006).

65 On Tito's five-year prison term cf. Djilas (1980: 31). Tito's fate, seemingly, is not atypical for leaders of socialist states. Ceaucescu was also imprisoned, just as Erich Honecker and numerous other communist leaders were during the first half of the 20th century. It is however understudied to what extent the repressive politics of "real socialist" states can be explained by biographical details of their leaders.

66 The ideal strategy of violent insurgency, as it is argued here, is the basis of most if not all armed groups' strategy after World War II. The core elements of this strategy were theoretically formulated during the age of the Napoleonic Wars, and their elements have been reformulated ever since in different versions. Gérard Chaliand (1994: 17) rightly points out that guerilla tactics are much older and might even be historically universal. Their organization into a theory of irregular warfare, however, occurred only in the 19th century by Clausewitz (1991 [1832]) and Lemière de Corvey (1823).

67 Among many other authors, Erich Maria Remarque has captured this experience in his novel, All Quiet on the Western Front (London 1929).

68 This is reported, for example, in accounts by civilians who lived in the zones where Museveni's "National Resistance Army" (NRA) operated in the early 1980s. Peasants tried to avoid contact as they perceived the rebels as state-like actors who should not be trusted. Support for the insurgents only grew when arbitrary repression by state forces increased considerably, cf. Schubert (2001: 141).
69 One certainly is that violence exerted by state forces as retaliation for alleged or real support of civilians can spoil the insurgents' legitimacy. It is noteworthy that Clausewitz had already calculated using overburdening counter-violence by state forces. "When people live together in villages, soldiers will be deployed into those most insecure or these villages may be plundered, burned etc." (1991 [1832]: 523).
One reason armed groups attack civilians, even from their own core constituency, is the competition between armed groups and other power agencies, cf. chapter 6.
70 With "emotions" I refer here to individual psycho-physic reactions, not to the mechanisms that rational-choice based authors have recently tried to conceptualize. To conceive, for example, of hatred as a "historically formed schema" as Peterson (2002: 63) does, means to leave the essentially situational quality of emotional forces in the explanation of violence and to locate it rather on a structural level. The same criticism applies to the definition of fear and rage as phenomena in which "cognition precedes emotion" (2002: 75). It might be useful to follow this track, but the argument here focuses on situational emotions as causes of delegitimizing excessive violence and cyclical consequences. On a very similar list of emotions in the use of excessive violence as "psychological foundations" cf. Chirot/MacCauley (2006: 61–81).
71 It is the merit of Stathis Kalyvas (2003) to have hinted at this fundamental insight into the dynamics of violence in war.
72 On rationalist explanations of revenge cf. the discussion in Salmon (2006).
73 The same author delivers a classical account of situational revenge. "When the popular colonel of the 12th Texas Cavalry was killed in a skirmish, a sergeant in the troop reported that the men were too much exasperated after the death of our colonel to take prisoners – they were shot down" (McPherson 1997: 149). On the mechanism of revenge and the Red Army in its war against fascist Germany cf. Merridale (2005: chap. 7).
74 David Keen (2005: 79) is quoting here Shakespeare's character Shylock from The Merchant of Venice, "And if you wrong us, shall we not revenge? […] The villainy you teach me I will execute, and it shall go hard but I will better the instruction".
75 On instances of this see Chapter 6.
76 I am drawing here on the work of Jago Salmon (2006), member of the Young Scholar Group, who conducted field research in Sudan in 2003. Literature on the PDF is extremely scarce.
77 I owe the insights into Arafat's symbolic language to Thomas Scheffler (1996: 121).
78 To call this legitimacy is somewhat misleading if the language of Weber is rigidly interpreted. For Weber, the meaning of the term went beyond all kinds of toleration, endurance, or indifference. His claim is that beyond material interest and other motivations of rulers, staff, and ruled, a stable political order must rely on something else, namely the subjective belief in the "rightness" of the established order. At least the staff, the administrative personnel, needs to think of the order as being binding. This is also what armed groups strive for.

It should be noted that legitimacy in that sense does not imply that observers of this belief need to share it. Theses of the sociological fact of legitimacy in any instance should never be understood as political judgments.

79 The most prominent study in this regard is certainly Hobsbawm/Ranger (1986), inspiring a number of single and comparative studies on the at times incremental, at times accelerated change of political traditions.

80 On the case of the Kurds cf. van Bruinessen (1992), Bozarslan (1997), and Picard (1999).

81 One could argue, therefore, that armed groups such as the Kurdish movements are facing the same problems and practical dilemmas Joel Migdal (1988) has analyzed for developing states. The leadership of armed groups has to rely on agencies of social power, in this case traditional authorities that at the same time threaten the integrity of the group. This dilemma applies equally to occupational regimes. Hashim (2006: 104–108) shows how the politics of integrative clientelism continued under the US occupation of Iraq.

82 See Picard (1996; 1997) on Lebanon, Martinez (1998) on Algeria, Larziellière (2004: 183) on the Palestinians, Kell (1995) on Indonesia, and Roy (2003) on the use of Islam as symbolic reference in general.

83 Such turns can be seen in the case of Robert Mugabe in the liberated Zimbabwe as well as in the Sandinista Movement in revolutionary Nicaragua and in the case of Yoweri Museveni in Uganda.

84 According to the results of the MAG database, in 80 percent of all cases, parts of the rural population back the insurgency, in 41 percent of the cases urban marginalized classes participated in armed groups. Reportedly, students were a considerable part of the followers in 51 percent of the cases.

85 One might, for example, think of the Interahamwe in Rwanda (Prunier 1998), the Revolutionary United Front in Sierra Leone (Richards 1996) or the Mooryan in Somalia (Marchal 1993).

86 On this interesting case of organizational learning in an armed group cf. Schubert (2001: 287), Ngoga (1998), and Weinstein (2007: 140).

87 Like other forms of legitimacy, charisma is a question of "subjective belief" among staff and followers. On the question of whether personal qualities of leaders actually need to correspond to these beliefs cf. the summarized discussion in Radkau (2005: 607).

88 Paradoxically, warrior charisma is often embedded into older, almost traditional imaginations of "social banditry", as John Allcock (2000: 392) has shown for the "hajduck"-tradition in the wars of the former Yugoslavia.

89 Source: interviews of the author conducted in Ziguinchor and Dakar, August and September 1994.

90 The ideas presented here are a reformulation of theses developed by Heinrich Popitz (1992: 185–232) and Trutz von Trotha (1994a). Whereas Popitz develops his ideas on comparative historical studies, von Trotha takes his material from his magistral study on the establishment of German colonial rule in West African Togo. Problems of occupational forces, I would argue, are identical for state armies and armed groups.

91 On the schools, courts, and hospitals the UNITA built in the area it controlled cf. Heywood (1989: 53), for the GAM, fighting in Indonesia, cf. Missbach (2005: 109), for

the LTTE cf. Radtke (2009: 103). Interestingly, however, the LTTE ran into difficulties when it attempted to change the traditional gender role patterns in Tamil society.
92 Cf. the sketch of these complex business networks in Prkic (2005).
93 The writings of Balandier (1982), Brunschwig (1983), and von Trotha (1994b) are telling in this regard.
94 That these adaptations worked in both directions, and that colonialism had strong effects on the colonizing states and societies as well, has often been overlooked. It is shown for example in Bancel et al. (2003). The ambiguity of the colonial situation is perfectly illustrated by the two prominent works of Frantz Fanon. While "Wretched of the Earth" (1965) stresses the boundaries between the two worlds of the colonial situation, "Black Skin, White Masks" (1967) tackles phenomena of acculturation, albeit with little sympathy. Yet these adaptations were not able to overcome the inherent contradictions of the colonial state. In the era of decolonization, the alien quality of the colonizers, however constructed, but identified by language, skin color, citizenship, and habits could nevertheless be instrumentalized by their former collaborators, the indigenous elites, to challenge their rule drawing on a simplifying dichotomy. European conquerors remained les blancs. For many post-colonial regimes, cultural belonging to their newly gained subjects certainly enhanced their first basic legitimacy.
95 As Goodwin (2003: 235 et passim) has convincingly shown, continuing government repression or indiscriminate violence can fuel insurgencies throughout wars. Rephrased in the language of this book, the mechanism of repression can be continuously at work during the war and is not always just an initial cause.
96 Groups like UNITA, NRA, and SPLA have maintained such training camps. Their function within the figuration, however, is ambiguous, as locations for education and disciplinary institutions simultaneously. On the topic of subjectivation taking place in these institutions, see also chapter six.
97 This rough summary is based on my own notes from the interview and is also supported by an anonymous text (1985) Abbot Diamacoune supposedly authored. The discourse of the MFDC is also analyzed by de Jong (2001), Marut (1994), and Faye (1994). On the conflict and its constructed ethnic underpinnings cf. Linares (1992) and Schlichte (1996, 170–202).
98 Alinsitowe Diatta was born in 1920 in the Casamance, had been working as a migrant laborer in Dakar and returned to the Casamance after several revelations had urged her to return home and perform sacrifices for the benefit of her community. She began sacrificing black bulls after which abundant rains were reported. Therefore she attracted many followers and began to contradict certain colonial policies like the enforced cultivation of groundnuts. The French colonial administration viewed her as a threat, condemned her to six years imprisonment, and deported her to French Sudan, contemporary Mali (de Jong 2001: 197f.).
99 That history and narration may serve political interest is certainly not a new insight. The critical academic discourse about historiography as a political tool for the creation of legitimizing narratives reaches well into the 19th century, as in the work of Gustav Droysen, cf. White (1987: 83ff.).
100 On the history of this concept, which dates back to the French Enlightenment, and on related practices in international politics cf. Heater (1994).

101 This quote is taken from the regular pamphlet of the MFDC Le Journal du Pays, no.1, August 1994, p. 2.
102 This has been stated for the program of Marxism by a number of authors. Karl Löwith (1953) has looked at the temporal structures of Marxism and their foundations in Judeo-Christian cosmologies. Carl Schmitt (1923) earlier stated that most basic concepts of political language are nothing more than secularized theological terms. Reinhard Koselleck (1985) has characterized notions such as revolution, democracy, progress, or reform as "concepts of movement" that share implicit temporalities with religious terms.
103 For a passionate study of charismatic time as a distinctive temporality of a post-revolutionary regime cf. Hanson (1997: esp. Chapter 1). This study converges with the use of Weber's categories developed here.
104 On this instance of a charismatic cycle cf. Martinez (1998) and Heristchi (2004).
105 The waning of the Partisan-myth is a recurrent theme of the entire literature on the causes of Yugoslavia's decay, see e.g. Allcock (2000) and Woodward (1995).
106 The term charisma is not accidentally a religious term. It was introduced into sociological language by Max Weber, who took it from Rudolph Sohm's work on the historical development of ecclesiastical law, cf. Kroll (2001). On the psychological micro-workings of charisma in religious fields see also Oakes (1997).
107 This phenomenon is known from all religions that use particular forms of organizations. The history of Christian churches is an endless procession of such reform movements. Monks in medieval times often felt ill at ease with the pomp and the richness of monasteries as they considered such pretension and luxury contrary to Rule of St. Benedict, the 6th Century book of precepts concerning the proper conduct of monastic life. The foundation of new orders like the Cistercians cf. Eberl (2002) and other orders, however, depended on individuals who were able to formulate programs and exert their will in an already dense and conflictive organization. Many attempts failed, because the new movements did not attract enough followers, lacked resources, or were not accepted by higher echelons of the Church. In a number of regards, the organizational dynamics of the Christian Church can be seen as analogous to many cyclic movements of political ideas and related secular movements.
108 The intellectual internationality of these times also becomes evident in the fact that Walter Rodney, author of the widely read book "How Europe Underdeveloped Africa" (1972), was teaching at the time in Dar-es-Salam. Rodney, a Guyana-born historian who had studied in Guyana, Jamaica, and Great Britain was known as a prominent pan-Africanist and promoter of the Black Power movement. While running for office in Guyanese elections in 1980, Rodney was killed in a bomb explosion.
109 The quotation is taken from an interview with this former vice president, Peter Naigow (cf. Ellis 1999: 83).
110 Nationalism was therefore a logical conclusion, even if in fact it often meant very small ethnic projects, cf. Gordadze (2003). Religious fundamentalist projects have so far proven ineffective in these settings. The attempt to use Wahhabist Islam as a mobilizing program in Chechnya thus met resistance by the population, cf. Tishkov (2004: 176ff.).
111 This basic logic is also seen in the quotations presented elsewhere in this book. Cf. the historical narrative of the Abbot Diamacoune in this chapter or the quote from the Charta of Hamas in the preceding chapter.

112 Some forms of support survived the end of the Cold War and became essential for many groups. Not being criminalized, for example, is an important pre-condition for exiled leaders, as the leadership of the Indonesian GAM, operating from Sweden, illustrates, cf. Missbach (2005).
113 On this globalized image of statehood and its constituting elements cf. Migdal/Schlichte 2005, on the process of its globalization cf. Reinhart (1999).
114 On the programs of armed movements in Latin America cf. Wickham-Crowley (1992), Le Bot (1994: 27ff.) and Goodwin (2003). On the idea of national self-determination in former French colonies cf. Chafer (2002) and the excellent case study by Joseph (1977). How secular political ideas merged with religious or even magical perceptions cf. Ellis/Ter Haar (2004).
115 On the politics of the Soviet Union with social-revolutionary movements cf. Breslauer (1992). On this aspect in US foreign policy cf. Woodward (2006). A general overview on the Cold War in the Third World is given by the contributions in Rüland/Hanf/Manske (2006). China's role in Asia during the Cold War is analyzed by Roberts (2006), and its engagement in Africa is investigated by Hutchinson (1976).
The rivalry between East and West had its sub-arenas as well. It could, for example, be observed in the competition between East and West Germany over alliances with African governments concerning mutual recognition, cf. Bley/Tetzlaff (1978). On the special case of France's relations with different African states and insurgencies cf. Bayart (1984) and Wauthier (1995). On the Cold War in Africa generally see Laïdi (1990).
116 The reason concepts such as "nation", "democracy", and "liberation" figure prominently in the names and discourses of armed groups lies in the temporality of these concepts. As Reinhart Koselleck (1985: 271–288) has shown, these "concepts of movement" (Bewegungsbegriffe) emerge in political discourse in a period when the future "opens" and they are successful not despite their polysemic character, but as a result of it.
117 This is the basic mechanism of the emergence of religious symbolism in political opposition in Algeria, cf. Martinez (1998), India, cf. Eckert (2005), Jaffrelot (1996), and Tunisia, cf. Hibou (2006). A recent summary of research being conducted in this field is Almond et al. (2003).
118 On these relations cf. Dorronsoro (2000: 230) and Rashid (2000: 170–182).
119 It is noteworthy that this turn happened simultaneously in different national academic settings. A pathbreaking volume was edited by Jean Chistophe Rufin and Christophe Jean (1996) whose theses were then popularized by Mary Kaldor (1998). An economic argument about the sustainable interest in continuing warfare also occurs in King (1997). More systemic lines of theorization were developed during the same timeframe in Germany by the social anthropologist Georg Elwert (1997) and a co-authored article by the author of this book cf. Genschel/Schlichte (1997). More influential were later articles by Keen (1998) and, most frequently referenced, Berdal/Malone (2000). The conceptual couple of "greed and grievance" became the anchor point of the World Bank's extensive research program on which a large number of studies dealing with this question were based. The most pronounced criticism of this reductionist approach can be found in Roland Marchal and Christine Messiant (2006; 2003). Both authors, in the "greed versus grievance debate" see a nouvelle problematique légitime that replaces the comparably

simplifying register of the interpretation of civil wars during the Cold War with a criminalizing discourse that ignores the political nature of its subject.
120 The idea of "incentive structures" has been at the core of most studies concerning the economy of war. It became prominent primarily as a result of the research undertaken on behalf of the World Bank cf. Collier and Hoeffler (2000; 2003). While the meaning of the term "economic" oscillates between alluding to econometric methodology and using micro-economic vocabulary, it is not altogether clear which economic theory has been used and developed in these studies. Apart from a distinction between peaceful protest and violent rebellion, a political dimension does not exist as for Collier, rebellion is per definitionem "organized crime", while the legitimacy of state violence seems unquestioned. Another forgotten dimension is global historical timing as economies have historical trajectories which play out differently, too, depending on global conditions.
121 For the latest version cf. Collier et al. (2003). For the most advanced work in this branch of research cf. Ron (2005). For a critical discussion cf. the contributions for the conference of the Social Science Research Council (2004).
122 Much of the more economically oriented research draws exclusively on numeric information, failing to take into account the broad variety of historic, anthropological, and sociological studies on the subject. Sometimes, it would seem, the subject is addressed as if it were taking place on another planet, with no possibility of a direct approach. See, however, the recent attempts of scholars to combine rational choice theory with serious field research, e.g. Weinstein (2007).
123 In this section of the chapter, I draw extensively on the study of Katrin Radtke (2009) on the taxation of diaspora communities by armed groups, cf. particularly her chap. 9.
124 The first to make this observation was, in all likelihood, Otto Hintze in his essay, Staatenbildung und Verfassungsentwicklung (1906), followed by Norbert Elias' study on the monopoly of taxation in his "Process of civilization" (first edited in 1939) and later by Charles Tilly (1992).
125 Note the precautionary remarks concerning this data as discussed above in chapter two. Figures on spin-off groups are particularly problematic due to the low number of cases.
126 This can be done in quite different ways as the work of Alpa Shah (2006) on the Naxalites in India shows in comparison with Katrin Radtke's study on the taxation of diaspora communities (2009).
127 The cases here include Arkan's and Seselj's volunteer guards in the wars of Yugoslavia, SLA (Lebanon), Interahamwe (Rwanda), National Guard and Mchedrioni (Georgia), Dostum's group in Afghanistan, and the Shan United Army (Myanmar).
128 On e.g. the role of US agencies in civil wars in Latin America cf. Grandin (2004: chap. 3).
129 These micro-dynamics on the regional level have long been neglected by scholars of international relations. See, for example on India's foreign policy cf. Mohan (2003) on China's support for insurgencies in India Dasgupta (1978), Israel's engagement in Central America and Southern Africa (Hunter 1987), or Otayek (1986) on Libya's role in Africa and Wauthier (1995) on France as its main competitor.
130 A perfect example of the dynamics sketched here very abstractly can be found in the case of Afghanistan. In a first phase the economy of the rentier state collapsed during the war after the late 1970s, when the conflict between a modernizing state and traditional society coincided with superpower competition and Pakistan's and Iran's regional

interests. The result was a system of localized predatory warlords that the Taliban transformed into a rentier state again that financed itself by an openly criminalized economy (Rubin 2000). Currently, the rentier state has not undergone significant change, except that a higher percentage of it income comes from foreign aid. All three elements, a sinking capital stock, informalization, and de-bordering become very evident in this case, as in any other extremely long war, such as in Angola or Myanmar or Liberia.

131 There is an abundant literature on economic collapse in times of civil wars. On contemporary cases cf. the contributions in Jean/Rufin (1996), van Acker (2004) on Northern Uganda, Ellis (1999) on Liberia, Le Billon (2005) on Angola, or Newberg (2005) on Afghanistan.

132 I am drawing here on distinctions that have been developed by the French sociologist Pierre Bourdieu for his explanation of continuing social inequality in post-war France. For a detailed theoretical discussion of these concepts cf. Bourdieu (1987).

133 They are, however, often not totally worthless. The most striking experience of the author concerning sinking capital stock in times of war was the sight of downed electricity poles in Liberia which, according to local accounts were brought down by soldiers of the Ecowas-intervention forces who removed the wire in order to sell it as scrap metal (author's observation, July 1997, Monrovia and Grand Cape Mount). More concrete and illuminative accounts on the dire consequences of a sinking capital stock in civil wars can be found in Nordstrom (2004). The impact of war on social structures, behavior, and mentalities has been formulated in Sorokin (1942).

134 These and the following theses apply only to intrastate wars. It can be argued that international wars exhibit similar tendencies. The states involved in greater international wars that are usually at the center of economic studies on international war, however, have quite different economic structures than most states affected by civil war that are considered in this study. As Götz Aly's study (2005) on the distribution of wealth through the Nazi war machinery has recently shown, there might be quite different mechanisms at work than the ones outlined here: Based on an enormous amount of material, Aly shows how the plundering of Europe was used in the Nazi war economy to bolster a welfare state during the war in Germany.

135 This, of course, does not mean that relations in camps are void of conflicts or violence cf. Crisp (2000). Situations between cases can differ enormously. Refugee camps can become safe havens for combatants, and they can turn into income sources for belligerents. On the various dynamics in refugee camps cf. the studies of Lischer (2005) and Jacobsen (2005). Generally, however, there is a loss of all types of capital. Despair prevails, and the endless time horizon of camp situations renders war participation as an exit option more likely. Roland Marchal's phrase that war participation can be understood as a "blind jump into a dreamt modernity" (2000: 174) is even more fitting here than under "normal" circumstances.

136 For example, the links between the blossoming war economy of the DR Congo and formal world markets have been documented by the United Nations (2001). As a consequence of this and other reports, a number of political campaigns have aimed at regulating war economies by targeting their beneficiaries in Western economies. One attempt to regulate the trade involving illegal exports from war zones was undertaken with the Kimberley Process Certification Scheme on the global gem market.

137 That applied, as an historic example, to the city of Hamburg during the Thirty Years War (1618–1648). Nowadays, the city of Beni-Lubero in North Kivu (DR Kongo) is a case in point cf. Raeymaekers (2004).
138 Again, it should be stressed here, international wars differ in this regard as the study of Aly (2005) and numerous other works have shown. Strong and authoritarian states are able to enforce an increase of production, often using coercion and forced labor for this end.
139 Cyprus played this role during the Lebanese civil war, and during the embargo against Serbia and Montenegro in the early 1990s; Bulgaria, Hungary, Romania, and even Turkey benefited from new opportunities for illegal trade cf. Bjelić (2003).
140 Paradoxically, the besiegers helped the besieged to prolong the stalemate, and politically, leaders on both sides developed an interest in the continuation of this situation. For the fragments of the JNA that became the army of the Bosnian Serbs and was besieging Sarajevo, the city became a trump card in the negotiations. For the Bosnians controlling the besieged city, it was crucial to keep the population within city boundaries. They therefore threatened citizens with prison terms if they attempted to leave the city (Burg/Shoup 1999: 177).
141 See the masterful study of Calas (1998) on Uganda's capital Kampala during war times, also covering the long-lasting effects of this experience.
142 David Keen (1998; 2000) has presented concise sketches of these mechanisms. See also King (1997) and Genschel/Schlichte (1998). The case of Somalia demonstrates well that traders in particular are extremely adaptive to both transitions, to war and to peace cf. Grosse-Kettler (2004).
143 According to one source, the revenues of Lebanese militias from their engagement in drug trafficking amounted to 600 million US Dollars annually in the 1980s, cf. Harris (1997: 207). On the relation between militias cf. Endres (2004), on the trajectory of the Forces Libanaises see Salmon (2006).
144 Sometimes, the creation of this scarcity is a deliberate policy of the opponent. The counter-insurgency strategy of "protected villages" in Northern Uganda, for example, is aiming not only at protecting civilians, but also at stripping a roaming armed group, the Lord's Resistance Army, of any accessible resource. Likewise, the strategy to remove and resettle large parts of civil populations was reportedly used in the war in Mozambique by the government in order to eliminate any possible support from the insurgent Renamo (Weissman 1996).
145 Mary Kaldor (1998) has suggested that these expansive strategies are also connected to an increase of opportunities in globalized world markets. Whether this is truly the case has not been investigated systematically despite the enormous talk on the subject.
146 On the relation between the war in Liberia and the emergence of the RUF cf. Abdullah/Muana (1998), the economic underpinnings of the Khmer Rouge's fate are given in Lechervy (1996).
147 On these interlinkings cf. the study by Lischer (2005). For a more phenomenological approach to the political form of the camp cf. Diken/Laustsen (2005). For detailed descriptions of the political economy of refugee camps cf. Crisp (1986; 2000).
148 An example for this was the struggle for control of the port of Buchanan during the Liberian civil war cf. Prkic (2005). The diamond zones in Sierra Leone and the oil-rich

enclave of Cabinda in Angola were central during the respective wars for the same reason.
149 The findings on the forms of taxation stem from interviews by Katrin Radtke (2009). Her research on the diaspora-link of armed groups, notably the EPLF and the LTTE was carried out in 2003 and 2004.
150 Such figures, as in the case of the PKK, should be considered with some reservations as there is no independent confirmation for what is always a daring estimate. On the economy of the UÇK cf. Andrees (2001) and Frank (2006).
151 Interview, Belgrade, March 2003. Šešelj has allegedly traveled to the United States in 1989 for a fund raising tour. While in the US he was, it is reported, given the title of "Duke of the Chetniks" by Momdjilo Djujić, a Chetnik leader who fought in World War II and fled to the United States after Communist Partisans had achieved control of Yugoslavia.
152 Interview of the author with former officer of the Yugoslav National Army, Belgrade, October 2003.
153 One might well think here of Weber's distinction between "to live FOR politics" in comparison to "live ON politics".
154 Alice claimed to be "obsessed" by Lakwena and other spirits, cf. the anthropological study of Heike Behrend (1999: 1).
155 Apart from the standard-setting study of Berend (1999) cf. Doom/Vlassenroot (1999) and van Acker (2004) on the LRA.
156 The sub-regional system of war that stretches from Southern Sudan to Burundi, including Rwanda, Uganda, and the East of the DR Congo cannot even be sketched here. Cf. however Prunier (2004) and Mamdani (2002) on the underpinnings and historical background. Prunier (2004: 364) claims that there had been no support for the SPLM/A by Uganda prior to 1993.
157 The policy of the Ugandan government towards the conflict is ambiguous. While on the one hand, numerous amnesties have been offered, the conflict was also "functional" for the regime as it could present itself as a bulwark against Islamic fundamentalism. Militarily, LRA should not be a challenge for Uganda's well-trained army of 50,000 troops, but no serious effort has been undertaken (Interview with Western Military Attachée, Kampala, October 2004).
158 On variations concerning how scarcity of resources and the organization of armed groups are causally connected cf. Weinstein (2007) and Kahl (2006).
159 Cf. Radu (2001), the PKK itself assessed the diaspora's contribution at 25 million US Dollars cf. Bozarslan (1996).
160 McCoy (1999: 142) notes that the flood of Burmese heroin on the US market and the ensuing price drop are related to the emergence of "heroin chic" in American youth culture in the 1990s. "Though few knew his name on the fashion ramps and/or the club floors, it was Khun Sa who made heroin chic happen". This example, among so many, demonstrates the close links between the allegedly remote informal economy and everyday life in Western metropoles.
161 Two changes seem to be crucial for this change of power relations. First, the conflict between two US institutions became arbitrable after the Cold War had ended. While the CIA was apparently inclined to use Khun Sa as a bulwark against communist encroachment in the region, the DEA wanted to depose him. After 1990 there were fewer argu-

ments for the former position (cf. Elliot 1993). Secondly, the power balance within Thailand had changed in the 1980s. The military lost its political grip, and that meant that Khun Sa's most important ally was weakened cf. McCoy (1999: 147).

162 Other cases of similar structures are the NPFL, dealt with already in chapter two cf. Prkic (cf. Prkic 2005; Ellis 1999) or the RUF in Sierra Leone, cf. Reno (1998) and Abdullah/Muana (1998).

163 This structural argument has been first made by Christopher Clapham in his analysis of African guerillas (1998: 11).

164 This insight also is old, cf. Simmel (1950: 356).

165 "Every domination both expresses itself and functions through administration. Every administration, on the other hand, needs domination, because it is always necessary that some powers of command be in the hands of somebody." (Weber 1978, II: 948).

166 On the two cases see Nissen (2003). The tendency to caudillismo at the top level of the FSLN is analyzed in Feinberg/Kurtz-Phenan (2006). On the case of the FLMN in El Salvador see also McClintock (1998).

167 The term "Tuareg" is an invention of foreigners of the late 19th century. This collective noun is attributed since then to a broad range of nomadic confederations with quasi-feudal structures moving and living in Algeria, Libya, Burkina Faso, Mali, and Niger. The following account is based on research carried out in Mali in the fall of 1994 (cf. Schlichte 1996: 128–168). Further detailed information on the historical background of the rebellion and its social underpinnings is given in Klute (1995), Bourgeot (1990, 1994), and Claudot-Hawad (1993). On the parallel rebellion in neighboring Niger cf. Salifou (1993). On the role of intellectuals in the rebellion cf. Lecoq (2004).

168 That "geography matters" for the organization of rebellions could be seen as a truism, known since Clausewitz' times. Recent research has started to re-examine the relation between physical geography and armed conflict. The findings, however, are not integrated theoretically, cf. Gates (2001) and Buhaug/Gates (2002).

169 Razzias had, in fact, continued even in the 1930s (Klute 1995: 65). On the reality of colonial rule in this extremely volatile and fluid social space cf. Bernus et al. (1993).

170 This local title is reportedly derived from the French *chomeur* (unemployed).

171 In Klute/von Trotha (2000) it is shown that, behind the official theater of peace negotiations, the actual political process was following old patterns of politics between the confederations. Both authors warn, however, that to exaggerate the role of these old patterns into a romantic exoticism would overlook the fact that social change does not allow this to be seen as a general model for peace settlements, be it in Africa or elsewhere.

172 The civil war in Chad is certainly one of the most understudied cases in the history of warfare. Many events and developments will probably never be reconstructed. For an overview cf. Balencie/de la Grange (1999: 481–514), a more detailed account is Buijtenhuijs (1987). The under-documentation of this case indicates how dubious data-sets on violent conflicts and their victims even of the last decades are, in fact.

173 On this case, too, literature is scarce, cf., however, Schraeder (1993) and Balencie/de la Grange (1999: 541–547).

174 In recent discussions on the explanation of different fates of insurgent movements, this historical dimension is regularly omitted. According to explanations that draw on rational choice concepts, it is rather the economic "endowment" of an armed group or in-

formation asymmetries that will account for the differences in the organization of armed groups (cf. Weinstein 2005). Different recruitment profiles would result from differences in the economic endowment of the initial group. In the absence of rich economic endowments, leaders attract new recruits by drawing on social ties to make credible promises about private rewards that will accompany victory. Opportunistic joiners would then tend to stay away from these movements (2005: 599). In a later work based on three cases (2007), Weinstein claims that this difference in endowments would also explain differences in the violent behavior of insurgent movements. It is, however, very questionable whether a theoretical model that conceives armed groups largely like corporations can, in fact, explain much of the variation. As argued throughout this book, sociological theories that include concepts like legitimacy, power, as well as the effects of violence, shame, guilt, and honor are much more promising to come to terms with this empirical variety.

175 This is particularly apparent in cases where entire groups of leaders share educational experiences such as military formation or attendance at the same universities and schools. Identical habitus are formed in a variety of institutions as a few examples can already demonstrate: In the case of the FSLN in Nicaragua only a small proportion of the leading *commandantes* had not studied at the National University at Managua (McClintock 1998: 251). In the case of Peru's *Sendero Luminoso*, the provincial university of Ayacucho became the nucleus for the radicalization of the group that had started as a splinter of Peru's communist party (McCormick 1990: 10). The *Mchedrioni*, a militia that formed in Georgia during the civil war in the early 1990s, used the criminal code of honor as rules for their internal functioning as many of its members had been in prison earlier, partly for political reasons (Sobaka 2003). In other post-Soviet conflicts, irregular war actors were to a large extent former state agents and employed the same rules in which they were socialized in Soviet institutions, as was the case with the Republican Guard in Moldova (Isachenko/Schlichte 2007). Another master example for the formation of a similar habitus through common socialization are, of course, the Taliban, cf. Rashid (2000).

176 Coser delineates this concept from Goffman's "total institutions" by stressing that "greedy institutions" such as the order of the Jesuits or Communist parties in the early 20th century do not need an identical location to maintain their boundaries. Communists and Jesuits alike were strongly discouraged from taking roots. No stable relationship outside the party was allowed. "Either the girl joins the party, or you drop her", a young German communist was told regarding his girlfriend (Coser 1974: 133). That military organizations must create a sort of life totality has been connected by Georg Simmel (1950: 359) with their quality of being "secret societies". This concept is much more apt than Goffman's to explain this trait of armed groups.

177 Hamas and Fatah are cases in point for this observation. The PKK, which became the arch-enemy of the strong and well-equipped Turkish military and intelligence apparatus, also developed similar techniques such as cover-names for its agents and a system of anonymous drivers and messengers to be used by its higher functionaries that disguised their official identity (Stein 1994: 92).

178 For the case of the SL cf. the study of Weinstein (2007: 251–258) and Del Pinho (1998), for the case FARC cf. Villamarin-Pulido (1996). Still the best account on this dynamic in

Mozambique's Renamo is Christian Geffray (1990). Cf. Kalyvas (2006) and Duyvesteyn/Angstrom (2005) for further sources.

179 The fear of punishment within the group often leads to the delegitimization of the insurgency altogether in the eyes of many members, as in the case of the *Group islamique armé* in Algeria (Martinez 1998). Within militias of the Yugoslav wars, similar developments took place.

180 It can hardly be stressed enough that charisma is a chronically unstable source of legitimacy as Weber repeatedly points out. It is typically accompanied by two problems, one is its dependency on repetitive proofs, and second is the problem of finding heirs for the position acquired. Weber, however, also stresses that the transformation of warrior charisma into more stable relations is possible, even during a war (1978, II: 1121).

181 The notorious problem of fragmentation during negotiations has been analyzed by Charles King (1997) and therefore does not need to be described here at length.

182 As was shown with the case of Liberia's NPFL in chapter two, this competition can assume violent forms which, of course, can lead to immediate fragmentation.

183 Literature on the recent developments in Chechnya is scarce, see however Tishkov (2004) and Gammer (2006).

184 On the complex relation between Kurdish parties and armed groups in Turkey, Syria, Iraq, and Iran cf. Bozarslan (1997). On the KDP in Iraq cf. Ahmad (1994), on KDP-Iran cf. Koohi-Kamali (2003: 178).

185 On this not very profoundly researched case cf. the still leading studies of Tucker (2000) and Smith (1991).

186 This is a lesson not only taught by the practical theorists of irregular warfare such as Mao (1961) and Guevara (1961), it has also been confirmed by empirical investigation, cf. Weinstein (2005; 2006). But this insight is highly intuitive as well.

187 The "conditioning" of soldiers is a managerial art in all armies. Its main aim is to assure that soldiers will not defect in combat situations. They shall no longer think of the alternatives to flee, to submit, or to posture. Modern military psychology sees the readiness to apply violence as the outcome of four parameters. These include a) the predisposition of the soldier, his education as well as his temperament, b) the demand of authority as well as the legitimacy of the authority, also depending on the proximity of its representative, c) the group absolution, i.e. the group's support for individual violent acts, and d) the "attractiveness" of the victim, i.e. its relevance for the operational goal and in the given situation (cf. Grossman 1995: 142ff).

188 Source: MAG database. The usual caveats apply, cf the remarks in the introduction.

189 This, however, did not exclude looting and further gross human rights violations for which Arkan's guard became notorious in that war, cf. Schlichte (2009).

190 These observations are taken from Teresa Koloma Beck's field research, cf. Beck/Schlichte (2006).

191 I am drawing here again on the work of Katrin Radtke who studied the mobilization of Tamil diaspora in Toronto and of Eritreans in Frankfurt on Main through the LTTE and the EPLF respectively (2009).

192 This technique is, of course, not unique to armed groups. It is a highly regular technique in all forms of government. I owe the expression to Joel Migdal's inspiring list of "politics of survival" (1988: 214).

193 On these politics of the NRA cf. Ngoga (1998: 92–101). The new institutions of the NRA were not set in place in the Northern region of Uganda, where the military politics of the NRA were much less benevolent.
194 In his comparative analysis of Cárdenas, Franco, and Perón, Georg Eickhoff (1999) has stated that charisma is here produced in practices that aim at acclamation.
195 Regarding this table, one must also bear in mind that it is based on a selection bias. Included in the sample are only those groups who are counted as war participants according to a qualitative definition. The sample, therefore, does not include a countless number of smaller groups which might have attempted to reach the stage of war actors but failed and were unrecorded in war statistics.
196 Note that the percentages in table 7 do not come from a representative sample. One criterion for the selection into the MAG data base was a minimum degree of documentation, see also a list of included cases in the appendix. Due to a selection bias caused by the differences in documentation, an unknown number of less successful groups remain unnoticed.
197 It might be necessary to recall the fact that most armed groups have fuzzy borders. The term "followers", therefore, has no clear boundary with the environment of an armed group.
198 Here the micro-politics of armed groups link up with the large structural narratives of chapter three. Political traditions of importance for the internal life of armed groups are, of course, not exclusively analogous to those of the state in which they come about. It is rather that the hybrid forms of rule that characterize post-colonial states will appear again in an armed group challenging this state. Armed groups can also, of course, include patterns that have not played a role in the respective state's functioning, and they can, as will be seen, only represent certain political traditions or rather new projects.
199 The creation of this "inescapability", as will be seen below, is crucial for the formation of armed groups, as it is has been for the formation of state armies, cf. e.g. Perlmutter (1977: 36).
200 It should be noted that this difference does not explain significant factors about the chances of political success of the group, defined as participation in formal political institutions (cf. Malthaner 2007). The reason for this might be that organizational capacity must first be weighed against the enemy's capacity and secondly, against the military strength an armed group might develop despite the fact that its organizational structure is relatively loose. In any case, there is no direct correlation between institutionalization and military success.
201 On the logic of patrimonial rule see Shmuel N. Eisenstadt (1973) and Médard (1991).
202 The notion of the "Big Man" is found in the anthropological work of Marshall Sahlins (1963). It has been used for the analysis of contemporary African politics by Médard (1992).
203 Patrimonial rule usually comes close to Weber's type of traditional rule in which the person exercising authority "is not a 'superior' but a personal master, his administrative staff does not consist mainly of officials but of personal retainers, and the ruled are not 'members' of an association but are either his traditional 'comrades' or his 'subjects'" (1978, I: 227).
204 On the trajectory of Dostum's forces cf. Giustozzi (2003) and Adamec (2005). I also thank Barbara Lemberger for additional information on the case. See also Balencie/de la

Grange (1999: 787f.). On the war in Afghanistan, cf. Dorronsoro (2000), Rubin (2000), and Rashid (2000).
205 It is noteworthy that Dostum's forces were among the few armed groups in Afghanistan that wore uniforms (cf. Rashid 2000: 112).
206 Dorronsoro (2000: 163–170) stresses the point that the same pressure of institutionalization developed among the factions of the Mujaheddin whose leaders also needed to reinforce their role as providers of arms and money with a legitimizing discourse.
207 For the development of the Eritrean resistance and especially for the trajectory of the EPLF cf. Pool (1998) and Radtke (2009). Radtke's study is based on 85 interviews with group members and expert observers in Sri Lanka and Eritrea and with organized and unorganized diaspora members in Canada and Germany.
208 On this category, all too often overlooked in the analysis of armed groups and profound political changes, cf. Migdal (1988: 272). For more detail on the EPLF and the regime change in Ethiopia in 1991 cf. Pool (1998: 19 and 32).
209 Cf. Pool (1998: 20 and 28) and Connell (1993).
210 A complete organization chart can be found in Leonhard (1988). Radtke (2009: 214) contains a chart of the diaspora organizations the EPLF developed. A very similar form of organization within a diaspora community developed among Turkish Kurds, cf. Watts (2004).
211 On the case of Moldova and the secessionist PMR cf. King (1995), Isachenko (2008), and Isachenko/Schlichte (2007).
212 It has been argued that this stability of Transnistria has largely been due to informal Russian support, and certainly this support plays an important role. It is, however, not sufficient to explain the persistence of this state, as Isachenko (2008) has argued. Furthermore, it is quite common for that many states, for their very existence, rely upon strong external allies. The case, therefore, is no exception.
213 In order to avoid misunderstandings, it might be helpful to look at the exact phrasing in which Weber defined power as, "the probability that one actor within a social relationship will be in a position to carry out his own will despite resistance, regardless of the basis on which this probability rests", while domination, according to him, is, "the probability that a command with a given specific content will be obeyed by a given group of persons" (1978, I: 53). Domination, in my interpretation of Weber, is institutionalized power.
214 As I did not discuss here the theoretical conncectivity of this understanding, a short remark must suffice. In a recent restatement of his widely discussed book, *Power: A radical view*, Steven Lukes has again argued that any theoretically satisfying concept of power cannot be restricted to "decisions" or the "rules of the game" but must take into consideration the very making of these rules, their production (2005: 28). His suggestion is completely in accord with the understanding promoted here. Power, as it is institutionalised and formed into domination, is precisely this order that determines the production of rules. This Weberian perspective, I would argue, is not incompatible with Norbert Elias', Michel Foucault's, and Pierre Bourdieu's conceptualization of the political. All these authors make a distinction between mere spontaneous forms of power and its institutionalized form, i.e. domination (cf. Lukes 2005: 89). Another very prominent understanding that strictly distinguishes power from violence (Arendt 1965), is certainly not reconcilable with the one promoted here.

215 This discussion became prominent with the contributions of Thomas Kuhn (cf. Lakatos 1974); it dates however back to the Kantian question of the *Ding an sich* and the early sociology of science by the Polish immunologist Ludwik Fleck (1981 [1935]).
216 One of the most frequently cited apocalyptic visions is that of Robert Kaplan (1994). Other pessimistic assessments came from Mary Kaldor (1998) and Martin van Creveld (1999). A good summary of the fears and dangers resulting from ongoing civil wars can be found in Mueller (2004: chap. 6).
217 For this typological summary, I am drawing on earlier publications; cf. Schlichte (2005), chapter two where further literature on cases can be found.
218 According to the war list in Gantzel/Schwinghammer (2000) the following wars can be summarized under the heading of wars of decolonisation (cf. list in the appendix): Indonesia (1945–49), Indochina (1946–54), Madagascar (1947–48); Malaysia (1948–60), Kenya (1952–56), Morocco (1952–56), Algeria (1954–62), Cameroon (1955–63), Cyprus (1955–59), Yemen (1963–67), Spanish-Morocco (1957–58), Tunisia (1961), Angola (1961–75), Guinea-Bissau (1963–74), Mozambique (1964–74), West Sahara (1975–91). For overviews on the period cf. Albertini (1987) and Wesseling (1997).
219 This has been observed by Christopher Clapham (1996: 242) for cases in sub-Saharan Africa but seems to be a much further ranging rule.
220 This type certainly cannot be sharply defined as a number of wars in neo-patrimonial settings and in former socialist states share some of its features. However, the wars in Mexico (1994), in Ethiopia (Oromo, 1976–93), in Turkey (1984–2001), in Indonesia (West-Irian, 1965–93, Aceh 1990–93), in India (Assam since 1990, Bodos since 1997), and in Iraq (Shiites 1991–95, Kurds 1974–98) come very close to the real type sketched here.
221 Already 20 of 24 wars waged in Latin America between 1945 and 2000 can be rubricated here, as well as the two parts of the Greek civil war (1944–45 and 1946–49), the war of the ANC in South Africa (1976–94), the war of the NPA in the Philippines (since 1970), wars in Yemen (1962–69), and in Laos (1975–79). On the general features of these wars cf. Wickham-Crowley (1992) and McClintock (1998).
222 On the pattern of patrimonial rule cf. Weber (1985: 580ff.). Eisenstadt (1973) and Médard (1991) have recoined it as neo-patrimonial, using the prefix "neo-" to indicate that this is rather a recent appropriation of colonial remnants, not a long-standing order. Wars in sub-Saharan Africa regularly follow the rules sketched here, but there are examples in other regions as well, e.g. in the Philippines (Mindanao since 1970) or in Afghanistan (since 1980).
223 On the persistence of statehood and a sociological understanding of statehood that allows for the analysis of the underlying dynamics cf. Migdal (2001) and Migdal/Schlichte (2005).
224 Regarding the unsettled issues of Cyprus and the separation of Eritrea from Ethiopia, according to international law, even secession was no exception.
225 Cf. Charles Taylor's contribution on the emergence of these "modern imaginaries" in the Western world (2004).
226 "Criminal" practices, as we would ahistorically label these activities today, accompanied the inception of all modern states. The colonial past and violence of wars waged in that process are the eminent proofs for this observation. For a selection of other historical evidence cf. the contributions in Heyman (1999) and Gerstenberger (1990).

227 Published originally in Zurich in 1939, while Elias was already an émigré, his work was not received with notable attention in social sciences until the 1970s; cf. Elias (1982, 1983).
228 Beginning with the work of Otto Hintze, this observation has been highlighted repeatedly by later scholars working on the sociology of the state. Theda Skocpol (1979) reinserted it into the debate on revolutions. Anthony Giddens (1985) stressed the conesquences of this mechanism for the development of public administration. And Charles Tilly (1992) highlighted the link between external warfare and the rise of new forms of state income.
229 On this image and its working in contemporary state formation cf. Migdal/Schlichte (2005).
230 For more evidence on similar developments in other historical spaces cf. Davis/Pereira (2003).
231 Most overviews of the global embeddings of regional political developments stress this point. For more detail on "the international politics of insurgency" in sub-Saharan Africa cf. Clapham (1996: chap. 9). Fred Halliday (2005: chap. 4 and 6) summarizes the patterns by which political violence in the Middle East was internationally embedded.
232 The most prominent result, of course, was the beginning of the war in Algeria, cf. Rioux (2004). The case shows other, more hidden, relations. World War II had cast a shadow of violence as well. Vo Nguyên Giap, the commanding general of the Viet Minh, had acquired a degree of his military expertise from US forces when fighting against Japan. There is no systematic study on the micro-consequences of World War II, but such a study would likely reveal that it was a catalyst period for the global spread of violence expertise, casting another shadow of violence.
233 These "liberation movements" – the dominant expression at the time – could draw not only on international legitimacy based on Resolution 1514 of the United Nations General Assembly from 1960 which declared "alien subjugation" as contrary to the Charter of the United Nations (cf. Clapham 1996: 209). Also, these groups benefited from external support – albeit merely ideally – in Western countries in which the icons and rhetoric of "Third World liberation" became part of a counterculture.
234 It is interesting to note that these linkages have not as yet been thoroughly investigated by scholars of political science. Historians who tried to summarize long-term developments in the 20th century have been much more apt to perceive the relevance of these remarkable networks, cf. Diner (1999) and Hobsbawm (1994: chap. 15).
235 On this history cf. the controversy between Bertrand Badie (1992) and Jean-François Bayart (1996). See also Reinhard (1999) and Migdal/Schlichte (2005).
236 Michel Foucault has masterfully analyzed the emergence and the practices of this "governmentality", i.e. the imaginative project of governing that characterizes modern states, cf. his lectures at the Collège de France (Foucault 2007).
237 This general statement, however, requires differentiation. The support of Saudi Arabia, for example, for the Taliban in Afghanistan follows a different rationale than the self-organized groups that occurred in Iraq since the invasion of 2003. Cf. Mamdani (2004) and Roy (2002) on the spread and international misperceptions of politicized Islam.
238 On the questionable bases of this arguments cf. Chandler (2006) and Keen (2005b).

239 On the influential definition of "state failure" cf. Goldstone et al. (2000). Among many others, the connection of civil war and transnational terrorism is maintained by Steven Krasner (2004).

240 How different and unconnected the trajectories of armed groups with Islamist orienttation have been is well elucidated by Larziellière (2003) and Martinez (2003). Meanwhile, this might have changed, but it is plausible to assume that their fusion is first and foremost the result of discursive shifts by their adversaries.

241 On the similarities between the processes of delegated violence and the proliferation of militias in Sudan and Iraq cf. Mamdani (2007). Earlier instances on the spread of factionalized violence in Chad and Sudan are described by Marchal (2006).

242 Cf. Paris (2002), Pugh (2003), Bliesemann de Guevara (2007), Keen (2005b), Chandler (2006), and Schlichte (2006).

243 On such constellations see Astri Suhrke (2006) on Afghanistan and Schlichte (2005a) on Uganda.

244 On the practices of policy-bending cf. Clapham (1996: 176).

# 9. Appendix: List of War Actors in Data Base

| Acronym | Group Name | Country |
|---|---|---|
| AFDL | Alliance des Forces Démocratiques pour la Libération du Congo | Zaire; Democratic Republic of Congo |
| ANA | Armenian National Army | USSR, Armenia/ Azerbaijan |
| ANF | Azerbaijan National Front | USSR, Armenia/ Azerbaijan |
| BCP | Burmese Communist Party | Myanmar |
| BPLF | Balochistan People's Liberation Front | Pakistan |
| BRA | Bougainville Revolutionary Army/ Bougainville Resistance Army | Papua New Guinea |
|  | Chechnya Rebels | Russian Federation |
| CPN | Communist Party of Nepal Maoist | Nepal |
|  | Dostum-Militia; Jowzjani-Troops; Junbishi-Troops | Afghanistan |
| ELN | Ejército de Liberación Nacional | Colombia |
| EPLF | Eritrean People's Liberation Front | Eritrea |
| ERP | Ejército Revolucionario del Pueblo | Argentina |
| EZLN | Ejército Zapatista de Liberación Nacional, Zapatistas | Mexico |
| FARC | Fuerzas Armadas Revolutionarias de Colombia | Colombia |
| FMLN | Frente Farabundo Martí de Liberación Nacional | El Salvador |
| FNL | Forces Nationales de Libération, Front National de Libération | Burundi |
| FPR | Front Patriotique Rwandais | Rwanda |

| | | |
|---|---|---|
| FRELIMO | Frente de la libertacao de Mocambique | Mozambique |
| FRETILIN | Frente Revolucionara do Timor Leste Independiente (Fretilin) | Indonesia |
| FRUD | Front pour la restauration de l'unité et de la démocratie | Djibouti |
| FSLN | Frente Sandinista de Liberación Nacional | Nicaragua |
| FULRO | Front Unifié de Lutte des Races Opprimées | Vietnam |
| GA | God's Army | Myanmar |
| GAM | Gerakan Aceh Merdeka/ Aceh-Sumatra National Liberation Front (ASNLF) | Indonesia |
| GIA | Groupe Islamique Armé | Algeria |
| | Harakat al-Muqawama al-Islamiyya (HAMAS) | Israel/Palestinian Territories |
| | Hizbollah | Lebanon |
| | Hutu-Militia | Rwanda |
| HVO | Hrvatsko vijece obrane | Yugoslavia/ Bosnia-Herzegovina |
| JKLF | Jammu and Kashmir Liberation Front | India |
| KDP | Kurdistan Democratic Party | Iraq |
| KDPI | Hezb-e Demokrat-e Kordestan, Kurdistan Democratic Party of Iran | Iran |
| KLF | Khalistan Liberation Force | India |
| KNU | Karen National Union | Myanmar |
| LTTE | Liberation Tigers of Tamil Eelam | Sri Lanka |
| | Ahmed Schah Masud; Jamiat-i-Islami | Afghanistan |
| MCHEDRIONI | Sakartvelos Mchedrioni | Georgia |
| MNLF | Moro National Liberation Front | Philippines |
| MQM | Muhajir Quami Movement | Pakistan |
| MRTA | Movimiento Revolucionario Túpac Amaru | Peru |
| MUSHALA | Mushala-Army | Zambia |

| | National Guard | Georgia |
|---|---|---|
| | Naxalites | India |
| NDF | National Democratic Front | Yemen |
| NPA | New Peoples Army | Philippines |
| NPFL | National Patriotic Front of Liberia | Liberia |
| NRM/A | National Resistance Movement/Army | Uganda |
| OLF | Oromo Liberation Front | Ethiopia |
| OPM | Organisasi Papua Merdeka, Organization for a free Papua | Indonesia |
| PIJ | Palestinian Islamic Jihad | Israel/ Palestinian Territories |
| PIRA | Provisional Irish Republican Army, Irish Republican Army (IRA) | Great Britain |
| PKK | Partiya Karkeren Kurdistan | Turkey |
| PLO | Palestine Liberation Organization | Israel/ Palestinian Territories |
| RGT | Republican Guard Transnistria | Moldova |
| RENAMO | Resistencia Nacional Moçambicana | Mozambique |
| RUF | Revolutionary United Front | Sierra Leone |
| SB | Shanti Bahini | Bangladesh |
| SG | Srpska Garda | Yugoslavia |
| SL/PCP | Frente Estudiantil Revolucionario por el Sendero Luminoso de Mariategui/ PCP-Sendero Luminoso | Peru |
| SLA | South Lebanon Army, South Lebanese Army | Lebanon |
| SNM | Somali National Movement | Somalia |
| SSDF | Somali Salvation Democratic Front | Somalia |
| SUA/TRC | Shan United Army (SUA); Tai Revolutionary Council (TRC); Mong Tai Army (MTA) | Myanmar |
| SWAPO | South West African People's Organization; People´s Liberation Army Namibia (PLAN) | Namibia |
| | Swiadists | Georgia |

|        | Taliban                                          | Afghanistan  |
|--------|--------------------------------------------------|--------------|
| TPLF   | Tigray People's Liberation Front                 | Ethiopia     |
| UÇK    | Ushtria Çlirimate e Kosovës                      | Yugoslavia   |
| MK     | Umkhonto we Sizwe                                | South Africa |
| UNITA  | União Nacional para a Independência Total de Angola | Angola    |
| UPC    | Union des Populations du Cameroun                | Cameroon     |
| UPC    | Union des Patriotes Congolais                    | DR Congo     |
| URNG   | Unidad Revolucionaria Guatemalteca-Revolutionäre | Guatemala    |
| USC    | United Somali Congress                           | Somalia      |
| UTO    | United Tajik Opposition                          | Tajikistan   |
| ZANU   | Zimbabwe African National Union                  | Rhodesia     |

# 10. List of Tables

| | | |
|---|---|---|
| Table 1: | Biographical characteristics of leaders | 35 |
| Table 2: | Features of staff members of armed groups | 36 |
| Table 3: | Milieus of followers of armed groups | 38 |
| Table 4: | Reported violence of armed groups against civilian population | 74 |
| Table 5: | Political programs of armed groups | 89 |
| Table 6: | Typology of funding forms of armed groups | 120 |
| Table 7: | Most often reported forms of funding of armed groups | 121 |
| Table 8: | Organizational features of armed groups | 165 |
| Table 9: | Appendix: List of War Actors in Data Base | 226 |

# 11. Bibliography

Abdelkah, Fariba (1999). *Being Modern in Iran*. London: C. Hurst & Co. Publishers.
Abdullah, Ibrahim/Muana, Patrick (1998). *The Revolutionary United Front of Sierra Leone. A Revolt of the Lumpenproletariat*. In: Christopher S. Clapham (ed.). African Guerrillas. 172–193. Oxford: James Currey.
Abelès, Marc (1991). *L'Anthropologie de l'Etat*. Paris: Payot.
Adamec, Ludwig (2005). *Historical Dictionary on Afghan Wars, Revolutions, and Insurgencies*. Lanham, MD: Scarecrow Press.
Ag Acheriff, Ammera (1993). *Aux dernières heures de la colonisation*. In: Edmond Bernus/Jean Clauzel (eds.). Nomades et commandants. Administration et sociétés nomads dans l'ancienne AOF. 207–214. Paris: Karthala.
Ahmad, Fadil (1994). *Die kurdische Befreiungsbewegung. Zwischen Stammeskultur und politischer Erneuerung*. Hildesheim-Achtum: Internationales Kulturwerk.
Albertini, Rudolf von (1987). *Europäische Kolonialherrschaft 1880–1940*. 3rd edition. Wiesbaden: Steiner Verlag.
Allcock, John (2000). *Explaining Yugoslavia*. New York: Columbia University Press.
Almond, Gabriel A./Appleby, R. Scott/Sivan, Emmanuel (2003). *Strong Religion. The rise of fundamentalism around the world*. Chicago: University of Chicago Press.
Aly, Götz (2005). *Hitlers Volksstaat. Raub, Rassenkrieg und nationaler Sozialismus*. Frankfurt am Main: Fischer.
Anastacijevic, Dejan (1996). *Tiger Ate Penguin* (transl.). In: Vreme (Belgrade), March 23, 1996.
Anderson, Lisa (1986). *The State and Social Transformation in Tunisia and Libya 1830–1980*. Princeton NJ: Princeton UP.
Andreas, Peter (2004). *The Clandestine Political Economy of War and Peace in Bosnia*. In: International Studies Quarterly, 48/1. 29–51.
Andrees, Beate (2001). *Die Kosovo-albanische Diaspora zwischen Krieg und Frieden*. In: WeltTrends, 9/32. 59–76.
Anonymus (1985). *La voix de la Casamance*. In: Politique africaine, no. 18. 127–138.
Appadurai, Arjun (2006). *Fear of Small Numbers. An essay on the geography of anger*. Durham and London: Duke University Press.
Apter, David (1997). Political Violence in Analytical Perspective. In: David Apter (ed.). *The Legitimization of Violence*. 1–32. Houndmills: Macmillan.
Arendt, Hannah (1965). *On Revolution*. New York: Compass Books.

— (1970). *On Violence*. London: Harvest Books

Badie, Bertrand (1992). *L'Etat importé. L'occidentalisation de l'ordre politique*. Paris: Fayard.

Bailey, F. G. (1969). *Stratagems and Spoils. A social anthropology of politics*. Oxford: Basil Blackwell.

Balancie, Jean Marc/de La Grange, Arnaud (eds.) (1999). *Monde rebelles. Guerres civiles et violences politiques*. Paris: Editions Michalons.

Balandier, Georges (1982). *Sociologie actuelle de l'Afrique noire. Dynamique sociale en Afrique centrale*. Paris: Presses Universitaires de France.

Bancel, Nicolas/Blanchard, Pascal/Vergès, Françoise (2003). *La République coloniale. Essai sur une utopie*. Paris: Albin Michel.

Barth, Fredrik (1969). *Ethnic Groups and Boundaries. The social organization of cultural difference*. Oslo: Universitetsforlaget.

Bašić, Natalija (1999). *»Krieg ist nun mal Krieg«. Porträt eines Kombattanten*. In: Mittelweg, 8/4. 5–19.

— (2003). *Krieg als Abenteuer. Feindbilder und Gewalt aus der Perspektive ex-jugoslawischer Soldaten*. Giessen: Psychosozial Verlag.

Bauman, Zygmunt (1991). *Modernity and Ambivalence*. Ithaca: Cornell University Press.

Bayart, Jean-François (1984). *La politique africaine de François Mitterand*. Paris. Karthala.

— (1985). *L'énonciation du politique*. In: Revue française de science politique, 35/3. 343–372.

— (ed.) (1996). *La greffe de l'Etat. Les trajectories du politique 2*. Paris: Karthala.

Bayreuther, Rainer (2005). Bürgerkrieg und Musik am Beispiel des Jugoslawienkonflikts. In Isabella von Treskow (ed.). *Bürgerkrieg. Erfahrung und Repräsentation*. 173–208. Berlin: Trafo.

Beck, Teresa K./Schlichte, Klaus (2006). *Nature and Civilization in the Habitus of the Warrior – Angola and Serbia*. Working papers Micropolitics 2/2006. Berlin: Humboldt University. September 22, 2007 http://www2.rz.hu-berlin.de/mikropolitik/downloads/Beck_Schlichte_01-07.pdf.

Behrend, Heike (1999). *Alice Lakwena & the Holy Spirits. War in Northern Uganda, 1986–1997*. Oxford: James Currey.

Berdal, Mats/Malone, David (2000). *Greed and Grievance. Economic agendas in civil wars*. Boulder, Col.: Westview Press.

Berman, Bruce/Lonsdale, Johen (1992). *Unhappy Valley. Conflict in Kenya and Africa*. London: James Currey.

Bernus, Edmond/Boilley, Pierre/Clauzel, Jean/Triaud, Jean-Louis (1993). *Nomades et commandants. Administration et sociétés nomades dans l'ancienne A.O.F.*. Paris: Karthala.

Bierschenk, Thomas/Olivier de Sardan, Jean Pierre (1997). *Local powers and distant state in rural Central African Republic*. In: The Journal of Modern African Studies, 35/3. 441–468.

Bjelić, Predrag (2003). *Turkish Economic Interests in the Western Balkans*. In: Review of International Affairs (Belgrade), 56/119. 44–53.

Bley, Helmut/Tetzlaff, Rainer (1978). *Afrika und Bonn. Versäumnisse und Zwänge deutscher Afrika-Politik*. Reinbek: Rowohlt.

Bliesemann-de Guevara, Berit (2008). *Material Reproduction and Stateness in Bosnia and Herzegovina*. In: Michael Pugh/Neil Cooper/Mandy Turner (eds.). Critical Perspectives on the Political Economy of Peacebuilding. Basingstoke: Palgrave (forthcoming).

Bloch, Marc (1994). *La société féodale*. First edition 1939. Paris: Albin Michel.

Bogner, Artur (2003). *Macht und die Genese sozialer Gruppen*. In: Sociologus, 53/2. 167–181.

Bollig, Michael (1991). *Intra- und interethnisches Konfliktmanagement in Nordwestkenia*. In: Thomas Scheffler (ed.). Ethnizität und Gewalt. 33–66. Hamburg: Deutsches Orient-Institut.

Bonwetsch, Bernd (1985). *Sowjetische Partisanen 1941–1944. Legende und Wirklichkeit des "allgemeinen Volkskrieges"*. In: Gerhard Schulz (ed.). Partisanen und Volkskrieg. Zur Revolutionierung des Krieges im 20. Jahrhundert. 92–124. Göttingen: Vandenhoeck & Ruprecht.

Bougarel, Xavier (1995). *Bosnie. Anatomie d'un conflit*. Paris: La Decouverte.

Bourdieu, Pierre (1985a). *Sociologie de l'Algérie*. First published 1958. Paris: Presses universitaires de France.

— (1985b). *The social space and the genesis of groups*. In: Theory and Society, 14/6. 723–742.

— (1987). *Distinction. A social critique of the judgement of taste*. Boston, Mass.: Harvard University Press.

Bourgeout, André (1990). *L'identité touareg: de l'aristocratie à la révolution*. In: Etudes rurales, n° 190. 129–162.

— (1994). *Révoltes et rébellions en pays touareg*. In: Afrique contemporaine, n° 170. 3–19.

Boveri, Margret (1970). *Tage des Überlebens. Berlin 1945*. München: dtv.

Bozarslan, Hamit (1996). *Kurdistan: économie de guerre, économie dans la guerre*. In: François Jean/Jean-François Rufin (eds.). Economies des guerres civiles. 104–146. Paris: Hachette.

— (1997). *La question kurde. Etats et minorités au Moyen-Orient*. Paris: Presse de Science Po.

Braudel, Fernand (1972). *The Mediterranean and the Mediterranean World in the Age of Philipp II*. 2nd vol.. New York, NY: Harper and Row.

Breslauer, George W. (ed.) (1992). *Soviet Policy in Africa: from the old to the new thinking*. Berkeley: University of California Press.

Breuer, Stefan (1994). *Bürokratie und Charisma. Zur politischen Soziologie Max Webers*. Darmstadt: Wissenschaftliche Buchgesellschaft.

Brubaker, Rogers (2004). *Ethnicity without Groups*. Boston, Mass.: Harvard University Press.

Brunschwig, Henri (1983). *Noirs et Blancs dans l'Afrique Noire Française ou comment le colonisé devient colonisateur.* Paris: Flammarion.
Brzoska, Michael (2004). *"New wars" discourse in Germany.* In: Journal of Peace Research, 41/1. 107–117.
Buhaug, Halvard (2006). *Relative Capability and Rebel Objective in Civil War.* In: Journal of Peace Research, 43/6. 691–708.
Buhaug, Halvard/Gates, Scott (2002). *The Geography of Civil War.* In: Journal of Peace Research, 39/4. 417–433.
Buijtenhuijs, Robert (1987). *Le Frolinat et les guerres civiles du Tchad (1977–1984).* Paris: Karthala.
Burg, Steven L./Shoup, Paul S. (1999). *The War in Bosnia-Herzegovina. Ethnic Conflict and International Intervention.* Armonk, NY: M.E. Sharpe.
Burnett, Cora (1999). *Gang violence as survival strategy in the context of poverty in Davidsonville.* In: Society in Transition, 30/1. 1–12.
Calas, Bernard (1998). *Kampala. La ville et al violence.* Paris: Karthala.
Callahan, Mary P. (2003). *Making Enemies. War and state building in Burma.* Ithaca, NY: Cornell University Press.
Cannadine, David (1983). *The Context, Performance and Meaning of Ritual: The British Monarchy and the "Invention of Tradition".* In: Terence Ranger/Eric Hobsbawm (eds.). The Invention of Tradition. 101–164. Cambridge: Cambridge University Press.
Cassirer, Ernst (1944). *The myth of the state. Philosophical foundations of political behaviour.* New Haven: Yale University Press.
Chafer, Toni (2002). *The End of Empire in French West Africa: France's successful decolonization?.* New York: Berg.
Chaliand, Gérard (1994). *Stratégies de la guérilla. De la Longue Marche à nos jours.* Paris: Payot & Rivages.
Chami, Saade N. (1992). *Economic Performance in a war-economy. The case of Lebanon.* In: Canadian Journal of Development Studies, 8/3. 325–336.
Chandler, David (2002). *From Kosovo to Kabul and Beyond. Human rights and international intervention.* London: Pluto Press.
— (2006). *Empire in Denial. The politics of state-building.* London: Pluto Press.
Chaudry, Kiren Aziz (1997). *The Price of Wealth. Economies and institutions in the Middle East.* Ithaca, NY: Cornell University Press.
Chesnais, Jean-Claude (1981). *Histoire de la violence.* Paris: Robert Laffont.
Chipaux, Françoise (2006). *L'offensive de l'OTAN dans le Sud afghan suscite le désarroi et la colère des villagois.* In: Le Monde, September 6, 2006.
Chirot, Daniel, and McCauley, Clark (2006). *Why Not Kill Them All? The logic and prevention of mass political murder.* Princeton NJ: Princeton University Press.
Clapham, Christopher (1996). *Africa and the International System. The politics of state survival.* New York: Cambridge University Press.
— (ed.) (1998). *African Guerrillas.* Bloomington, Ind.: Indiana University Press.

Claudot-Hawad, Hélène (1993). *Histoire d'un enjeu politique: la vision évolutionniste des événements touaregs 1990–1992*. In: Politique africaine, no. 50. 132–140.

Clausewitz, Carl von (1991). *Vom Kriege*. First edition 1832. Berlin: Ullstein.

Collier, Paul (2000). *Greed and Grievance in Civil War?*. Policy Research Working Paper. Washington DC: World Bank.

Collier, Paul et al. (2003). *Breaking the Conflict Trap: Civil War and Development Policy*. Washington DC: World Bank.

Collins, Randall (1986). *Weberian Sociological Theory*. New York: CUP.

Colović, Ivan (2002). *The Politics of Symbol in Serbia. Essays in political anthropology*. London: C. Hurst & Co. Publishers.

Connell, Dan (1993). *Against All Odds: a Chronicle of the Eritrean Revolution*. Trenton NJ: Red Sea Press.

Coser, Lewis A. (1974). *Greedy Institutions. Patterns of undivided commitment*. New York: Free Press.

Constantin, François (1986). *Sur les modes populaires d'action diplomatiques, affaires de famille et affaires d'Etat en Afrique orientale*. In: Revue Française de Science Politique, 36/5. 672–694.

Coquery-Vidrovitch, Catherine/Moniot, Henry (1984). *L'Afrique noire de 1800 à nos jours*. Paris: Presses universitaires de France.

Crewe, Emma, and Harrison, Elizabeth (1998). *Whose development? An ethnography of aid*. London, New York: Zed Books.

Crisp, Jeff (1986). *Ugandan Refugees in Sudan and Zaire: The Problem of Repatriation*. In: African Affairs, 85/339. 163–180.

— (2000). *A State of Insecurity : The political economy of violence in Kenya's refugee camps*. In: African Affairs, n° 99. 601–632.

Dasgupta, Biplab (1978). *The Naxalite Movement: an epilogue*. In: Social Scientist, 6/12. 3–24.

Davis, Diane E., and Pereira, Anthony (eds.) (2003). *Irregular Armed Forces and Their Role in Politics and State Formation*. New York: Cambridge University Press.

De Jong, Ferdinand (2001). *Modern Secrets. The power of locality in Casamance, Senegal*. Amsterdam: University of Amsterdam Press.

Del Pino, Ponziano (1998). *Family, Culture, and 'Revolution': Everday Life with Sendero Luminoso*. In: Stefe J. Stern (ed.). Shining and Other Paths: War and Society in Peru, 1980–1995. 159–178. Durham: Duke University Press.

Derluguian, Georgi M. (2005). *Bourdieu's Secret Admirer in the Caucasus. A world-system biography*. Chicago: Chicago University Press.

Dessler, David (1991). *Beyond Correlation: Toward a causal theory of war*. In: International Studies Quarterly, 35/3. 337–355.

Diken, Bülent/Laustsen, Carsten Bagge (2005). *The Culture of Exception. Sociology facing the camp*. London: Routledge.

Diner, Dan (2000). *Das Jahrhundert verstehen. Eine universalhistorische Deutung*. Frankfurt am Main: Fischer Verlag.

Diop, Momar Coumba/Diouf, Mamadou (1990). *Le Sénégal sous Abdou Diouf. Etat et société.* Paris: Karthala.

Djilas, Milovan (1980). *Tito. Eine kritische Biographie.* Wien: Molden.

Doom, Ruddy/Vlassenroot, Koen (1999). *Kony's Message: A New Koine? The Lord's Resistance Army in Northern Uganda.* In: African Affairs, 98/390. 5–36.

Dorronsoro, Gilles (2000). *La revolution afghane. Des communistes aux tâlebân.* Paris: Karthala.

Dryland, Estelle (2000). *Migration and Resettlement: the emergence of the Muhajir Qaumi Mahaz.* In: South Asia, 23/2. 111–142.

Duby, Georges (1996). *Féodalité.* Paris: Gallimard.

Duyvesteyn, Isabelle/Angstrom, Jan (eds.) (2005). *Rethinking the Nature of War.* Abingdton: Frank Cass.

Eberl, Immo (2002). *Die Zisterzienser. Geschichte eines europäischen Ordens.* Stuttgart: Thorbeke Verlag.

Eckert, Julia (2005). *Whose State is it? Hindu-nationalist violence and populism in India.* In: Klaus Schlichte (ed.). The dynamics of states. The formation and crises of state domination. 41–70. Aldershot: Ashgate.

— (ed.) (2008). *The Social Life of Anti-Terrorism Laws. The war on terror and the classification of the "dangerous other".* New Brunswick: Transaction Publishers.

Eickhoff, Georg (1999). *Das Charisma der Caudillos. Cárdenas, Franco, Perón.* Frankfurt am Main: Vervuert.

Eisenstadt, Shmuel N. (1973). *Traditional Patrimonialism and Modern Neopatrimonialism.* Beverly Hills, Cal.: University of California Press.

Elbert, Thomas/Rockstroh, Brigitte/Kolassa, Iris-Tatjana (2006). *The Influence of Organized Violence and Terror on Brain and Mind: A Co-constructive perspective.* In: Paul B. Baltes/Patricia Reuter-Lorenz/Frank Rösler (eds.). Lifespan Development and Brain. The perspective of biocultural co-constructivism. 326–349. Cambridge: Cambridge University Press.

Elias, Norbert (1982). *The Process of Civilization.* Vol. 1–2. Oxford: Blackwell.

— (1983a). *The Court Society.* Oxford: Blackwell.

— (1983b). *Über den Rückzug der der Soziologie auf die Gegenwart.* In: Kölner Zeitschrift für Soziologie und Sozialpsychologie, 6/1. 29–40.

— (1987). *Die Gesellschaft der Individuen.* Frankfurt am Main: Suhrkamp.

— (1990). *Studien über die Deutschen. Machtkämpfe und Habitusentwicklung im 19. und 20. Jahrhundert.* Frankfurt am Main: Suhrkamp.

— (1991). *Was ist Soziologie?.* Weinheim: Juventa.

— (2003). *Figuration.* In: Bernhard Schäfers (ed.). Grundbegriffe der Soziologie. 8th edition. 86–91. Opladen: Leske und Budrich.

Elliot, Patricia (1993). *A Life in the Drug Trade.* In: Saturday Night (Toronto), 108/10. 17.

Ellis, Stephen/Ter Haar, Gerrie (2004). *Worlds of Power. Religious thought and political practice in Africa.* New York: Oxford University Press.

Ellis, Stephen (1999). *The Mask of Anarchy. The destruction of Liberia and the religious dimension of an African Civil War.* London: C. Hurst & Co. Publishers.

Elster, Jon (1999). *A plea for mechanisms.* In: Peter Hedström/Richard Swedberg (eds.). Social Mechanisms. An analytical approach to social theory. 45–73. Cambridge: Cambridge University Press.

Elwert, Georg (1997). *Gewaltmärkte. Beobachtungen zur Zweckrationalität der Gewalt.* In: Trutz von Trotha (ed.). Soziologie der Gewalt. Kölner Zeitschrift für Soziologie und Sozialpsychologie (special issue). 133–152.

— (2003). *The Socio-Anthropological Interpretation of Violence.* In: Wilhelm Heitmeyer/ John Hagan (eds.). The International Handbook of Violence Research. 291– 290. Dordrecht: Kluwer Academic Publishers.

Endres, Jürgen (2004). *Wirtschaftliches Handeln im Krieg. Zur Persistenz des Milizsystems im Libanon (1975–1990).* Wiesbaden: VS.

Enzensberger, Hans Magnus (1993). *Aussichten auf den Bürgerkrieg.* Frankfurt am Main: Suhrkamp.

Euskirchen, Markus (2005). *Militärrituale. Analyse und Kritik eines Herrschaftsinstruments.* Köln: Papyrossa.

Fairbanks, Charles H. (1995). *The Postcommunist Wars.* In: Journal of Democracy, 6/4. 18–34.

Fanon, Frantz (1965). *The Wretched of the Earth.* New York: Grove Press.

— (1967). *Black Skin, White Masks.* New York: Grove Press.

Favarel-Garrigues, Gilles (1999). *Privatisation et changement politique en Russie soviétique.* In: Béatrice Hibou (ed.). La privatisation des Etats. 247–284. Paris: Karthala.

Faye, Ousseynou (1994). *L'instrumentalisation de l'histoire et de l'ethnicité dans le discours séparatiste en Basse Casamance.* In: Afrika-Spektrum, 29/1. 65–77.

Fearon, James D./Laitin, David D. (2003). *Ethnicity, Insurgency, and Civil War.* In: American Political Science Review, 97/1. 75–90.

Feinberg, Richard/Kurtz-Phelan, Daniel (2006). *Nicaragua between Caudillismo and Modernity. The Sandinista Redux?.* In: World Policy Journal, Summer 2006.76–84.

Ferguson, James (1987). *The Anti-politics Machine. Development, depoliticization, and bureaucratic power.* Cambridge: Cambridge University Press.

Filkins, Dexter (2006). *Armed Groups Propel Iraq Toward Chaos.* The New York Times, May 24, 2006.

Fleck, Ludwig (1981 [1935]). *Genesis and Development of a Scientific Fact.* Chicago: University of Chicago Press.

Foucault, Michel (1995). *Discipline and Punish: the birth of the prison.* New York: Pantheon.

— (2007). *Security, Territory, Population. Lectures at the College de France.* London: Palgrave-Macmillan.

Frank, Cornelia (2006). *Die UÇK im Kosovo – Aufstieg, Konsolidierung, Transformation.* In: Jutta Bakonyi/Stephan Hensell/Jens Siegelberg (eds.). Gewaltordnungen bewaffneter Gruppen. Ökonomie und Herrschaft nichtstaatlicher Akteure in den Kriegen der Gegenwart. 167–178. Baden-Baden: Nomos.

Frijda, Nico H. (1993). *The Lex Talionis: on Vengeance.* In: Stephanie H. M. van Goozen et al. (eds.). *Essays on Emotion Theory.* 263–289. Hillsdale NJ: Lawrence Erlbaum Associates

Gammer, Moshe (2006). *From Chechen Revolution to Jihad.* In: Moshe Gammer. *The Lone Wolf and the Bear. Three Centuries of Chechen Defiance of Russian Rule.* 200–218. London: C. Hurst & Co. Publishers.

Gantzel, Klaus Jürgen/Schwinghammer, Torsten (2000). *Warfare Since the Second World War.* New Brunswick: Transaction Publishers.

Gates, Scott (2001). *Recruitment and Allegiance. The microfoundations of rebellion.* In: Journal of Conflict Resolution, 46/1. 111–130.

Geffray, Christian (1990). *La cause des armes au Mozambique. Anthropologie d'une guerre civile.* Paris: Karthala.

Genschel, Philipp/Schlichte, Klaus (1998). *Civil War as a Chronic Condition.* In: Law and State, 58. 107–123.

George, Sudhir Jacob (1994). *The Bodo Movement in Assam.* In: Asian Survey, 34/10. 878–892.

Gerstenberger, Heide (1990). *Subjektlose Gewalt. Theorie der Entstehung bürgerlicher Staatsgewalt.* Münster: Verlag Westfälisches Dampfboot.

Ghanem, As'ad (2001). *The Palestinian Regime. A "partial democracy".* Portland, Oreg.: Sussex Academic Press.

Giddens, Anthony (1985). *The Nation-State and Violence. Volume Two of a Contemporary Critique of Historical Materialism.* Cambridge: Polity Press.

Girard, Réné (1977). *Violence and the Sacred.* Baltimore MD: Johns Hopkins University Press.

Giustozzi, Antonio (2003). *Respectable Warlords? The politics of state-building in post-Taleban Afghanistan.* Working paper n° 33. Crisis states programme series. London: Development Research Centre, London School of Economics and Political Science.

Goethe, Johann Wolfgang von (1957). *Poems of Goethe. A sequel to Goethe, the lyrist.* Translated and with an introduction by Edwin H. Zeydel. Chapel Hill: University of North Carolina Press.

Goldstone, Jack et al. (2000). *State Failure Task Force Report 2000: Phase III Findings.* July 12, 2007 http://www.cidcm.umd.edu/publications/publication.asp?pubType=paper&id=9.

Gomez, Nikki Rivera (2005). *Coffee and dreams on a late afternoon: tales of despair and deliverance in Mindanao.* Diliman, Quezon City: University of the Philippines Press.

Goodwin, Jeff (2001). *No Other Way Out. States and revolutionary movements, 1945–1991.* Cambridge: Cambridge University Press.

Gordadze, Thornike (2003). *Les nouvelles guerres du Caucase (1991–2000) et la formation des Etats postcommunistes.* In: Pierre Hassner/Roland Marchal (eds.). Guerres et sociétés. Etat et violence après la Guerre froide. 371–402. Paris: Karthala.

Grandin, Greg (2004). *The Last Colonial Massacre. Latin America in the Cold War.* Chicago, Il.: University of Chicago Press.

Grenier, Yvon (1999). *The Emergence of Insurgency in El Salvador. Ideology and Political Will.* Pittsburgh: Pittsburgh University Press.

Grosse-Kettler, Sabine (2004). *External actors in stateless Somalia. A war economy and its promoters.* BICC-paper n° 39. Bonn: Bonn International Centre for Conversion. March 22, 2007 http://www.bicc.de/publications/papers/paper39/content.php.

Grossman, Dave (1996). *On Killing. The psychological cost of learning to kill in war and society.* Boston, New York: Back Bay Books.

Guevara, Ernesto (1961). *Guerilla Warfare.* New York: MR Press.

Halliday, Fred (2005). *The Middle East in International Relations. Power, politics and ideology.* New York: Cambridge University Press.

Hamzeh, A. Nazir (2004). *In the Path of Hizbollah.* Syracuse, NY: Syracuse University Press.

Hanf, Theodor (1990). *Koexistenz im Krieg. Staatszerfall und Entstehen einer Nation im Libanon.* Baden-Baden: Nomos.

Haq, Farhat (1995). *Rise of the MQM in Pakistan.* In: Asian Survey, 35/11. 990–1016.

Hanson, Stephen E. (1997). *Time and Revolution. Marxism and the design of Soviet Institutions.* Chapel Hill, NC: University of North Carolina Press.

Harik, Judith Palmer (2004). *Hezbollah. The changing face of terrorism.* London: Tauris.

Harris, William W. (1997). *Faces of Lebanon. Sects, wars and global extensions.* Princeton, NJ: Markus Wiener Publishers.

Hashim, Ahmed S. (2006). *Insurgency and counter-Insurgency in Iraq.* Ithaca, NY: Cornell University Press.

Heater, Derek (1994). *National Self-Determination. Woodrow Wilson and his legacy.* New York: St. Martin's Press.

Heitmeyer, Wilhelm/Hagan John (eds.). *The International Handbook of Violence Research.* Dordrecht: Kluwer Academic Publishers.

Hellmann-Rajanayagam, Dagmar (1994). *The Tamil Tigers: Armed Struggle for Identity.* Stuttgart: Steiner.

Heristchi, Claire (2004). *The Islamist Discourse of the FIS and the Democratic Experiment in Algeria.* In: Democracy, 11/4. 111–132.

Herrington, Stuart A. (1982). *Silence Was a Weapon. The Vietnam War in the villages. A personal perspective.* Novato, Cal: Presidio Press.

Heyman, Josiah McC. (ed.) (1999). *States and Illegal Practices.* New York: Berg Publishers.

Heywood, Linda (1989). *Unita and Ethnic Nationalism in Angola.* In: Journal of Modern African Studies, 27/1. 47–66.

Hibou, Béatrice (2006). *La force de l'obéissance. Economie politique de la répression en tunisie.* Paris: La Découverte.

Hinton, Alexander Laban (2004). *Why did you kill? The Cambodian genocide and the dark side of face and honor.* In: Nancy Scheper-Hughes/Philippe Bourgeois. Violence in War and Peace. 157–168. London: Blackwell.

Hintze, Otto (1970 [1906]). *Staatsverfassung und Kriegsverfassung.* In: Otto Hintze. Staat und Verfassung, Gesammelte Abhandlungen zur allgemeinen Verfassungsgeschichte. 52–83. Göttingen: Vandenhoeck und Ruprecht.

Hobsbawm, Eric (1959). *Primitive Rebels. Studies in the archaic forms of Social Movement in the 19th and 20th centuries.* New York, NY: Norton.

— (1996). *The Age of Extremes. A history of the World, 1914–1991.* New York: Vintage Books.

Hopkins, A.G. (ed.) (2001). *Globalisation in World History.* London: Pimlico.

Horkheimer, Max (1937). *Traditionelle und kritische Theorie.* In: Zeitschrift für Sozialforschung, 6/2. 245–294.

Huband, Mark (1998). *The Liberian Civil War.* London, Portland, Oreg.: Frank Cass.

— (1998). *Warriors of the Prophet. The struggle for Islam.* Boulder, Col.: Westview Press.

Humphreys, Macartan/Weinstein, Jeremy M. (2006). *Handling and Manhandling Civilians in Civil War.* In: American Political Science Review, 100/3. 429–447.

Hunter, Jane (1987). *Israeli Foreign Policy: South Africa and Central America.* Boston, Mass.: South End Press.

Huntington, Samuel P. (1968). *Political Order in Changing Societies.* New Haven, Conn: Yale University Press.

— (1996). *The Clash of Civilizations and the Remaking of World Order.* New York: Simon and Schuster.

Hutchison, Alan (1976). *China's African Revolution.* Boulder, Col.: Westview Press.

Imbusch, Peter (2002). *The Concept of Violence.* In: Wilhelm Heitmeyer/John Hagan (eds.). The International Handbook of Violence Research. 35–52. Dordrecht: Kluwer Academic Publishers.

Isachenko, Daria (2008). *Production of Recognised Space: State-building practices of Northern Cyprus and Transdniestria.* In: Journal of Intervention and Statebuilding. Special issue on post-conflict spaces, May 2008.

Isachenko, Daria/Schlichte, Klaus (2007). *The crooked ways of state-building: How Uganda and Transnistria muddle through the international system.* Working Papers Micropolitics 1/2007. Berlin: Humboldt University. September 17, 2007 http://www2rz.hu-berlin.de/mikropolitik/downloads/07-04_Crooked_ways.pdf.

Jacobsen, Karen (2005). *The Economic Life of Refugees.* Bloomfield, CT: Kumarian Press.

Jean, François/Rufin, Jean-Christophe (eds.) (1996). *Economy des guerres civiles.* Paris: Hachette.

Joas. Hans (2000). *Krieg und Werte. Studien zur Gewaltgeschichte des 20. Jahrhunderts.* Weilerswist: Velbrück.

Johannès, Franck (2007). *Paralysies libanaises.* In : Le Monde, January 25, 2007, pp. 22–23.
Johnson, Douglas (1998). *The Sudan People's Liberation Army and the Problem of Factionalism.* In: Christopher Clapham (ed.). African Guerrillas. 53–72. Oxford: James Currey.
Joseph, Richard (1977). *Radical Nationalism in Cameroon. Social Origins of the U.P.C. Rebellion.* Oxford: Oxford University Press.
Judah, Tom (2000). *The Serbs. History, myth and the destruction of Yugoslavia.* New Haven, Conn.: Yale University Press.
Kahl, Colin H. (2006). *States, Scarcity, and Civil Strife in the Developing World.* Princeton, NJ: Princeton University Press.
Kaldor, Mary (1999). *Neue und alte Kriege.* Frankfurt am Main: Suhrkamp.

Kalyvas, Stathis (2001). *"New" Wars And "Old" Wars: a valid distinction?.* In: World Politics, 54/1. 99–118.
— (2003). *The Ontology of "Political Violence": Action and Identity in Civil Wars.* In: Perspectives on Politics, 1/3. 475–494.
— (2006). *The Logic of Violence in Civil War.* New York: Cambridge University Press.
Kantorowicz, Ernst H. (1997). *The King's Two Bodies: a study in mediaeval political theology.* Princeton, NJ: Princeton University Press.
Kaplan, Robert (1994). *The Coming Anarchy. How scarcity, crime, overpopulation, tribalism, and disease are rapidly destroying the social fabric of our planet.* In: The Atlantic Monthly, February 1994.
— (1996). *The Ends of the Earth. A journey at the dawn of the 21st century.* New York: Random House.
Kapferer, Bruce (1997). *Remythologizing Discourse: State and Insurrectionary Violence in Sri Lanka.* In: David Apter (ed.). The Legitimization of Violence. 159–188. Houndmill: Macmillan.
Kasfir, Nelson (2005). *Guerillas and civilan participation: the National Resistance Army in Uganda, 19881–86.* In: Journal of Modern African Studies, 43/2. 271–296.
Keen, David (1994). *The Benefits of Famine. A political economy of famine and relief in Southwestern Sudan, 1983–1989.* Princeton, NJ: Princeton University Press.
— (1998). *The Economic Functions of Violence in Civil War.* Adelphi-Paper 320, International Institute for Strategic Studies. Oxford: Oxford University Press.
— (2000). *Incentives and Disincentives for Violence.* In: Mats Berdal/David Malone (eds.). Greed and Grievance. Economic agendas in civil wars. 19–41. Boulder, Col.: Lynne Rienner.
— (2005a). *Conflict and Collusion in Sierra Leone.* Oxford: James Currey.
— (2005b). *Endless war? Hidden functions of the "War on terror".* London: Pluto Press.
Kell, Tim (1995). *The Roots of the Acehnese Rebellion, 1989–1992.* Ithaca, NY: Cornell Modern Asia Project.

Kennes, Erik (2003). *Essai biographique sur Laurent Désiré Kabila.* With Munkana N'Ge. Paris: L'Harmattan.
Kepel, Gilles (2004). *The War for Muslim Minds. Islam and the West.* Cambridge, Mass.: Belknap Press.
Kessler, Richard J. (1989). *Rebellion and Repression in the Philippines.* New Haven, NJ.: Yale University Press.
King, Charles (1995). *Post-Soviet Moldova: A borderland in transition.* London: Royal Institute of International Affairs.
— (1997). *Ending Civil Wars.* Adelphi-Paper 308, International Institute for Strategic Studies. Oxford: Oxford University Press.
— (2004). *The Micropolitcs of Social Violence.* In: World Politics, 56. 431–455.
Klute, Georg (1995). *Hostilités et alliances. Archéologie de la dissidence des Touaregs au Mali.* In: Cahiers d'Etudes africaines, 35/1. 55–71.
Klute, Georg/von Trotha, Trutz (2000). *Wege zum Frieden. Vom Kleinkrieg zum parastaatlichen Frieden im Norden von Mali.* In: Sociologus, 50/1. 1–36.
Koohi-Kamali, Farideh (2003). *The Political Development of the Kurds in Iran: Pastoral Nationalism.* New York: Palgrave Macmillan.
Koselleck, Reinhard (1979/1985). *Futures Past. On the semantics of historical time.* Cambridge, Mass.: MIT Press.
Krasner, Stephen (2004). *Sharing Sovereignty. New Institutions for collapsed and failing states.* In: International Security, 29/2. 85–120.
Krippendorff, Ekkehart (1994). *Staatlich organisierte Gewalt: Das Militär in den USA.* In: Hans Joas/Wolfgang Knöbl (eds.). Gewalt in den USA. 286–299. Frankfurt am Main: Fischer.
Kroll, Thomas (2001). *Max Webers Idealtypus der charismatischen Herrschaft und die zeitgenössische Charisma-Debatte.* In: Edith Hanke/Wolfgang J. Mommsen (eds.). Max Webers Herrschaftssoziologie. 47–72. Tübingen: Mohr.
Kunze, Thomas (2000). *Nicolae Ceausescu. Eine Biographie.* Berlin: Ch. Links Verlag.
Laïdi, Zaki (1990). *The Superpowers and Africa: the constraints of a rivalry, 1960–1990.* Chicago: University of Chicago Press.
Laitin, David (2001). *Rebellion in the Former Soviet Union.* In: Comparative Political Studies, 34/8. 839–861.
Lakatos, Imre (ed.) (1974). *Criticism and the Growth of Knowledge.* Cambridge: Cambridge University Press.
Larzillière, Pénélope (2003). *Tchétchénie: le jihad reterritorialisé.* In: Critique internationale, 20/July 2003. 151–164.
— (2004). *Etre jeune en Palestine. Voix et regards.* Paris: Balland.
Le Billon, Philippe (2005). *Resource Wealth and Angola's Uncivil Wars.* In: Cynthia J. Arnson/William I. Zartman (eds.). Rethinking the Economy of War. The intersection of need, creed, and greed. 107–139. Baltimore, MD: The Johns Hopkins University Press.

Le Bot, Yvon (1994). *Violence de la modernité en Amérique latine. Indianité, société et pouvoir.* Paris: Karthala.

Lechervy, Christian (1996). *L'économie des guerres cambodgiennes: accumulation et dispersion.* In: Christophe Jean/Jean-Christophe Rufin (eds.). Economies des guerres civiles. 189–232. Paris: Hachette.

Lecocq, Baz (2004). *Unemployed Intellectuals in the Sahara: The Teshumara Nationalist Movement and the Revolutions in Tuareg Society.* In: International Review of Social History, 49. 87–109.

Leitenberg, Milton (2006). *Deaths in Wars and Conflicts between 1945 and 2000.* Ithaca, NY: Cornell Peace Studies Program.

Lemière de Corvey, Jean-Frédéric-Auguste (1823). *Des partisans et des corps irréguliers: Ou manière d'employer avec avantage les troupes-légères, quelque soit leur dénomination: partisans, voltigeurs, compagnies-franches, guérillas, et généralement toute espèce de corps-irreguliers, contre des armées disciplinées.* Paris: Anselin et Pochard.

Lemke, Thomas (2001). *Max Weber, Norbert Elias und Michel Foucault über Macht und Subjektivierung.* In: Berliner Journal für Soziologie, 11/1. 77–95.

Leonhard, Richard (1988). *Popular Participation in Liberation and Revolution.* In: Lionel Cliffe/Basil Davidson (eds.). The Long Struggle of Eritrea for Independence and Constructive Peace. 105–135. Nottingham: Spokesman.

Lewis, Ioan M. (1965). *A Modern History of Somaliland. From nation to state.* New York: Praeger.

Lieven, Anatol (1998). *Chechnya. Tombstone of Russian Power.* New Haven, Conn.: Yale University Press.

Linares, Olga F. (1992). *Power, Prayer, and Production. The Jola of Casamance, Senegal.* Cambridge Studies in Social and Cultural Anthropology. Cambridge: Cambridge University Press.

Lindenberger, Thomas/Lüdtke, Alf (eds.) (1995). *Physische Gewalt. Studien zur Geschichte der Neuzeit.* Frankfurt am Main: Suhrkamp.

Lintner, Bertil (1999). *Burma in Revolt. Opium and insurgency since 1948.* Bangkok: Silkworm Books.

Lischer, Sarah Kenyon (2005). *Dangerous Sanctuaries. Refugee camps, civil war, and the dilemmas of humanitarian aid.* Ithaca, NY: Cornell University Press.

Löwith, Karl (1953). *Weltgeschichte als Heilsgeschehen. Die theologischen Voraussetzungen der Geschichtsphilosophie.* Stuttgart: Kohlhammer.

Lukes, Steven (2005). *Power. A radical view.* 2nd edition. London: Macmillan.

Macher, Riek (1995). *South Sudan: A history of political domination – a case of self-determination.* University of Pennsylvania, African Studies Center. December 28, 2005 http://www.africa-upenn.edu/Hornet/sd_machar.html.

Malcom Klein (1995). *The American Street Gang. Its nature, prevalence and control.* Oxford: Oxford University Press.

Malthaner, Stefan (2007). *The "Armed Groups Database": Aims, sources and methodology.* Working Paper Micropolitics 2/2007. September 17, 2007 http://www2.rz.hu-berlin.de/mikropolitik/downloads/working_paper_02_07_malthaner_database.pdf.

Mamdani, Mahmood (1996). *Citizen and Subject. Contemporary Africa and the legacy of late colonialism.* Princeton, NJ: Princeton University Press.

Mamdani, Mahmood (2002). *African States, Citizenship, and War: a case-stuy.* In: International Affairs, 78/3. 493–506.

— (2004). *Good Muslim, Bad Muslim. America, the Cold War, and the Roots of Terror.* New York: Pantheon.

— (2007). *The Politics of Naming: Genocide, civil war, insurgency.* In: London Review of Books, March 8, 2007.

Mao, Tse-Tung (1961). *On Guerilla Warfare.* New York: Praeger.

Marchal, Roland (1993). *Les mooryans de Mogadiscio. Formes de la violence dans un espace urbain en guerre.* In: Cahiers d'Etudes Africaines, 130. 295–320.

— (2000). *Atomisation des fins et radicalisme des moyens. De quelques conflits africains.* In: Critique internationale, 6/Winter 2000. 159–175.

— (2003). *Conclusions.* In: Roland Marchal/Pierre Hassner (eds.). Guerres et sociétés. Etat et violence après la Guerre Froide. 573–589. Paris: Karthala.

— (2006). *Chad/Darfur: How two crises merge.* In: Review of African Political Economy, 33/109. 467–482.

Marchal, Roland/Messiant, Christine (1997). *Les chemins de la guerre et de la paix. Fins de conflit en Afrique orientale et australe.* Paris: Karthala.

— (2003). *Les guerres civiles à l'ère de la globalisation. Nouvelles réalités et nouveaux paradigmes.* In: Critique internationale, 18/January 2003. 91–112.

— (2006). *Une lecture symptomale de quelques théorisations récentes des guerres civiles.* In: Lusotopie, 13/2. 3–46.

Markakis, John (1987). *National and Class Conflict in the Horn of Africa.* Cambridge: Cambridge University Press.

Marseille, Jacques (1984). *Empire colonial et capitalisme français. Histoire d'un divorce.* Paris: Albin Michel.

Marte, Fred (1994). *Political Cycles in International Relations. The Cold War and Africa, 1945–1990.* Amsterdam: VU University Press.

Martinez, Luis (1998). *La guerre civile en Algérie.* Paris: Karthala.

— (2003). *Le cheminement singulier de la violence islamiste en Algérie.* In: Critique internationale, 20/July 2003. 79–95.

Marut, Jean-Claude (1994). *Le mythe.* In: François George Barbier-Wiesser (ed.). Comprendre la Casamance. Chronique d'une intégration contrastée. 19–26. Paris: Karthala.

Mattick, Hans W./Caplan, Nathan (1967). *Stake Animals, Loud-Talking, and Leadership in Do-Nothing and Do-Something Situations.* In: Malcolm W. Klein (ed.). Juvenile Group in Context. Theory, research and action. 106–119. Englewood Cliffs, NJ: Prentice Hall.

Mayntz, Renate (2004). *Mechanisms in the Analysis of Macro-Social Phenomena.* In: Philosophy of the Social Sciences, 34/2. 237–259.

Mazower, Mark (2002). *Violence and the State in the Twentieth Century.* In: The American Historical Review, 107/4. 1158–1178.

Mazrui, Ali A. (ed). (1977). *The Warrior Tradition in modern Africa.* Leiden: Brill.
— (1977a). *Soldiers as Traditionalizers: Military Rule and the Reafricanization of Africa.* In: Ali A. Mazrui (ed.). The Warrior Tradition in modern Africa. 236– 256. Leiden: Brill.
— (1977b). *The Warrior Tradition and the Masculinity of War.* In: Ali A. Mazrui (ed.). The Warrior Tradition in modern Africa. 69–80. Leiden: Brill.
McClintock, Cynthia (1998). *Revolutionary Movements in Latin America. El Salvador's FMLN & Peru's Shining Path.* Washington, D.C.: United States Institute of Peace Press.
McCormick, Gordon H. (1990). *The Shining Path and the Future of Peru.* Santa Monica: Rand Corporation.
McCoy, Alfred W. (1999). *Requiem for a Drug Lord: State and Commodity in the Career of Khun Sa.* In: Josiah McC. Heyman (ed.). States and Illegal Practices. 129–167. Oxford: Berg.
McKenna, Thomas (1999). *Muslim Rulers and Rebels. Everyday politics and armed separatism in the Southern Philippines.* Berkeley, Cal.: University of California Press.
McPherson, James M. (1997). *For Cause and Comrades. Why men fought in the civil war.* New York: Oxford University Press.
Médard, Jean-François (ed.) (1991). *Etats d'Afrique noire. Formations, mécanismes et crise.* Paris: Karthala.
— (1992). *Le »Big Man« en Afrique. Esquisse d'analyse du politicien entrepreneur.* In: Année sociologique, 1992. 167–192.
Mennell, Stephen (1998). *Norbert Elias. An introduction.* Dublin: University College Dublin Press.
Merridale, Catherine (2005). *Ivan's war. The Red Army 1939–1945.* London: Faber and Faber.
Mertens, Ilja (2000). *Von einer 'inneren Angelegenheit', die auszog, das Fürchten zu lehren. Transstaatliche politische Mobilisierung und das 'Kurdenproblem'.* In: Thomas Faist (ed.). Transstaatliche Räume – Politik, Wirtschaft und Kultur in und zwischen Deutschland und der Türkei. 159–199. Bielefeld: Transkript.
Milivojevic, Marko (1998). *Entries "paramilitary/irregular forces": "Vojislav Seselj", "Vukasin Draskovic", "Zeljko Raznatovic".* In: John B. Allcock/Marko Milivojevic/John H. Horton (eds.). Conflict in the Former Yugoslavia. An encyclopedia. Denver, Col.: ABC-Clio.
Middleton, John (1971). *Some effects of colonial Rule among the Lugbara.* In: Victor Turner (ed.). Colonial rule in Africa, vol. 3. 6–48. Cambridge: Cambridge University Press.
Migdal, Joel S. (1988). *Strong Societies and Weak States. State-society relations and state capabilities in the Third World.* Princeton, NJ: Princeton University Press.
— (2001). *State in Society. Studying how states and societies transform and constitute one another.* Cambridge: Cambridge University Press.

Migdal, Joel S./Schlichte, Klaus (2005). *Rethinking the State.* In: Klaus Schlichte (ed.). *The Dynamics of States. The formation and crisis of state domination.* 1–48. Aldershot: Ashgate.

Mills, C. Wright (1956). *The Power Elite.* London: Oxford University Press.

Mishal, Shaul/Sela, Avraham (2006). *The Palestinian Hamas: vision, violence, and coexistences.* New York: Columbia University Press.

Missbach, Antje (2005). *Freiheitskämpfer oder Geschäftemacher? Der bewaffnete Kampf der Gerakan Aceh Merdeka (GAM) unter Berücksichtigung klassischer und neuerer Guerillatheorien.* Berlin: Berlin Studies on Southeast Asia.

Mohan, Raja C. (2003). *Crossing the Rubicon: the shaping of India's new foreign policy.* New York: Palgrave Macmillan.

Mommsen, Wolfgang J./Osterhammel, Jürgen (eds.) (1986). *Imperialism and After. Continuities and discontinuities.* London: German Historical Institute.

Mueller, John (1999). *The Remnants of War.* Ithaca, NY: Cornell University Press.

Münkler, Herfried (1994). *Politische Bilder, Politik der Metaphern.* Frankfurt am Main: Fischer.

— (2002a). *Über den Krieg. Stationen der Kriegsgeschichte im Spiegel ihrer theoretischen Reflexion.* Weilerswist: Velbrück.

— (2002b). *Die neuen Kriege.* Reinbek: Rowohlt.

Museveni, Yoweri Kaguta (1997). *Sowing the Mustard Seed. The struggle for freedom and democracy in Uganda.* London: Macmillan.

Nabuguzi, Emmanuel (1991). *Le magendo en Ouganda.* In: Politique africaine, no. 42. 134–140.

Nedelmann, Birgitta (1997). *Gewaltsoziologie am Scheideweg. Die Auseinandersetzungen in der gegenwärtigen und Wege der künftigen Gewaltforschung.* In: Trutz von Trotha (ed.). Soziologie der Gewalt. Kölner Zeitschrift für Soziologie und Sozialpsychologie (special issue). 59–84.

Newberg, Paula R. (2005). *Surviving State Failure: Internal war and regional conflict in Afghanistan's Neighborhood.* In: Cynthia J. Arnson/William I. Zartman (eds.). Rethinking the Economy of War. The intersection of need, creed, and greed. 206–233. Baltimore, MD: The Johns Hopkins University Press.

Nissen, Astrid (2003). *La transformacion de los grupos armados en El Salvado y Nicaragua.* Paper presented at the 51st Congreso Internacional de Americanistas. Santiago de Chile, July 14, 2003.

Ngoga, Pascal (1998). *Uganda: The National Resistance Army.* In: Christopher Clapham (ed.). African Guerrillas. 91–106. Oxford: James Currey.

Nordstrom, Carolyn (1995). *War on the Front Lines.* In: Carolyn Nordstrom (ed.). Fieldwork under Fire. Contemporary studies of violence and survival. 129–153. Berkeley: University of California Press.

— (2004). *Shadows of War. Violence, power, and international profiteering in the 21st century.* Berkeley, Cal.: University of California Press.

Norkus, Zenonas (2005). *Mechanisms as miracle makers? The rise and inconsistencies of the "mechanisms approach" in social science and history.* In: History and Theory, 44/October 2005. 348–372.

Nzongola-Ntalaja, Georges (2002). *The Congo From Leopold to Kabila. A people's history.* London: Zed Books.

Oakes, Len (1997). *Prophetic Charisma. The psychology of revolutionary religious personalities.* Syrakuse, NY: Syrakuse University Press.

Oneal, John R./Russett, Bruce M. (1997). *The Classical Liberals Were Right: Democracy, interdependence, and conflict, 1950–1985.* In: International Studies Quarterly, 41/2. 267–294.

Önis, Ziya (1991). *The Logic of the Developmental State.* In: Comparative Politics, vol. 24. 109–126.

Orywal, Erwin (1996). *Die Ehre der Gewalt: Recht und Rache in Balutschistan.* In: Erwin Orywal/Aparna Rao/Michael Bollig (eds.). Krieg und Kampf. Die Gewalt in unseren Köpfen. 61–72. Berlin: Reimer.

Otayek, Réné (1986). *La politique africaine de la Libye.* Paris: Karthala.

Palonen, Kari (1993). *Introduction: from policy and polity to politicking and politicization.* In: Kari Palonen/Tuijva Parvikko (eds.). Reading the Political. Exploring the Margins of Politics. 6–16. Tampere: The Finnish Political Science Association.

Paris, Roland (2002). *International Peacebuilding and the "mission civilisatrice".* In: Review of International Studies, 28/4. 637–656.

Parsons, Talcott (1963). *On the concept of power.* Proceedings of the American Philosophical Society, 107. 232–262.

Peristiany, J. G. (ed.) (1966). *Honour and Shame. The values of Mediterranean Society.* Chicago: Chicago University Press.

Perlmutter, Amos (1977). *The Military and Politics in Modern Times. On Professional, Praetorians, and Revolutionary Soldiers.* New Haven, Conn.: Yale University Press.

Peterson, Roger D. (2002). *Understanding Ethnic Violence. Fear, hatred, and resentment in 20th century Eastern Europe.* Cambridge: Cambridge University Press.

Pewzner, Evelyne (ed.) (2005). *Temps et espaces de la violence.* Chilly-Mazarin: Editions Sens.

Picard, Elizabeth (1996). *Liban: La matrice historique.* In: François Jean/Jean-Christophe Rufin (eds.). Economies des guerres civiles. 62–103. Paris: Hachette.

— (1997). *The Lebanese Sh'ia and Political Violence in Lebanon.* In: David Apter (ed.). The Legitimization of Violence. 189–233. Houndmills: Macmillan.

— (1999). *Les Kurdes et l'autodétermination. Une problématique légitime á l'épreuve de dynamiques sociales.* In: Revue française de science politique, 49/3. 421–442.

— (2002). *La violence milicienne et sa légitimation religieuse.* In: Thomas Scheffler (ed.). Religion between Violence and Reconciliation. 319–332. Würzburg: Ergon-Verlag.

Pirouet, Louise (1977). *Armed Resistance and Counter-Insurgency. Reflections on the Anya Nya and Mau Mau Experience.* In: Ali A. Mazrui (ed.). The Warrior Tradition in modern Africa. 197–214. Leiden: Brill.

Pool, David (1998). *The Eritrean People's Liberation Front.* In: Christopher Clapham (ed.). African Guerrillas. 19–35. Bloomington, Ind.: Indiana University Press.

Popitz, Heinrich (1992). *Phänomene der Macht.* 2nd edition. Tübingen: Mohr.

Posen, Barry, R. (1993). *The Security Dilemma and Ethnic Conflict.* In: Michael E. Brown (ed.). Ethnic Conflict and International Security. 103–124. Princeton, NJ: Princeton University Press.

Prkic, François (2005). *The Phoenix State: War economy and state formation in Liberia.* In: Klaus Schlichte (ed.). The Dynamics of States. The formation and crisis of state domination. 115–136. Aldershot: Ashgate.

Prunier, Gérard (1998). *Rwanda. History of a Genocide.* London: C. Hurst & Co. Publishers.

— (2004). *Rebel Movements and Proxy Warfare: Uganda, Sudan and the Congo (1986–99).* In: African Affairs, 103/412. 359–383.

— (2005). *Darfur. The ambiguous genocide.* Ithaca, NY: Cornell University Press.

Pugh, Michael (2003). *Protectorates and Spoils of Peace: intermestic manipulations of political economy in South-East Europe.* In: Dietrich Jung (ed.). Shadow Globalization, ethnic conflict and new wars. A political economy of intra-state wars. 47–69. London: Routledge.

Radkau, Joachim (2005). *Max Weber. Die Leidenschaft des Denkens.* München: Hanser.

Radtke, Katrin R. (2005). *From Gifts to Taxes: The mobilization of Tamil and Eritrean diaspora in intrastate warfare.* Working Paper Micropolitics 2/2005. March 12, 2007 http://www2.hu-berlin.de/mikropolitik/?area=publikationen.

Radtke, Katrin R. (2006). *Von der Gabe zur Steuer. Die Mobilisierung der Diaspora zur Finanzierung der Bürgerkriege in Sri Lanka und Eritrea.* PhD-thesis submitted to the Faculty of Philosophy, Humboldt-University, Berlin.

Radtke, Katrin 2009: *Mobilisierung der Diaspora. Die moralische Ökonomie der Bürgerkriege in Sri Lanka und Eritrea.* Frankfurt am Main: Campus.

Radu, Michael (2001). *The Rise and Fall of the PKK.* In: Orbis, 45/1. 47–64.

Raeymakers, Timothy (2004). *The Political Economy of Beni-Lubero.* In: Koen Vlassenroot/Timothy Raeymakers (eds.). Conflict and Social Transformation in Eastern DR Congo. 61–80. Gent: Academia Press.

Ramirez, Philippe (2004). *Maoism in Nepal. Towards a comparative perspective.* In: Michael Hutt (ed.). Himalayan "People's War". Nepal's maoist rebellion. 225–242. London: C. Hurst & Co. Publishers.

Ranstorp, Magnus (1994). *Hizbollah's Command Leadership: its structure, decision-making and relationship with Iranian Clergy and institutions.* In: Terrorism and Political Violence, 6/3. 303–339.

Rashid, Ahmed (2000). *Taliban. Militant Islam, oil, and fundamentalism in Central Asia.* New Haven, Conn.: Yale University Press.

Reemtsma, Jan Philipp (2006). *Die Natur der Gewalt als Problem der Soziologie.* In: Mittelweg 36, 15/5. 2–25.

— (2008). *Vertrauen und Gewalt. Versuch über eine besondere Konstellation der Moderne.* Hamburg: Hamburger Edition.

Remington, Robin Alison (1997). *State Cohesion and the Military*. In: Melissa K. Bokovoy/Jill A. Irvine/Carol S. Lilly (eds.). State-Society Relations in Yugoslavia, 1945–1992. 61–78. New York: St. Martin's Press.

Reinhard, Wolfgang (ed.) (1999). *Verstaatlichung der Welt. Europäische Staatsmodelle und außereuropäische Machtprozesse*. München: Oldenbourg.

Rénique, José Luis (1998). *Apogee and Crisis of a "Third Path": Mariateguismo, "people's war", and counterinsurgency in Puno*. In: Steve J. Stern (ed.). Shining and Other Paths: War and society in Peru 1980–1995. 307–340. Durham NC: Duke University Press.

Reno, William (1998). *Warlord Politics and African States*. Boulder, Col.: Lynne Rienner.

Reuter, Jens (1994). *Die Wirtschaftskrise der BR Jugoslawien. Reformen im Schatten von Krieg, Embargo und schleppender Transformation*. In: Südosteuropa, 43/8. 478–491.

Richani, Nazih (2002). *The Political Economy of War and Peace in Colombia*. Albany, NY: State University of New York Press.

Richards, Paul (1996). *Fighting for the Rainforest. War, youth and resources in Sierra Leone*. London: Heinemann.

Rioux, Jean-Pierre (2004). *Les Français et la guerre des deux Républiques*. In: Mohammed Harbi/Benjamin Stora (eds.). La guerre d'Algérie, 1954–2004. La fin de l'amnésie. 17–26. Paris: Laffont.

Robben, Antonius (2004). *The Fear of Indifference: Combatants' anxieties about the political identity of civilians during Argentina's dirty war*. In: Nancy Scheper-Hughes/Philippe Bourgeois (eds.). Violence in War and Peace. An anthology. 200–206. London: Blackwell.

Roberts, Priscilla (2006). *Behind the Bamboo Curtain. China, Vietnam, and the world beyond Asia*. Stanford, Cal.: Stanford University Press.

Rodney, Walter (1972). *How Europe undeveloped Africa*. London: Bogle-L'Ouverture.

Romero, Mauricio (2003). *Reform and Reaction. Paramilitary groups in contemporary Colombia*. In: Diane E. Davis/Anthony W. Pereira (eds.). Irregular armed forces and their role in politics and state formation. 178–208. Cambridge: Cambridge University Press.

Rouquié, Alain (1987). *The Military and the State in Latin America*. Berkeley: University of California Press.

Roy, Olivier (2003). *Globalized Islam. The search for a new Ummah*. New York: Columbia University Press.

Rubin, Barnett R. (2000). *The Political Economy of War and Peace in Afghanistan*. In: World Development, 28/10. 1789–1803.

Rufin, Jean-Christophe (1999). *Le temps rebelles*. In: Jean-Marc Balancie/Arnaud de la Grange (eds.). Mondes rebelles. Guerres civiles et violences politiques. L'encyclopédie des conflits. 13–34. Paris: Michalon.

Rufin, Jean-Christophe/Jean, François (eds.) (1996). *L'économie des guerres civiles*. Paris: Hachette.

Rüland, Jürgen/Hanf, Theodor/Manske, Eva (eds.) (2006). *U.S. Foreign Policy Toward the Third World. A post-Cold War assessment.* Armonk, NY: M.E. Sharpe.

Rzehak, Lutz (2004). *Die Taliban im Land der Mittagssonne. Geschichten aus der afghanischen Provinz.* Wiesbaden: Reichert.

Sahlins, Marshall (1963). *Poor Man, Rich Man, Big Man. Chief: Political types in Polynesia and Melanesia.* In: Comparative Studies in Society and History, 5. 288–303.

Said, Edward (1978). *Orientalism.* New York: Pantheon Books.

Salifou, André (1993). *La question touarègue au Niger.* Paris: Karthala.

Salmon, Jago (2004). *Massacre and Mutiliation: Understanding the Lebanese Forces through their use of violence.* Paper presented at the workshop "Techniques of violence in Civil War". PRIO, Oslo, August 20–21. July 22, 2006 http://www.prio.no/cscw/micro/techniques/paper_sal mon.pdf.

— (2006). *MilitiaPolitics. The formation and organisation of irregular armed forces in Sudan (1985–2001) and Lebanon (1975–1991).* PhD-thesis submitted to the Faculty of Philosophy, Humboldt-University, Berlin.

Sapir, Jacques (1995). *Crise et transition en URSS et en Russie.* In: Robert Boyer/Yves Sillard (eds.). Théorie de la regulation. L'etat des savoirs. 435–442. Paris: La Decouverte.

Scharpf, Fritz W. (1993). *Coordination in Hierarchies and Networks.* In: Fritz W. Scharpf (ed.). Games in Hierarchies and Networks. Analytical Approaches to the study of governance approaches. 125–165. Boulder, Col.: Westview Press.

— (2000). *Institutions in Comparative Policy Perspective.* In: Comparative Political Studies, 33/6–7. 762–787.

Scheffler, Thomas (1996). *Worte, Taten, Bilder. Gewaltkult und Realpolitik im palästinensischen Nationalismus.* In: Erwin Orywal/Aparna Rao/Michael Bollig (eds.). Krieg und Gewalt. Die Gewalt in unseren Köpfen. 121–133. Wiesbaden: Reimer.

— (1999). *Religion, Violence and the Civilizing Process. The case of Lebanon.* In: Jean Hannoyer (ed.). Guerres civile. Èconomies de la violence, dimension de la civilité. 163–186. Paris: Karthala.

Scheper-Hughes, Nancy/Bourgois, Philippe (eds.) (2004). *Violence in War and Peace. An anthology.* London: Blackwell.

Schievelbusch, Wolfgang (2003). *Die Kultur der Niederlage. Der amerikanische Süden 1865, Frankreich 1871, Deutschland 1918.* Frankfurt am Main: Fischer.

Schlichte, Klaus (1996). *Krieg und Vergesellschaftung in Afrika. Ein Beitrag zur Theorie des Krieges.* Hamburg: Lit.

— (2005a). *Uganda – a State in Suspense.* In: Klaus Schlichte (ed.). The Dynamics of States. The formation and crises of state domination. 161–182. Aldershot: Ashgate.

— (2005b). *Der Staat in der Weltgesellschaft. Politische Herrschaft in Afrika, Asien und Lateinamerika.* Frankfurt am Main: Campus.

— (2006). *Neue Kriege oder alte Thesen? Wirklichkeit und Repräsentation kriegerischer Gewalt in der Politikwissenschaft.* In: Anny Geis (ed.). Den Krieg überdenken.

Kriegesbegriffe und Kriegstheorien in der Kontroverse. 111–132. Baden-Baden: Nomos.

— (2009). *Na krilima patriotisma – on the wings of patriotism. Delegated and spin-off violence in Serbia.* In: Armed Forces and Society, (forthcoming).

Schmitt, Carl (1923). *Römischer Katholizismus und politische Form.* Heilerau: Hegner.

— (1922). *Politische Theologie. Vier Kapitel zur Lehre von der Souveränität.* Berlin: Duncker & Humblot.

Schräder, Peter J. (1993). *Ethnic Politics in Djibouti: From 'Eye of the Hurrikane' to 'Boiling Cauldron'.* In: African Affairs, 92/367. 203–221.

Schröder, Günther/Korte, Werner (1986). *Samuel Kanyon Doe, der People's Redemption Council und die Macht. Vorläufige Anmerkungen zur Anatomie und Sozialpsychologie eines Putsches.* In: Robert Kappel/Werner Korte/Friedegrund Mascher (eds.). Liberia. Underdevelopment and political rule in a peripheral society. 103–144. Hamburg: Institute for African Studies.

Schubert, Frank (2001). *War came to our place. Eine Sozialgeschichte des Krieges im Luwero-Dreieck, Uganda 1981–1986.* Unpublished PhD-thesis. Department of History, University of Hannover.

— (2006). *"Guerillas Don't Die Easily": Everyday Live in Wartime and the Guerrilla Myth in the National Resistance Army in Uganda, 1981–1986.* In: International Review for Social History, 51. 93–111.

Schulze, Kirsten E. (2004). *The Free Aceh Movement (GAM): Anatomy of a seperatist movement.* Washington, DC: East-West Center.

Sekulić, Milisav (2001). *Na krilima patriotisma. Borci Rakovice u ratovima od 1990 do 1999.* Belgrade: no publisher.

Shah, Alpa (2006). *Markets of Protection. The 'Terrorist' Maoist Movement and the State in Jharkand, India.* In: Critique of Anthropology, 26/3. 297–314.

Shepler, Susan (2005). *Globalizing Child Soldiers in Sierra Leone.* In: Sunaina Mira/Elisabeth Soep (eds.). Youthscapes. The popular, the national, the global. 119–133. Philadelphia, Penn.: University of Pennsylvania Press.

Showalter, Dennis E. (1993). *Caste, Skill, and Training: The Evolution of Cohesion in European Armies from the Middle Ages to the Sixteenth Century.* In: The Journal of Military History, 57/3. 407–430.

Silber, Laura/Little, Allan (1996). *Yugoslavia. The death of a nation.* London: Penguin.

Sidel, John T. (1999). *Capital, Coercion and Crime. Bossism in the Philippines.* Stanford, Cal.: Stanford University Press.

Siegelberg, Jens (1994). *Kapitalismus und Krieg. Eine Theorie des Krieges in der Weltgesellschaft.* Hamburg: Lit.

Simmel, Georg (1950). *The Sociology of Georg Simmel.* Translated, edited and with an introduction by Kurt H. Wolff. Glencoe, Ill.: The Free Press.

Smith, Martin (1991). *Burma – Insurgency and the politics of ethnicity.* London/New York: no publisher.

Skocpol, Theda (1979). *States and Social Revolutions.* Cambridge: Cambridge University Press.

Sobaka (2003). *Sobaka Dossier – Jaba Ioseliani*. Diacritica Press and Sobaka Online Magazine. June 24, 2006 http://www.diacritica.com/sobaka/dossier/ioseliani.html.

Social Science Research Council (2004). *The economic analysis of conflict: problems and prospects*. Conference, 19–20 April 2004, Washington D.-C.. March 8, 2007 http://programs.ssrc.org/gsc/gsc_activities/globalization_conflict/conflictagenda/.

Soeters, Joseph L. (2005). *Ethnic Conflict and Terrorism. The origins and dynamics of civil wars*. London: Routledge.

Sofsky, Wolfgang (1996). *Traktat über die Gewalt*. Frankfurt am Main: Fischer.

— (1997). *The Order of the Terror: the concentration camp*. Princeton N.J.: Princeton University Press.

Sorokin, Pitirim A. (1942). *Man and Society in Calamity. The effects of war, revolution, famine, pestilence upon human mind, behavior, social organization and cultural life*. New York: E. P. Dutton.

Stavans, Ilan (1993). *Two Peruvians*. In: Transition, 61. 18–39.

Stern, Steve J. (ed.) (1998). *Shining and other Paths. War and Society in Peru, 1980–1995*. Durham, NC: Duke University Press.

Stein, Gottfried (1994). *Endkampf um Kurdistan? Die PKK, die Türkei und Deutschland*. München: MVG.

Stietencron, Heinrich von (1995). *Töten im Krieg. Gundlagen und Entwicklungen*. In: Heinrich von Stietencron/Jörg Rüpke (eds.). Töten im Krieg. 17–38. Freiburg: Alber.

Suhrke, Astri (2006). *The Limits of State Building in Afghanistan. The role of international assistance*. Bergen: Christian Michelsen Institute.

Swamy, Narayn M.R. (2002). *Tigers of Sri Lanka: From boys to guerrilla*. Colombo: Vijitha Yapa Publications.

Taylor, Charles (2004). *Modern Social Imagineries*. Durham, NC: Duke University Press.

Tilly, Charles (1992). *Coercion, Capital, and European States. Ad 990-1992*. Cambridge: Cambridge University Press.

— (2001). *Mechanisms in political processes*. In: Annual Review of Political Science, no. 4. 21–41.

Tishkov, Valery (2004). *Chechnya: Life in a War-Torn Society*. Berkeley, Cal.: University of California Press.

Tocqueville, Alexis de (1978). *Der alte Staat und die Revolution*. First published 1856. München: dtv.

Tönnies, Ferdinand (1991). *Gemeinschaft und Gesellschaft. Grundbegriffe der reinen Soziologie*. First published 1887. Wiesbaden: Wissenschaftliche Buchgesellschaft.

Tripp, Charles (2000). *A History of Iraq*. Cambridge: Cambridge University Press.

Tsurayev, Kazbek (2005). *Chechen Rebells Name Successor*. In: Caucasus Reporting Service (CRS), No. 278. July 27, 2006 http://www.iwpr.net/?p=crs&s=f&o=239814&apc_state=henicrsc 14650e422b187cae86eab39b7d647b3.

Tucker, Shelby (2000). *Among Insurgents: Walking through Burma*. London/New York: Tauris.
Tyrell, Hartmann (1980). *Gewalt, Zwang und die Institutionalisierung von Herrschaft: Versuch einer Neubestimmung von Max Webers Herrschaftsbegriff*. In: R. Pohlmann (ed.). Person und Institution. Helmut Schelsky gewidmet. 59–92. Würzburg: Könighausen und Neumann.
United Nations (2001). *Report of the Panel of Experts on the Illegal Exploitation of Natural Resources and other Forms of Wealth of the Democractic Republic of the Congo*. S/2001/357. New York: United Nations Security Council.
Uzoigwe, Godfrey N. (1977). *The Warrior and the State in Pre-colonial Africa: Comparative perspectives*. In: Ali A. Mazrui (ed). The Warrior Tradition in modern Africa. 20–46. Leiden: Brill.
Vagts, Alfred (1959). *A History of Militarism*. New York: Merridian.
van Acker, Frank (2004). *Uganda and the Lord's Resistance Army: The new order no one ordered*. In: African Affairs, 103/412. 335–357.
van Acker, Frank/Vlassenroot, Koen (2001). *Les "maï-maï" et les functions de la violence milicienne dans l'est du Congo*. In: politique africaine, no. 84. 103–116.
van Bruinessen, Martin (1992). *Agha, Shaikh and State: the social and political structures of Kurdistan*. London: Zed Books.
Van Creveld, Martin (1991). *On Future War*. London: Brassey.
— (1999). *The Rise and Decline of the State*. Cambridge: Cambridge University Press.
Vigne, Randolph (1987). *SWAPO of Namibia: a movement in exile*. In: Third World Quarterly, 9/1. 85 -107.
Villamarín Pulido, Luis Alberto (1996). *In Hell. Guerrillas that devour their own. The story of a former member of the FARC (Colombian Revolutionary Armed Forces)/Johnnny*. Bogotha: Author.
Von Trotha, Trutz (1994a). *"Streng aber gerecht" – "hart, aber tüchtig". Über Formen von Basislegitimität und ihre Ausprägung am Beginn staatlicher Herrschaft*. In: Wilhelm G. Möhlig/Trutz von Trotha (eds.). Legitimation von Herrschaft und Recht. 69–90. Köln: Köppe Verlag.
— (1994b). *Koloniale Herrschaft. Zur soziologischen Theorie der Staatsentstehung am Beispiel des "Schutzgebietes Togo"*. Tübingen: Mohr.
— (1999). *Formen des Krieges. Zur Typologie kriegerischer Aktionsmacht*. In: Sighard Neckel/Michael Schwab-Trapp (eds.). Ordnungen der Gewalt. Beiträge zu einer politischen Soziologie der Gewalt und des Krieges. 71–95. Opladen: Leske und Budrich.
Volkov, Vadim (2002). *Violent Entrepreneurs. The use of force in the making of Russian capitalism*. Ithaca, NY: Cornell University Press.
Wade, Robert H. (2005). *Failing States and Cumulative Causation in the World System*. In: International Political Science Review, 26/1. 17–36.
Waldmann, Peter (1978). *Caudillismo als Konstante der politischen Kultur Latenamerikas?*. In: Richard Konetzke et. al. (ed.). Jahrbuch für Geschichte von Staat, Wirtschaft und Gesellschaft Lateinamerikas, vol. 15. 191–207.

— (1989). *Ethnischer Radikalismus. Ursachen und Folgen gewaltsamer Minderheitenkonflikte.* Opladen: Westdeutscher Verlag.
— (2000). *Rache ohne Regeln.* In: Mittelweg 36, 9/6. 4–25.
Walter, Barbara F. (1997). *Designing Transitions from Violent Civil War.* Paper presented at the annual meeting of the American Political Science Association. Washington, DC.
Walter, Barbara F. (2003). *The Critical Barrier to Civil War Settlement.* In: International Organization, 51. 335–364.
Walter, Barbara F./Snyder, Jack (eds.) (1999). *Civil Wars, Insecurity, and Interventions.* New York: Columbia University Press.
Walter, Eugene V. (1969). *Terror and Resistance. A study of political violence.* New York: Oxford University Press.
Wartenberg, Thomas E. (1990). *The Forms of Power. From domination to transformation.* Philadelphia: Temple University Press.
— (1995). *Situated Social Power.* In: Thomas E. Wartenberg (ed.). Rethinking Power. 79–101. Albany NY: State University of New York Press.
Waterbury, John (1993). *Exposed to innumerable Delusions. Public Enterprise and State Power in Egypt, India, Mexico, and Turkey.* Cambridge: Cambridge University Press.
Watts, Nicole F. (2004). *Institutionalizing Virtual Kurdistan West: Transnational Networks and Ethnic Contention in International Affairs.* In: Joel S. Migdal (ed.). Boundaries and belonging: states and societies in the struggle to shape identities and local practices. 121–147. Cambridge: Cambridge University Press.
Wauthier, Claude (1995). *Quatre presidents et l'Afrique.* Paris: Seuil.
Weber, Max (1958). *From Max Weber. Essays in Sociology.* Translated, edited and with an introduction by H. H. Gerth and C. Wright Mills. New York: Oxford University Press.
— (1978). *Economy and Society. An outline of interpretive sociology.* Edited by Guenther Roth and Claus Wittich, Vol. 1–2. Berkeley, Cal.: University of California Press.
— (1985). *Wirtschaft und Gesellschaft. Grundriß der verstehenden Soziologie.* Tübingen: Mohr.
— (2000). *Political Writings.* Edited by Peter Lassmann and Ronald Speirs. New York: Cambridge University Press.
Weigert, Stephen L. (1996). *Traditional Religion and Guerrilla Warfare in Modern Africa.* London: Macmillan.
Weinstein, Jeremy M. (2005). *Resources and the Information Problem in Rebel Recruitment.* In: The Journal of Conflict Resolution, 49/4. 598–624.
— (2007). *Inside Rebellion. The politics of insurgent violence.* Cambridge, Mass.: Cambridge University Press.
Weissman, Fabrice (1996). *Mozambique: la guerre du ventre.* In: François Jean/Jean-Christophe Rufin (eds.). Economies des guerres civiles. 319–342. Paris: Hachette.

Wesseling, Hendrik L. (1999). *Imperialism and Colonialism. Essays on the History of the European Expansion.* Westport, Conn.: Greenwood.

White, Hayden (1987). *The Content of the Form. Narrative discourse and historical representation.* Baltimore MD: The Johns Hopkins University Press.

Wickham-Crowley, Timothy P. (1992). *Guerrillas & Revolution in Latin America. A Comparative Study of Insurgents and Regimes since 1956.* Princeton, New Jersey: Princeton University Press.

Wiesel, Elie (2006). *Night.* First edition Paris 1958. New York: Hill and Wang.

Woo-Cummings, Meredith (ed.) (1999). *The Developmental State.* Ithaca, NJ: Cornell University Press.

Woodward, Barbara (1995). *Balkan Tragedy: Chaos and dissolution after the Cold War.* Washington, D.C.: Brookings Institution.

Woodward, Peter (2006). *US Foreign Policy and the Horn of Africa.* Aldershot: Ashgate.

Young, John (1997). *Peasant Revolution in Ethiopia. The Tigray People's Liberations Front 1975–1991.* Cambridge: Cambridge University Press.

Zitelmann, Thomas (1993). *Violence, pouvoir symbolique et mode de representation des Oromo.* In: politique africaine, no. 50. 45–58.

# Social Science

Felix Kolb
**Protest and Opportunities**
The Political Outcomes of Social Movements
2007, 341 pages, ISBN 978-3-593-38413-9

Karolina Karr
**Democracy and Lobbying in the European Union**
2007, 209 pages, ISBN 978-3-593-38412-2

Stefani Scherer, Reinhard Pollak,
Gunnar Otte, Markus Gangl (eds.)
**From Origin to Destination**
Trends and Mechanisms in Social Stratification Research
2007, 323 pages, ISBN 978-3-593-38411-5

Johannes Harnischfeger
**Democratization and Islamic Law**
The Sharia Conflict in Nigeria
2008, 283 pages, ISBN 978-3-593-38256-2

Helmut Willke
**Smart Governance**
Governing the Global Knowledge Society
2007, 222 pages, ISBN 978-3-593-38253-1

Michael Dauderstädt, Arne Schildberg (eds.)
**Dead Ends of Transition**
Rentier Economies and Protectorates
2006, 249 pages, ISBN 978-3-593-38154-1

Mehr Informationen unter
www.campus.de

**campus**
*Frankfurt · New York*